# Book of Days '70s

# Book of Days '70s

## A Day-by-Day Look at the POP CULTURE MOMENTS That Made History

**HARVEY SOLOMON & RICH APPEL**

METRO BOOKS
NEW YORK

## Dedication

*To Rachel and Sarah: born in the 70s, breathtakingly beautiful,*
*and we never dressed you in polyester. Real. (HS)*

*To Melody and Jordan, who at 10 and 14 are already more prolific writers*
*than I'll ever be. And to Jane—ahead of these 366, the best date of all. (RA)*

© 2009 by Tell Tale Press, Inc.

This 2009 edition published by Metro Books,
by arrangement with Tell Tale Press, Inc.

Cover design: Jim Sarfati
Cover art © Kelvin Wakefield/iStockphoto.com
Interior concept design: Charles Kreloff
Interior layout and design: Anthony White

Metro Books
122 Fifth Avenue
New York, NY 10011

ISBN: 978-1-4351-0470-9

Printed and bound in China

10 9 8 7 6 5 4 3 2 1

CD Track Listing

1. Walk on the Wild Side—Lou Reed (Lou Reed/Mick Ronson).
Time: 4:13. ℗1972 Sony Music Entertainment.

2. Lady Marmalade—LaBelle (B. Crewe/K. Nolan). Time: 3:14.
℗1974 Sony Music Entertainment.

3. I Want You to Want Me (Live)—Cheap Trick (Rick Nielsen). Time: 3:44.
℗1979 Sony Music Entertainment.

4. Frankenstein—The Edgar Winter Group (Edgar Winter). Time: 4:44.
℗1972 Sony Music Entertainment.

5. What I Did for Love (from *A Chorus Line*)—Priscilla Lopez & Company
(Marvin Hamlisch/Edward Kleban). Time: 3:43.
℗1975 Sony Music Entertainment.

6. The Devil Went Down to Georgia—The Charlie Daniels Band
(Charlie Daniels/Fred Edwards/Jim Marshall/Charlie Hayward/Tom Crain/
Taz DiGregorio). Time: 3:34. ℗1979 Sony Music Entertainment.

7. More Than a Feeling—Boston (Tom Scholz). Time: 4:45.
℗1976 Sony Music Entertainment.

**Sony Music**

CUSTOM MARKETING GROUP

# Contents

# Introduction

Collectibles like pet rocks, Rubik's cubes, and lava lamps. Clothes like leisure suits, hot pants, fake furs, designer bodysuits, cowl neck sweaters, and platform shoes. Home goods like beanbag chairs, Crock-Pots, waterbeds, and avocado green appliances. Munching Pringles, chugging Boone's Farm Apple Wine, chewing Pop Rocks candy. Wearing shag haircuts and mullets, clunky gold chains, and granny glasses. Watching the Fonz and R2-D2, listening to eight-tracks, dancing to disco, shouting "breaker, breaker" into CB radios, the decade's revolutionary mobile devices. And smiley face stickers plastered everywhere. Ah, for the good old kitschy 1970s—"strange, feverish years" wrote David Frum in *How We Got Here: The 70's*.

So bring on transcendental meditation, jogging, Rolfing, est, yoga, "finding your inner child," and primal therapy. Author Thomas Wolfe coined the phrase the "me decade," which later morphed into the "me generation," obsessed with "changing one's personality, remaking, remodeling, elevating, and polishing one's very self…and observing, studying, and doting on it."

It's time to focus on number one, because what's happening all around is tough and getting tougher—inflation, recession, the energy crisis, Vietnam, Watergate—and the nation's leaders sure aren't helping. Richard Nixon, the first president in the seventies, resigned in disgrace. Replacement Gerald Ford became better known for bumbling and bumping into things than enacting meaningful policy. Jimmy Carter, well intentioned but ultimately ineffectual, paved the way for the Reagan '80s.

## Turbulence and Transition

No wonder the idealism and optimism of the '60s took a sharp turn toward disillusionment. The naïve Woodstock generation's hopes for peace and love fell victim to harsh economic and political realities: National Guardsmen gunning down students at Kent State; long lines at gas stations; a president who campaigned on a law and order platform breaking the law. "There is a bright side to everything," said impersonator David Frye at his Nixonian best. "My administration has taken crime out of the streets and put it in the White House where I can keep an eye on it."

Technology, actually, helped everyone keep an eye on everything. Towering twins—video technology and satellite transmission—brought live reporting of events into living rooms from even the remotest corners on earth: the Yom Kippur war, the launch of Skylab, the Munich Olympics massacre, the mass suicide at Jonestown, the Three Mile Island near nuclear meltdown, Americans held hostage in Iran. All with unprecedented immediacy and urgency. The "global village" first suggested by Marshall McLuhan in his 1964 bestseller, *Understanding Media,* had arrived, but rather than unifying, it often provoked fear and animosity.

Perhaps as a reaction to dispiriting news, escapism rose to new heights—especially embodied in the decade's love affair with earlier, simpler times. "Where were you in '62?" asked *American Graffiti,* director/co-writer George Lucas' box-office smash. The wave of nostalgia swept from the silver screen (with *Grease,* too) to the small screen with the '50s-set *Happy Days* and several spin-offs. And then, naturally enough, it flooded the pop charts.

## From ABBA to Zappa

Wolfman Jack parlayed an appearance in *American Graffiti* into a successful career with radio and television gigs like NBC's *Midnight Special.* Retro sounding and looking Sha Na Na played Woodstock, appeared in *Grease,* and hosted a syndicated TV show for five years. Icons of the 1950s Elvis Presley and Rick Nelson embarked on comebacks with hits like "Burning Love" and "Garden Party," respectively, while '60s doo-woppers the Four Seasons clicked with "December 1963 (Oh, What a Night)." Current artists scored with throwback hits like Elton John's "Crocodile Rock" and Loggins & Messina's "Your Mama Don't Dance."

Yet this infatuation with the past represented but a fraction of the decade's astoundingly diverse sounds. It was goodbye Joplin, Hendrix, and Morrison, hello Clapton, Springsteen, and Marley. "Every possible influence reared its ugly and pretty head," wrote Bob Hansen in *25 Years of Rock & Roll.* "The great '60s explosion—both creative and destructive—was over."

Mirroring the Beatles' breakup in 1970, rock 'n' roll splintered into many subgenres. Soft rock surged with Bread and America alongside mellow sounds from the Carpenters, John Denver, and Olivia Newton-John. The Eagles, arguably the decade's biggest act, championed country rock with enormous hits like "Hotel California." Rock assumed a Southern accent with the Allman Brothers, ZZ Top, and Lynyrd Skynrd, the latter producing the anthemic classic "Free Bird," a tribute to the late Duane Allman. Soul continued to sizzle with artists like Marvin Gaye, Isaac Hayes, and a hip, happening weekly TV showcase, *Soul Train.*

Hard rock reenergized with Led Zeppelin and Pink Floyd, the latter producing the era-defining album *Dark Side of the Moon.* Shock rock emerged with Alice Cooper, Frank Zappa, and Iggy Pop, along with heavy metal's Black Sabbath, Grand Funk Railroad, and Rush paving the way for one of the decade's most influential movements: punk. The Clash challenged the Sex Pistols as the rawest rockers around, though the stridency spread through the likes of Patti Smith ("Because the Night") and the Ramones ("I Wanna Be Sedated").

Striking a less anarchic but equally outrageous note, glam rock shocked sensibilities with a purposely over-the-top, sexually ambiguous and/or androgynous look and feel. David Bowie led the charge, followed by Queen and its flashy front man, Freddie Mercury, delivering a multi-layered "Bohemian Rhapsody" and the double-sided "We Are the Champions/We Will Rock You." "I won't be a rock star," said Mercury. "I will be a legend."

Another, less self-promoting legend emerged to introduce America—and the world— to a fresh, rhythmic beat: reggae. From the slums of Kingston, Jamaica, dread-locked Bob Marley of the Wailers rose to iconic sta-tus with an insistent, bass-driven roots and rock sound that incorporated social and political messages. Fueled by the prodigious consumption of ganja (spliffs, mon), Marley's albums brimmed with songs about struggle and freedom like "I Shot the Sheriff" and "No Woman, No Cry"—"Good friends we have, oh, good friends we've lost, along the way..." Cancer took his life far too soon in 1980; his posthu-mous compilation album *Legend* remains the best-selling reggae album ever.

Yet while reggae never occupied more than a narrow niche, another overseas act delivered an accessible, chartbusting commer-cial sound. The Swedish quartet ABBA, abhorred by the critics and adored by the masses, became the decade's biggest inter-national pop act with hypnotic hits like "Waterloo," "Mamma Mia," "Fernando," and "Dancing Queen." Their brisk, upbeat sound meshed nicely with disco, the driving force that late in the decade eclipsed anything that rock had to offer.

Disco music contained no political message or flower power ideals, just an escapist, pulsating, nonstop sexual beat. From steamy early Barry White love anthems like "Never, Never Gonna Give Ya Up" to countless breathy disco divas to the pack-aged success of the Village People and their timeless "Y.M.C.A.," disco thumped and humped on and on. Dubbed "Queen of the Discos," Donna Summer delivered hits like "Love to Love You Baby" and "Bad Girls," the latter of which critic Stephen Holden said "cheerfully evokes the trash-flash vitality of tawdry disco dolls cruising down the main drag on a Saturday night." She had lots of company on Saturday night alongside the Bee Gees, who artfully reinvented their sound with a nonstop barrage of dance hits. Their soundtrack for *Saturday Night Fever*, with "Stayin' Alive" and "Night Fever," embodied the hedonistic disco era.

## Cinematic Comeback

*Saturday Night Fever* and *Grease* rocked the big screen. Other music/movie cross-overs included the Who's *Tommy*, a belated *Hair* (musical: 1968; movie: 1979), Bette Midler's theatrical bow as a feverish Joplin-like diva in *The Rose*, and a sleeper turned enduring cult classic, *The Rocky Horror Picture Show*.

Movies made a big comeback in the '70s, reversing the declining theater audiences that had accompanied the rise of television. New technologies helped propel the big screen to fresh prominence in sight (Panavision), sound (Dolby), and spectacle. The latter came via computer-generated, jaw-dropping special effects in blockbusters like *Jaws*, *Star Wars*, and *Close Encounters of the Third Kind*, sending the careers of Steven Spielberg and George Lucas into outer space. Disaster movies struck too with the *Towering Inferno*, *Poseidon Adventure*, and *Airport*.

Escapism certainly had its place, but so too did realism. Urban crime hit its mark with films like *Mean Streets*, *Taxi Driver*, *Dirty Harry*, *The French Connection*, and *The Warriors*, and spun off "blaxploitation" action flicks with black heroes like *Shaft* and *Foxy Brown*. But criminal intent drew its richest canvas in the form of Francis Ford Coppola's landmark *Godfather* movies. The first two busted box-office records and won Oscars for best picture, the only time a sequel has ever won film's top honor. Just like Mario Puzo's book broke publishing records, the film series clamped a vise grip on the culture's collective imagination—giving moviegoers, truly, an offer they couldn't refuse. "[It's] an epic of crime, sung in the plain idiom of the streets," wrote Geoffrey Wolff in *The Washington Post* of the original novel. "A world of cunning and treachery where power is a function of a leader's ability to seem to say one thing while he intends to perform the opposite."

Realism also scored with a trio of well-received films that revisited the horrors of Vietnam: *Coming Home*, *The Deer Hunter*, and *Apocalypse Now*. But movies weren't all about cynicism and alienation. Woody Allen mined a comedic mother lode that culminated with *Annie Hall*, a surprise Oscar winner for best picture over favored *Star Wars*. Mel Brooks contributed *Blazing Saddles* and other laugh riots. "We are not interested in polite titters," said one of Brooks' favorite players, Gene Wilder. "We want the audience rolling on the floor and falling about."

Following his turn in *Diamonds are Forever*, Sean Connery turned over the 007 mantle to Roger Moore for four more '70s James Bond extravaganzas. Unknown Sylvester Stallone vaulted into cinema's top ranks with *Rocky*. But when it came to leading men, no one topped taciturn Clint Eastwood. The only star to place in the list of top ten actors in both '70 and '79 (rating second both times), he began the decade starring in and making his directorial debut in *Play Misty for Me*, proceeded to own the role of maverick cop (Dirty) Harry Callahan, and finished with 1979's second highest-grossing movie, *Every Which Way But Loose*. Along the way Eastwood delivered one of film's most quoted lines while confronting a sprawled bank robber in *Dirty Harry*: "I know what you're thinking. 'Did he fire six shots or only five?' Well, to tell you the truth, in all this excitement I kind of lost track myself. But being as this is a .44 Magnum, the most powerful handgun in the world, and would blow your head clean off, you've got to ask yourself one question: 'Do I feel lucky?' Well do ya, punk?"

## Small Screen, Big Change

Television felt lucky, and played some hunches that paid off handsomely. Since its cinematic rivals had always enjoyed far greater latitude in portraying risky and risqué subject matter, the home medium decided to gamble on some edgier material. The most stunning successes first emerged not with dramas but sitcoms. Two endured considerable pre-launch network trepidation and tepid starts to catch fire, winning multiple Emmy and other awards, and achieving landmark status.

CBS's *All in the Family* wound up the top-rated show for five seasons straight, centered around the home life of a bigoted archconservative patriarch (Carroll O'Connor) and his sweet, ever understanding wife (Jean Stapleton). The show consistently tackled difficult topics like abortion, child abuse, death, impotence, integration, prejudice, premarital sex, racism, rape, and more, handling them with uncommon, affecting grace. "'All in the Family' changed the course of television comedy," wrote Tim Brooks and Earle Marsh in *The Complete Directory to Primetime Network and Cable TV Shows*. "It brought a sense of harsh reality to a TV world which previously had been populated largely by homogenized, inoffensive characters and stories that seemed to have been laundered before they ever got on the air."

An even more outlandish premise matched that audacity, and then some. Set in the Korean War, *M\*A\*S\*H* offered a tart, topical correlation to the raging Vietnam War. CBS had just ended the six-year run of *Hogan's Heroes*, set in a Nazi POW camp, but that show emphasized traditional broad, bland fun. Injecting life-and-death reality into the general craziness at a battlefront hospital, CBS's *M\*A\*S\*H* (spun off from a motion picture) ran for eleven years, nearly four times longer than the conflict it depicted. Co-creator Larry Gelbart called it a labor of love. "It's nice not to see that love go unrequited," he said at the Emmys. Its two-and-a-half-hour finale in 1983 drew the largest television audience ever, a record that stands more than a quarter century later.

Other sitcoms of note: *All in the Family* spin-offs *Maude* and *The Jeffersons*; *The Mary Tyler Moore Show*, featuring television's first independent, single working woman; sexually daring *Three's Company*; flashback faves *Happy Days* and *Laverne & Shirley*; and zany *Mork & Mindy*, which introduced breakout star Robin Williams.

Dramatically, television delivered lots of cops: *Baretta, Cannon, CHiPS, Hawaii Five-O, Kojak, McCloud, The Mod Squad, Police Woman, The Rockford Files, Starsky and Hutch*, and more. *Charlie's Angels* epitomized the scantily clad "jiggle TV" trend pioneered by ABC's Fred Silverman, (in)famously nicknamed "the man with the golden gut," whose Midas touch propelled perennial third place ABC to #1 late in the decade.

At the exact opposite end of the spectrum, CBS and NBC found success in wholesome family dramas *The Waltons* and *Little House on the Prairie*, respectively. *Marcus Welby, M.D.* and *Medical Center* covered the medical beat, though no one could resuscitate the fading variety except the versatile star and strong ensemble cast of *The Carol Burnett Show*. Television's costliest risks paid its biggest dividends. ABC's captivating slave drama *Roots* confirmed the power of the miniseries, becoming the most-watched show in TV history to date. Expensive, lavish "event" miniseries boomed, with *Rich Man, Poor Man* and *Holocaust, The Big Event*, filling crucial ratings sweeps periods and winning passels of Emmy awards. The golden age continued nonstop into the '80s with *Shogun, The Thorn Birds, Lonesome Dove*, and more.

While movies and music captured Saturday night fever—and Elton John made Saturday night all right for fighting—NBC made Saturday night all right for watching. *Saturday Night Live* turned late night date night into an institution, single-handedly making it (reasonably) cool to stay home on Saturday night. It capitalized less on outrage and more on outrageous with an edgy blend of satire, skits, star hosts, and top-shelf musical guests. With razor sharp writing and a resident troupe of "Not Yet Ready For Prime-Time Players" including Chevy Chase, John Belushi, Dan Aykroyd, and Gilda Radner, the show generated instant water cooler buzz.

From adults to kids, television made another everlasting contribution with *Sesame Street*. Amidst a wasteland of commercial dross for children, producer Joan Ganz Cooney fashioned a show that presented math and English in an entertaining format that was never preachy or boring. With Jim Henson's Muppets contributing to fun, fast-paced segments, it became a milestone that made a difference for generations present and future.

Just like the movies had whiz-bang special effects, television had a techie edge too: cable. New gold rush days of franchising led to the wiring of America with coaxial cable as cable systems sprung up in urban and suburban markets. Programming burgeoned, with dozens of satellite-delivered national networks offering record choices in news, sports, movies, and entertainment targeting general and niche audiences.

The rise and reach of television, both cable and broadcast, sounded a death knell for life—*Life* magazine, that is. The general audience icon expired as a weekly in 1972, following the demise of *Look* the year before. Ironically, in their wake the largest circulation and most profitable magazine left in America was *TV Guide*.

## Division, Diversity, Depth

Sandwiched between the epochal, epic '60s and the careerist, "greed is good" credo of the '80s (Michael Douglas in *Wall Street*), the '70s invariably get a bad rap. It's easy to ridicule the decade's bad hair, ridiculous polyester and spandex fashions, and vapid disco beat. Easy, but wrong, because the '70s transformed America as much as, if not more than, the '60s. "The United States experienced a remarkable makeover," wrote Boston University professor Bruce J. Schulman in *The Seventies*. "Its economic outlook, political ideology, cultural assumptions, and fundamental social arrangements changed.... We live in their shadows."

Social movements flourished, bringing civil rights, women's rights, gay rights, Native American rights, and environmentalism to new heights. Even the depths of Watergate delivered not only unprecedented political change, but a legacy that lives on—the "gate" suffix that's now attached to every political imbroglio.

Yes, the much-maligned '70s reinvented America—for better and worse. We've assembled a flavorful day-by-day recounting of its greatest hits—as well as a generous helping of more obscure yet elucidating incidents and tidbits that help define the decade. From the long and winding road, to running on empty, to changes in latitude, changes in attitude, to hot stuff. Enjoy the ride.

**Harvey Solomon and Rich Appel**

JANUARY

## JANUARY

### 1972

The nascent women's liberation movement, propelled in the 1960s by Betty Friedan's provocative best-seller *The Feminine Mystique*, gets a major boost today as a special Spring Preview issue of *Ms.* magazine sells 300,000 copies in eight days. Created by pioneering feminist author (and onetime Playboy bunny) Gloria Steinem, it presents a slick, sophisticated strike against the status quo. "Most women's magazines," she says, "simply try to mold women into bigger and better consumers." Inaugural story subjects include abortion, lesbianism, the inequality of marriage, and the male chauvinism of the English language, encapsulated in the magazine's name that presents a bold alternative to the standard descriptors "Miss" and "Mrs." *Ms.* makes its monthly debut in July, and within a year recoups its initial investment—much to the dismay of doubting pundits like newsman Harry Reasoner, who opines, "I'll give them six months before they run out of things to say."

## JANUARY 2

### 1974

Slow down, you're movin' too fast: the open road narrows a bit today as President Nixon signs a bill mandating a maximum national highway speed of 55 m.p.h. States have sixty days or less to respond, and those that don't will lose federal funds for highway construction. So get with the program that experts estimate will save 200,000 barrels of oil a day. "With an attitude of respect and mutual concern," says Nixon, "the social and economic impacts of the energy crisis can be minimized." With conservation the new norm, several newspapers run the front-page story with a photo of a man giving his restaurant coworkers a ride in a horse-drawn cart. Today's average price for a gallon of leaded gasoline? Fifty-three cents. Unleaded won't come along until 1975.

# JANUARY

**1970** The end is near. As the rift among The Beatles widens, three members—George Harrison, Paul McCartney, and Ringo Starr—gather at Abbey Road Studios. Over the next two days they'll record "I Me Mine," Harrison's bitter take on their impending breakup. It's the last time The Beatles ever record together. The song appears on *Let It Be*, their fitful final album remixed by producer Phil Spector and released in May. The album hints at the unraveling, and the title track later wins an Oscar for original song. Meanwhile John Lennon and Yoko Ono, off on holiday in Denmark, issue a statement on New Year's Day: "We believe that the last decade was the end of the old machine crumbling to pieces. And we think we can get it together, with your help. We have great hopes for the new year."

# JANUARY

## 1971

The show must go on—only an hour earlier. Today Broadway producers shift curtain time from the traditional 8:30 p.m. to 7:30. They hope the change boosts business, especially among suburban theatergoers worried about late-night city crime. Local restaurateurs are worried too, afraid that the earlier start time will cut into their dinner crowds. "It's an experiment—we all hope it works," says irrepressible producer David Merrick (*Hello Dolly*, *42nd Street*), adding, "I've found that if you have a hit play, you can put it on at 4 a.m. and get an audience." So while early reviews are decidedly mixed, by season's end theaters enjoy a 17 percent increase in ticket sales, and the move to turn back the hands of time is hailed as an unqualified success.

# JANUARY

## 1970

A favored election slogan of the president also applies to daytime drama: Nixon's the one. After moving from writing for *Guiding Light* and *Another World* to creating and producing *One Life to Live*, Agnes Nixon lives up to her nickname: Queen of the Soaps. Today the soap dispenser branches out with *All My Children*, giving ABC not only another breakout daytime soap, but one catering to the prized younger demo. The torrid and topical series soon expands to a full hour, and two years later actress Mary Fickett wins the first Emmy for a daytime performer. Her role as an anti–Vietnam War protestor troubles ABC execs, but the award mollifies them—though not as much as the show's ratings success. The long-running soap steams along with eternal vixen Erica Kane, played deliciously by Susan Lucci, who carries an unenviable record of eighteen straight Emmy Award losses until she breaks the streak in 1999.

**JANUARY 1974** Even in Great Britain the producers thought it wouldn't find an audience, so the program sat unreleased for more than a year. Who's interested in a show about goings-on in a turn-of-the-century, upper-crust household? Turns out lots of people, so a couple years after strong native success, the multilayered *Upstairs, Downstairs* makes its stateside debut tonight on PBS's *Masterpiece Theatre*. Produced by ITV, a commercial competitor to the BBC, it portrays the disparate lives of not only the masters upstairs but the servants below—both of whom contend with rigorous class distinctions. "To the upper classes, this probably was the peak of English life," says host Alistair Cooke (see Oct. 5). "For the poor working classes, there was no future unless you were lucky enough to get on the household staff." *Upstairs, Downstairs* goes on to become PBS's most successful miniseries ever, and the public broadcasting network continues its strategy of premiering new series in January, far from the commercial networks' much-ballyhooed fall openings.

# JANUARY

**1970** After volunteering his land last August for the instantaneously legendary Woodstock music festival, dairy farmer Max Yasgur becomes a national hero to many. "I never expected this festival to be so big," says Yasgur. "But if the generation gap is to be closed, we older people have to do more than we have done." Today some local people, i.e., disgusted neighbors, sue him for $35,000 in property damage caused by the more than 400,000 carousing kids who traipsed through. Next year Yasgur himself successfully collects an insurance settlement payment, and sells his farm soon thereafter. He dies of a heart attack in 1973 at the age of fifty-three.

# JANUARY

**1972** Clifford's folly: One of the most outrageous literary hoaxes in history evaporates today with the telephonic appearance of reclusive billionaire Howard Hughes. In a three-hour conference call with reporters he'd talked with years before, the zealously private Hughes refutes his involvement with writer Clifford Irving's forthcoming high-profile McGraw-Hill biography. The elaborate scheme of Irving, his wife, and researcher Richard Suskind turns out to be a modern-day film noir replete with forged documents, Swiss bank accounts, purported live interviews all over the globe, hoodwinked forensic handwriting analysts, lawyers, and an embarrassed publisher. A media circus erupts, and an unrepentant Irving holds out with crumbling denials until finally coming clean three weeks later. He returns the advance and later serves a year and a half in jail.

# JANUARY

**1976** Living vicariously through its fictional characters and fictionalized historical figures like Harry Houdini, Sigmund Freud, and Emma Goldman, readers make author E.L. Doctorow's *Ragtime* a runaway best-seller. With a vibrant turn-of-the-century setting, it becomes a book-of-the-month club selection and delights critics, too. "There is no longer any such thing as fiction and nonfiction," says Doctorow. "There is only narrative." Hollywood options the rights, at first for Robert Altman (*Nashville*), though it'll be Milos Forman who directs the 1982 film for producer Dino De Laurentiis. Today the National Book Critics Circle gives *Ragtime* its inaugural award for fiction. Doctorow will again receive the award exactly thirty years later, for *The March*.

# JANUARY 10

**1972** The smoking battle heats up today with the issuance of the toughest government report ever on the hazards of secondhand smoke. "There is no disagreement," says the US surgeon general. "Cigarette smoking is deadly." No disagreement, if you discount, say, the Tobacco Institute, which fires back by denouncing the report as unfair and misleading. Emboldened antismoking activists have been turning up the heat with a ban on TV ads, mandatory nonsmoking sections on all domestic flights, and special package-label warnings for pregnant women. Big Tobacco obfuscates at every turn, but its secret memos, later made public, expose the hypocrisy. "Tobacco products, uniquely, contain and deliver nicotine, a potent drug with a variety of physiological effects," an internal R.J. Reynolds document divulges.

## AMERICA LOVES IT LOUD

Years before the term "reality television" came into vogue came the pioneering Loud family of Santa Barbara, California. In 1973, they agreed to put their daily lives under the microscope—or more accurately, before the camera—for *An American Family*, a groundbreaking twelve-hour PBS documentary. On January 11, America watched entranced as this messy real-life drama began to unfold: squabbles, spats, husband Bill's philandering (which triggered the couple's divorce). "It's as new and as significant as the invention of drama or the novel," said anthropologist Margaret Mead on television verité, "a new way in which people can learn to look at life." The next week, wife Pat visited eldest son Lance, the first openly gay person ever on American television, in New York City. Controversial and complex, *An American Family* remains an unequaled watershed television event.

> **As I was coming out of the closet, our car was hurtling over an embankment.**
>
> —Lance Loud

# JANUARY

## 1975

On the stage at Woodstock, raspy rocker Joe Cocker got by with more than a little help from tens of thousands of his friends. A master at converting others' compositions into his own, he'd already scored with two Beatles songs—the aforementioned "With a Little Help from My Friends" and "She Came in Through the Bathroom Window"—as well as with Leon Russell's "Delta Lady," Dave Mason's "Feelin' Alright," and his first Top Ten hit in the US, the remake of The Box Tops' "The Letter." Today Cocker hits the charts with, surprise surprise, the tender ballad "You Are So Beautiful," which in the weeks to follow becomes his biggest solo recording, winning him a whole new set of fans. In the coming year he duets on *Saturday Night Live* with John Belushi, gamely playing along as the actor does his (in)famous Cocker impersonation. But the notoriously hard-living singer thrives and survives, while the lampooning Belushi is the one who buys the farm in 1982 with a drug overdose.

"Some people thought we were presenting Archie as a false character— President Nixon thought we were making a fool out of a good man."

—Carroll O'Connor

# JANUARY 12

**1971** The stereo-typical sitcom of wholesome, homogenized families undergoes a shattering shift with Norman Lear's *All in the Family*. Bigoted archconservative patriarch Archie Bunker (Carroll O'Connor) mixes it up with just about everyone, from his long-haired, "dumb Pollock" son-in-law (Rob Reiner) to his dim but sweet "dingbat" wife (Jean Stapleton). "The best teevee comedy since the original *The Honeymooners*," raves *Variety*. "It must be seen to be believed." The show takes a couple months to catch on but quickly becomes TV's #1 series for five straight years, winning multiple awards and spinning off future successes like *Maude* and *The Jeffersons*.

# JANUARY 13

**1976** An imperious (aren't most of them?) impresario. Larger than life. Outspoken. And could drink most anybody under the table. Today Boston Opera cofounder Sarah Caldwell becomes the first woman to conduct (Verdi's *La Traviata*) at New York's Metropolitan Opera House. "Her whole life was one big improvisation," says longtime friend and opera singer Beverly Sills, "most of it inspired." Through the years Caldwell's theatrical staging helps create both fierce fans and detractors, while her financial irresponsibility leads to constant money troubles. Yet today's pioneering first caps a recent trifecta that includes appearing on the cover of *Time* magazine and leading a historic program of music by female composers held at the New York Philharmonic and sponsored by *Ms.* magazine.

## GOING OVERBROAD

In January 1972, local law enforcement swooped into a small Albany, Georgia, theater and arrested its manager on obscenity charges. The crime? Showing director Mike Nichols's recently released *Carnal Knowledge*. Instantly, the case became a lightning rod for the controversial film, which features sexually charged couplings among Jack Nicholson, Ann-Margaret (who was nominated for an Oscar for her role), Art Garfunkel, and Candice Bergen. While theater manager Billy Jenkins was tied up in court for the next year and a half, the film enjoyed a great run and made headlines in both the arts and business sections. In *Jenkins v. Georgia*, the US Supreme Court finally overturned the decisions of the lower courts—which ruled that the film constituted obscene material—and called Georgia's obscenity statutes "constitutionally overbroad, and therefore facially invalid." Overbroad, indeed. And they say the judiciary has no sense of humor.

# JANUARY 14

## 1972

Trying to get more competitive in the sitcom race, NBC is crazy as a Foxx. Redd Foxx, that is, the raunchy nightclub comedian recruited to star in *All in the Family* producer Norman Lear's adaptation of another British comedy, *Steptoe and Son*. On these shores it premieres tonight as *Sanford and Son*, with Foxx as a widowed, crotchety junkyard owner. Content with his plain little business, he mixes it up regularly with his go-getter of a son/business partner Lamont (Demond Wilson). It doesn't take much for ol' man Sanford to fake a heart attack ("Elizabeth! I'm comin' to join ya!"), either when Lamont threatens to end the partnership or, later in the series, when "ugly" Aunt Esther gets on his bad side. "It's impossible," says *TV Guide*, "despite his outrageous disreputableness, not to love him." In ratings, *Sanford* is no junker but a Top Ten hit from the get-go and for its entire five-season run.

# JANUARY 15

**1974** Perennial third-place finisher ABC proves that rock 'n' roll is really here to stay, welcoming the first of many *Happy Days* with the premiere of its new 1950s-based sitcom. Redhead Ron Howard (Opie on *The Andy Griffith Show*) stars, fresh off his success in director George Lucas's Eisenhower-era box-office smash, *American Graffiti*. But while the series initially focuses on Richie (Howard) and fellow high school pals, it really takes off by expanding the role of resident cool cat Arthur Fonzarelli (Henry Winkler), a.k.a. "The Fonz." His trademark "aaaayyys" and thumbs-ups help shoot the series to #1 in its third season, a performance that propels ABC to #1 in primetime for the first time ever. *Happy Days* spins off several other sitcoms, most successfully the Penny Marshall–Cindy Williams costarrer *Laverne & Shirley*.

**TRENDSETTER**

## UNDER A PIGSKIN MOON

The first nighttime Super Bowl aired in January 1972 on CBS, with a face-off between the Miami Dolphins and the Dallas Cowboys, who had lost the previous year's contest against the Baltimore Colts. Live from Tulane Stadium in New Orleans, the first Super Bowl under the lights was also the coldest ever, at a chilly 39°F. While the Cowboys had an added boost from starting quarterback Roger Staubach, the Dolphins had strategy help from President Nixon, who placed a late-night call to Dolphins coach Don Shula several weeks before the game to suggest a pass play. It didn't work, like most else for Miami that night, as the Cowboys cruised to a 24-3 victory. CBS scored a victory, too: the game garnered the highest ratings of any TV program to date. Miami would return the next season en route to back-to-back Super Bowl wins backboned by QB Bob Griese and running backs Larry Csonka and Jim Kiick. Then the Steel Curtain of Pittsburgh descended for four titles between 1975 and 1980.

# 16

**1976** She's a little bit country, he's a little bit…purple? From tonight's premiere on, few episodes of *Donny and Marie*—one of the last musical variety hours on primetime—go by without Marie Osmond poking fun at brother Donny's purple socks. The singing siblings take their cues from Sonny and Cher's recently departed, similarly formatted show: opening monologue with lots of good-natured joshing, fast-paced comedy skits, celebrity guests (Paul Lynde more often than not), and lots of musical numbers. Next year the clean-cut song-and-dance show takes yet one more cue from Sonny and Cher: Marie begins wearing glamorous outfits by showy designer Bob Mackie, who formerly did the honors for Cher— and Carol Burnett on her variety hour, too.

# JANUARY

**1971** O say, can you see...what's going on? Marvin Gaye kicks off Super Bowl V at Miami's Orange Bowl with the national anthem. It's a rare public sighting of the Motown star, who'd disappeared for nearly a year following the death of his singing partner, Tammi Terrell, of a brain tumor. Gaye briefly pursued the idea of a career in pro football, trying out unsuccessfully for the Detroit Lions. Still, he made new friends and invited several players into the studio, where they contributed background vocals on his unconventional single, "What's Going On." A 180-degree departure from his once sweet soul sound, the song so shocks Motown honcho Berry Gordy that he initially refuses to release it. After he relents, the *What's Going On* album produces three consciousness-raising Top Ten hits—the title track plus "Mercy Mercy Me (The Ecology)" and "Inner City Blues (Make Me Wanna Holler)"—driving Gaye's career to new heights. It all comes crashing down on April 1, 1984, the day before his forty-fifth birthday, when his father shoots him to death after an altercation.

# JANUARY

**1971** As Bob Dylan might say, you've gotta lot of nerve. One of the costs of fame, the influential singer/songwriter learns today, is the obsessive fan. A scruffy, self-styled "Dylanologist" who'd previously rumaged through Dylan's trash bags surreptitiously records a phone call with the reclusive musician. It soon appears briefly on Folkways Records as "Bob Dylan v. A.J. Weberman: The Historic Confrontation" until threats of legal action cause its quick withdrawal. "If I wasn't Bob Dylan," the singer says later, "I'd probably think Bob Dylan has a lot of answers myself." While his hectoring of Dylan brings the eccentric and radical Weberman his greatest notoriety, he later uses his garbology (his word) skills on other famous people like Norman Mailer.

# JANUARY

**1977** When Florida's Dade County passes an ordinance prohibiting discrimination on the basis of sexual orientation, Anita Bryant's off and ranting. "Homosexuals cannot biologically reproduce," cries the singer and spokeswoman for Florida orange juice (but not for long). "Therefore, they must recruit our children." With all the ingredients of a potboiler—sex and religion, with Bryant even breaking into "Battle Hymn of the Republic"—her Save Our Children campaign propels gay issues to newfound prominence. She publishes an autobiography, subtitled "The Survival of Our Nation's Families and the Threat of Militant Homosexuality." Several months later Dade voters repeal the law, and communities nationwide similarly vote to curb gay rights. Bryant's successes, however, inspire her opponents to unite against her. They organize a boycott of Florida orange juice and mount a comeback. The later defeat of a California initiative sends her forces reeling, and as the losses pile up, Bryant's career takes a nosedive from which it never recovers.

# JANUARY 20

**1978** At the peak of his considerable powers, savvy network TV programmer Fred Silverman has vaulted ABC from third place to first. With hits like *Three's Company* and *Charlie's Angels* (derisively dubbed "Jiggle TV"), he demonstrates the same Midas touch he showed earlier as a CBS producer with *All in the Family* and *The Waltons*, a performance that won him the job running ABC. Today the executive *Time* magazine famously calls "the man with the golden gut" jolts Hollywood as he bolts for NBC. But the third time isn't a charm. Shows like *Supertrain* and *Hello, Larry* bomb infamously. Relations sour so much with late-night franchise *Saturday Night Live* that John Belushi gleefully parodies Silverman on air: "When I took over NBC eleven short months ago," says Belushi, "I inherited shows that even I considered stupid and inane! I said to myself, 'If only I had a *Mork & Mindy*, if only I had a *New Newlywed Game*'...." Silverman's gone within a couple years, and so is the golden glow, but he does develop future hits like *Hill Street Blues* and *The Facts of Life*.

# JANUARY 21

**1978** How deep is Oscar's love for *Saturday Night Fever*? Not very. Today the film receives a paltry lone nomination, a best actor nod for John Travolta's portrayal of disco king Tony Manero. The ultimate snub comes in the original song category, where Academy of Motion Picture Arts and Sciences voters ignore all of the Bee Gees' chart-topping million-selling songs from the movie

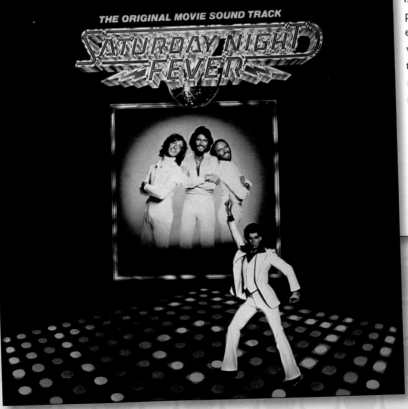

like "Stayin' Alive" and "How Deep Is Your Love." A spokesman for the producer grouses that the Academy consists of "retired violinists who probably still play 78s on their Victrolas." Interestingly, the movie itself is based on a *New York* magazine article later exposed as largely fictional. Nevertheless, its storyline embeds itself into popular culture, igniting the box office, dance floor gyrations, and dubious fashion choices for years to come.

# JANUARY 22

## 1973

Unimpressed with what he'd seen while scouting undefeated champ Joe Frazier (26-0), one of George Foreman's handlers advises, "George, drop that hammer on him." Tonight the young, three-to-one underdog unleashes an old-fashioned whuppin' on Smokin' Joe, who'd previously beaten Muhammad Ali. Knocking him down time and time again in the first round and into the second, Foreman finishes with a perfect right uppercut. Of the historic fight, which is still written about today, ESPN remarks, "The punch lifted the fireplug form of Frazier straight up in the air, defying gravity, like a tree stump pulled out of the ground." The referee stops the fight at 1:35, instantly silencing the pundits' snickering criticism that Big George's undefeated record (37-0) was not so impressive when you considered whom he'd beaten. Cable subscribers see the power-packed main event on new network HBO (see Nov. 8), in its first televised boxing match.

# JANUARY

## 23

**1977** Unsure of its potential, ABC schedules the expensive twelve-hour miniseries over eight consecutive nights, figuring that if it's a flop at least it will be over soon. Instead, Alex Haley's complex, compelling slave drama *Roots* captivates America and becomes the most-watched show in TV history to date. Featuring a rich, ethnically diverse ensemble cast and a star-making turn by young LeVar Burton as Kunta Kinte, *Roots*-mania envelops the country. Based on Haley's Pulitzer Prize–winning novel, it goes on to win nine Emmys and a Peabody Award. Half the country's population, one hundred million people, tune in to the January 30 finale. *Variety* notes the perils of broadcast TV: "The production and performances are strong....It was a bit disconcerting to cut from the anguished screams of a mother whose oldest son had been enslaved to a blurb for Ben-Gay, for use 'when pain is at its worst.'"

# JANUARY

## 24

**1970** Since inventor Robert Moog (rhymes with "vogue") pioneered the electric synthesizer in the late 1960s, it's had an enormous impact on music. With Walter Carlos's Grammy-winning *Switched on Bach* album plus his work on the soundtrack for *A Clockwork Orange*, along with The Beatles' "I Want You (She's So Heavy)" from *Abbey Road,* Moog becomes synonymous with the synthesizer. As a graduate student he'd studied and sold many kits for the theremin, a synthesizer precursor perhaps most notable for its use on The Beach Boys' "Good Vibrations." Today Moog introduces a $2,000 portable Mini-Moog synthesizer, transporting the sounds from the studio to the concert hall—or perhaps some venue less grand. "By 1974 or so," says Moog, "having a Mini-Moog would make it a lot easier to get a job playing the local Ramada Inn."

## JANUARY 25

**1973** It's a dog's life: *National Lampoon* runs its most (in)famous magazine cover this month, a shot of a docile pooch with a gun to its head and the tagline, "If You Don't Buy This Magazine We'll Kill This Dog." Notorious for such gleefully tasteless humor, the magazine was founded three years back by several ex-editors of the *Harvard Lampoon*. Tonight it branches beyond its print roots as its Woodstock (dubbed Woodchuck) parody *Lemmings* opens off Broadway after a successful run at a local NYC club. The stage show spoof combines "peace, love, and music" with mass suicide, much to the approval of Farmer Yasser. "Long hair, short hair," he enthuses, "what the hell's the difference once the head's blowed off?" John Belushi and Chevy Chase deliver tantalizing performances two years before the premiere of *Saturday Night Live*. Real artists and archetypes alike get the satirical treatment, such as the Motown Manifestos' danceable rendition of a Marx/Engels composition, "Papa Was a Running-Dog Lackey of the Bourgeoisie."

## JANUARY 26

**1977** Bohemian poetess and early underground punk-rock priestess Patti Smith slowly begins making a name for herself with a discordant, fevered sound. Moving from playing in small clubs like New York's CBGB, she opens tonight in Tampa for Bob Seger & the Silver Bullet Band (red hot with "Night Moves"). But mid-set the hyperactive singer makes a bad night move by gyrating and falling offstage, fracturing two vertebrae and sustaining head lacerations that require twenty-two stitches to close. "I got a big plaster cast on my neck," she says later, "and a Sex Pistols haircut." After a period of enforced recuperation she releases her most commercial album, *Easter,* with a more straightforward rock sound that includes "Because the Night," her biggest single, cowritten with Bruce Springsteen. It came about because while Patti was laying down her album, the Boss was in the studio next door recording *Darkness on the Edge of Town.*

## JANUARY 27

**1974** Playing a swaggering street punk in director Martin Scorsese's visceral, violent *Mean Streets*, Brooklyn native Harvey Keitel is making quite the name for himself. Tonight he shows a completely different, more beneficent side while dining at Sardi's in New York. Film critic Hollis Alpert, cofounder of the National Society of Film Critics, is eating nearby with his wife, Joan Alpert, when she begins choking on a piece of steak and loses consciousness. Quick-thinking Keitel leaps to her aid, holding her upside down until she coughs up the food—not exactly the Heimlich maneuver (see June 14), but effective. Meanwhile, *Mean Streets* is also helping launch the careers of its director and another young bad boy, Robert De Niro.

# WE INTERRUPT THIS PROGRAM...

Out they walked onto the White House stage: eight women in pale-blue gowns, eight men in light-blue blazers. It was the Ray Conniff Singers, an establishment sound for an establishment crowd celebrating the fiftieth anniversary of *Reader's Digest* on January 28, 1972. Outside, the antiwar protests may have been reverberating, but inside...well, tonight they were in the White House, too, in the unexpected form of singer Carol Feraci. Before the first song could even begin she unfurled a banner that read, "Stop the Killing." Then she launched into a lecture: "President Nixon, stop bombing human beings, animals, and vegetation. You go to church on Sundays and pray to Jesus Christ. If Jesus Christ were here tonight, you would not dare to drop another bomb. Bless the Berrigans and bless Daniel Ellsberg." The audience sat stunned. Conniff, a longtime Nixon supporter, got the group to launch into a song, but the audience had already turned. They kick Feraci out, and the media is unleashed. "Look What She Did to His Song!" cried one newspaper. Though her notoriety faded almost instantly, Feraci's brazen stunt foreshadowed Nixon's future fall.

## JANUARY 28

**1978** It's the perfect pair, for light escapist fare. With Tattoo's cry of "dee plane...dee plaaaaaane!" the first trio of celebrity-heavy guests arrive on remote, alluring *Fantasy Island*. The ABC romantic drama opens tonight following the cruise comedy *The Love Boat*. Both come from prolific producer Aaron Spelling, whose mesmerizing hold over Saturday night confounds ABC's competitors for the next few years. The island's mysterious overseer (Ricardo Montalban) makes sure his guests' dreams come true, with help from midget servant Tattoo (Herve Villechaize). Never is it mentioned whether guest accommodations include anything made of fine Corinthian leather—a much-parodied phrase from Montalban's commercials for the luxury Chrysler Cordoba that earns him as much, if not more, fame than his acting career.

## JANUARY 29

**1979** Reading, writing, and...rifles?! Long-haired Brenda Ann Spencer, 16, wanted a radio for Christmas. Her father gave her a rifle instead. Today she opens fire at the elementary school across the street from her San Diego home, killing two—the principal and a janitor—and wounding eight. When asked why she did it, Spencer replies with a shrug, "I don't like Mondays." Budding punk rocker Bob Geldof reads the story and quickly pens a song for his band, the Boomtown Rats. "I Don't Like Mondays" shoots to #1 in the UK and many other countries, but in the United States reaches only #73 after many stations refuse to play it. Previously an unheard of and unimagined horror, the lethal youthful rampage sadly proves to be the first of many. "With every school shooting," Spencer (who is serving twenty-five years to life) says later, "I feel partially responsible. What if they got their idea from what I did?"

**1971** "We never, evah, do anything nice and easy…" So warns Tina Turner at the outset of "Proud Mary," a remake of the original, sorta sleepy Creedence Clearwater Revival tune that's become a staple of wedding bands everywhere. Ike and Tina torch the number with a raucous, rip-roaring treatment that hits the charts today, on the way to becoming the biggest hit in their stormy fifteen-year career together. Five years later, Tina proves that personally she doesn't do anything nice and easy either when she abruptly splits from abusive, manipulative manager/husband Ike. When he first discovered Tina (born Anna Mae Bullock) in the late 1950s, she might have indeed been "A Fool in Love," the title of their first single. But out on her own, after battling through some long, tough years Tina re-emerges in the early 1980s, bigger and better than ever, with "What's Love Got to Do with It" and a solo career that eclipses all earlier efforts.

**1974** She may be a little slip of a thing, but she's really hard to miss. She's Cicely Tyson, and she has a huge effect on America's consciousness with the debut of the CBS special, *The Autobiography of Miss Jean Pittman*. It tells a fictionalized tale of a 110-year-old former slave recalling her life in a series of flashbacks from the Civil War to the civil rights movement of the 1960s. Tyson convincingly plays her character at a multitude of ages, generating universal acclaim. In May that translates into two Emmy Awards, winning actress of the year (for a special) and lead actress in a drama, over a strong field of Carole Burnett, Katharine Hepburn, Cloris Leachman, and Elizabeth Montgomery. The special wins seven more awards including for director and screenplay, a triumph that *Variety* says "overshadowed everything else in the annual event."

# FEBRUARY

## 1976

"The miniseries has arrived!" trumpets the *New York Daily News* as ABC premieres its ambitious twelve-hour *Rich Man, Poor Man*. Adapted from novelist Irwin Shaw's best-seller, it begins tonight with the first of six two-hour movies. Costarring a relatively unknown trio—Susan Blakely, Nick Nolte, and Peter Strauss—the blockbuster smartly mixes in recognizable guest stars (like Ed Asner and Fionnula Flanagan, who each win Emmys) and reinvigorates the art of adapting books into topical, soapy serials. It generates huge ratings and helps usher in a golden age of miniseries a full year before *Roots* arrives and rewrites the record books. Nominated for a record twenty-three Emmy nominations, it's somewhat snubbed by the Academy with only four wins, but returns next season with Book II.

# FEBRUARY

## 1973

Sizzling onscreen in gay Paree, *Last Tango in Paris* hits a roadblock in Rome. An obscenity case has yanked it from all Italian cinemas, threatening costars Marlon Brando and Maria Schneider with eight-month prison terms. Today a court in Bologna lifts the ban and acquits all defendants, including director Bernardo Bertolucci, of obscenity charges. The X-rated film continues to enrage and enthrall, with feminists pillorying the sexual humiliation of its lead actress, the unknown Schneider, in a role nixed by French leading ladies Dominique Sanda and Catherine Deneuve. Complex and confounding, the film features a ferocious turn by notoriously difficult Brando under the director's firm hand. "I think that what he was feeling," says Bertolucci of Brando's graphic role, "was the intense horror—and fascination—of the intrusion upon his intimacy."

# FEBRUARY

## 1973

Portentous, prodigious rock—can you dig it? The Moody Blues's "Nights in White Satin," one of the most classic "classic rock" songs of all time, has become, five years after its original release, the biggest hit of their career. No longer the raw R&B British Invasion band from Birmingham ("Go Now!"), the Moodies shuffled their lineup, adding catalyst Justin Hayward after the departure of Denny Laine (now in Paul McCartney's post-Beatles group Wings). A new, lush symphonic sound generated an ambitious concept album, *Days of Future Passed*, recorded with the London Festival Orchestra. But the album's anthem, "Nights in White Satin," proved too futuristic for American Top 40 radio in 1967. Not the case in 1972, though, when the Moodies' record label re-released the single after the group enjoyed a string of hit albums and singles in America. They follow the #2 hit with the song hitting the pop chart today: "I'm Just a Singer (in a Rock and Roll Band)," from their just-released seventh album *Seventh Sojourn*. The hard-driving rocker is the Moody Blues's last big hit for nearly a decade, as the singers in this rock and roll band decide to part ways until a reunion—this time for good—in 1978.

**MEANWHILE...**

## THE WORST OF HEARST

From unknown, pampered heiress to notorious celebrity bank robber—the strange saga of Patricia Hearst, age nineteen, began on February 4, 1974, when she was kidnapped from her Berkeley, California, apartment by a little-known urban guerrilla group called the Symbionese Liberation Army. Blanket media coverage erupted as talk of prisoner swaps and ransoms swirled. Soon, a photo of a gun-toting Hearst and stories of her participation in a bank robbery turned her from kidnappee to fugitive. Arrested eighteen months later for bank robbery, Hearst claimed coercion, but her famed defense attorney, F. Lee Bailey, presented a weak case. After she was convicted she served twenty-two months in prison before being pardoned by President Carter.

**❝Given the choice of being released...or joining the forces of the Symbionese Liberation Army and fighting for my freedom and the freedom of all oppressed people, I have chosen to stay and fight.❞**

—Patty Hearst

# FEBRUARY 4

**1970** He's a gruff, tough son of a...gun. He's General George S. Patton, of whom actor George C. Scott makes a commanding presence in the rousing movie *Patton*. Others who'd vied for the role included Robert Mitchum, Burt Lancaster, Lee Marvin, Rod Steiger, and John Wayne—tough guys all. Scott soon proves that his gruff persona extends beyond the screen. Universally praised for his bravura turn, the cantankerous Scott wins and then famously declines the Oscar. Today, though, it's all smiles as he, Karl Malden, and General Omar Bradley, a production consultant, attend its premiere. The film delivers a strong patriotic message at a time when the Vietnam War is growing increasingly unpopular. President Nixon watches it several times before announcing his plans to send troops into Cambodia beginning next month.

# FEBRUARY 5

**1972** Whatever happened to the "friendly skies"? Five airplanes have been hijacked since January 1, a sharp increase over last year's total of twenty-five. Optional screenings have proved ineffective, as has putting anonymous air marshals on domestic flights. "It's been a farce since its inception," grouses one unnamed airline executive. So today the Federal Aviation Administration institutes the first mandatory screening of passengers and their baggage on all domestic and foreign flights by US airlines. "A majority of the air piracies committed recently would have been prevented had the system been used to the fullest extent possible," says an FAA administrator. Its components include weapon detection devices, body searches, the requirement for passengers to show identification, and psychological profiling. Air travel is never the same again.

**1970** In a Los Angeles court, lawyers reveal for the first time that The Beatles' lyrics "helter skelter" had been scrawled in blood at the scene of the grisly deaths of pregnant actress Sharon Tate, wife of director Roman Polanski (*Rosemary's Baby*), and four others. The sensationalistic, circus-like story takes a new, odd turn as it now delves into the mind of Beatles-obsessed ringleader Charles Manson. Lawyers threaten to subpoena John and Paul, and while that doesn't happen their song "Helter Skelter" is later played during the trial. After the Manson family convictions, the prosecuting district attorney writes a tell-all book entitled *Helter Skelter: The True Story of the Manson Murders*.

# FEBRUARY

# 7

**1974** Return with us now to those thrilling days of yesteryear...when cowboys punched out their horses, gunslingers regularly hit the sauce, and Howard Johnson's had only one flavor of ice cream. Yes, it's *Blazing Saddles*, a skewed view of the Wild West as only Mel Brooks could see it. His uproarious tale features an ensemble cast including Harvey Korman as villainous Hedley Lamarr, Cleavon Little as a most unlikely sheriff, Madeline Kahn as seductress Lily von Shtupp, Gene Wilder, Slim Pickens, and others. Before the year's out Brooks debuts another monster big-screen comedy, the spoof *Young Frankenstein*. Later he sets his sights on Alfred Hitchcock with *High Anxiety*, and then the pre-talkie era with *Silent Movie*. Most enduringly, after seeing *Blazing Saddles*, eating a pot of beans will never be the same.

# FEBRUARY

**1976** "You talkin' to me?" Robert De Niro explodes and implodes in Martin Scorsese's disturbing, violent *Taxi Driver*. Writer Paul Schrader (who'll later team again with Scorsese for *Raging Bull*) paints a dark, brooding setting with matching characters that symbolize America's alienated urban jungle. "New York may have changed," writes *Time Out*, "but *Taxi Driver* is as powerful and painful as ever." The strong supporting cast includes Cybill Shepherd, Harvey Keitel, and, most controversially, thirteen-year-old Jodie Foster as a child prostitute. The film wins the prestigious Palme d'Or at Cannes, and De Niro takes the New York Film Critics Circle award. His manic performance is definitely not to be confused with that of his pal Danny DeVito in the forthcoming 1978 sitcom *Taxi*.

# FEBRUARY

**1973** Shot on a shoestring budget, independent filmmaker Perry Henzell's visceral *The Harder They Come* introduces reggae music to a worldwide audience. Featuring charismatic Jimmy Cliff as a budding singer turned outlaw, it offers a richly nuanced slice of the music- and ganja-drenched life of gritty Kingston, Jamaica, mon. Since some of its characters' thickly accented English proves difficult to decipher, it even adds English subtitles to some scenes. But what's instantly discoverable to all is its hypnotic reggae beat, with a killer soundtrack including Cliff doing the title track and two more, "You Can Get It If You Really Want" and "Many Rivers to Cross," plus Toots & the Maytals, Desmond Dekker, and others. A tough, crude, unforgettable opening salvo that lays bare the roots of a music about to introduce its first superstar, Bob Marley (see July 16).

# FEBRUARY 10

**1977** Live music—with no strings attached! Rock 'n' roll singers didn't always prance about on stage. Or if they did, they could easily become entangled in their microphone cords. Today *Rolling Stone* magazine touts rock's newest high-tech handheld: the wireless mike, soon joined by the wireless guitar hookup. Acts like Aerosmith, the Rolling Stones, Styx, and Neil Young snap 'em up. "The wireless microphone has been around since the late 1940s," says John Nady, an inventor who helped perfect the miniaturized devices. "They were two feet long, they had tubes in them, and the audio quality was terrible." Soon major manufacturers like Shure, AKG, Sennheiser, and others leap into the market, with prices going down and sales going up.

# FEBRUARY

**||||** **1975** Partners and politics mix as Hal Ashby's frothy *Shampoo* opens. Warren Beatty stars as a seductive hairdresser sorting out amorous adventures—amid Julie Christie, Goldie Hawn, Carrie Fischer, and Oscar-winner Lee Grant—all on the eve of Richard Nixon's election as president in 1968. Against the real-life backdrop of Watergate and Nixon's astounding resignation six months earlier, the sharp satire of social and sexual mores proves especially, deliciously topical. Moviegoers make it the year's fourth-highest-grossing film, behind *Jaws, One Flew Over the Cuckoo's Nest,* and *The Rocky Picture Horror Show.*

# FEBRUARY

**||2** **1975** Something sinister lurks behind a blissful suburban facade in *The Stepford Wives,* the film based on Ira Levin's chilling best-seller. And that something sears into popular culture vernacular now and forever as a term for blind, thoughtless obedience—what new suburbanites Katharine Ross and Paula Prentice discover when moving to the quaint Connecticut town of Stepford. Inferior sequels milking the unsettling premise follow, though master storyteller Levin (*Rosemary's Baby*) pushes on to new frights. "[His] suspense is beautifully intertwined with everyday incidents," writes one reviewer. "The delicate line between belief and disbelief is faultlessly drawn." Next Levin delivers a dose of reconstituted Nazism in *The Boys from Brazil,* as well as the elaborate puzzler *Deathtrap,* each of which spawns feature films.

MEANWHILE...

## MEETING THE BOTTOM LINE

Disproving his lone Top 10 chart success, "Right Place Wrong Time," Mac Rebennack (a.k.a. Dr. John) made The Bottom Line—which opened on February 12, 1974—the right place at the right time, as it quickly ascended to become the Big Apple's top club venue. Jaded New Yorkers who thought they'd seen it all were in for an unprecedented jolt of psychedelic blues voodoo as the bearded longhair, sporting a feathered headdress and Technicolor robes, prowled the stage sprinkling tinsel and singing, "They call me Dr. John, the night tripper, the gris-gris man..." from the song "Gris-Gris Gumbo Ya-Ya." The glittery audience included Mick Jagger, Carly Simon, and James Taylor (who went on to play Carnegie Hall while his younger brother Livingston stayed here). Odd couple Stevie Wonder and Johnny Winter even joined the New Orleans boogie man on stage for some impromptu jamming. Within a couple months, the club was attracting an eclectic musical mix including Canned Heat, Elvin Bishop, Average White Band, Jerry Reed, and jazz rocker Billy Cobham.

# FEBRUARY

# 13

**1971** After 1970 witnesses the breakup of The Beatles, Simon and Garfunkel, and Crosby, Stills, Nash & Young, many fear there'll be no big-selling recording acts this year. Into the void leaps bubblegum pop of those oh-so-cute-and-perky Osmonds whose "One Bad Apple" is one smash, topping the chart for five weeks beginning today. Drawing inevitable comparisons to the high-steppin', harmonizing Jackson Five, the Osmonds continue to rack up hits while breakout brother Donny simultaneously scores with solo songs like "Go Away Little Girl" and "Puppy Love." Discovered on Andy Williams's TV variety series, the bubbly group sells nearly eleven million records by years' end. Other melodious, family-oriented entertainers include The Cowsills and David Cassidy and the Partridge Family ("I Think I Love You").

# LIKE MOTHER, LIKE DAUGHTER

o one was hotter in 1972 than Liza Minelli, who netted both an scar for *Cabaret* (which was released in February) and an Emmy r her television special *Liza with a Z*. Taped at *New York's* Ly- um Theater, her sizzling live performance featured standards like God Bless the Child" and pop numbers like "Son of a Preacher an." "Minnelli has such gaiety and electricity that she becomes a ar before our eyes," gushed *New Yorker* critic Pauline Kael. "She still Judy Garland's daughter, but now she is her own voice." Bob osse was equally—if not more—hot, as he successfully re-created e decadence, debauchery, and desperation of the original *Cabaret* n the big screen. The film swept eight Oscar categories, including irecting (beating out Francis Ford Coppola's *The Godfather*, which nly won three). Fosse later completed an unprecedented Triple rown, adding a Tony for *Pippin* before the year was out. He capped e decade with another musical tour de force, his autobiographical *ll That Jazz*.

## FEBRUARY 1972 14

Nostalgia has a way of ebbing and flowing, and on this night it becomes a torrent as *Grease* opens at New York's Eden Theater. The circa late-1950s rock musical features Barry Bostwick and Carole Demas, and though critics aren't too enthusiastic, the public is. With its angsty adolescent love, slicked-up gangs, and class (not classroom) conflict, it's a junior *West Side Story* with a lot less weight but plenty of groovy rock 'n' roll. Though it wins no Tony Awards, it runs clear into the 1980s and becomes Broadway's longest-running musical 'til being eclipsed by *A Chorus Line*. Six years later a movie version fuels the *Grease* fire, solidifying the status of *Saturday Night Fever* star John Travolta and elevating song-and-dance partner Olivia Newton-John. The big-screen *Grease* becomes 1978's top box office draw, featuring three songs whose success spills over to the pop charts—"You're the One That I Want," "Hopelessly Devoted to You," and, interestingly enough, "Grease"—none of which were in the stage original.

## FEBRUARY 1977 15

Appearing on the *Today* show to promote her latest book. Meeting with chemists to discuss her new cosmetics line. Showing her apartment in anticipation of moving to a larger one. All activities in a typical week for entrepreneurial designer Diane von Furstenberg, who nevertheless kept her daily twenty-minute exercise routine this morning before sitting down with a newspaper reporter. Her marriage to Prince Egon von Furstenberg brought her royalty, family (two children), wealth, and the desire to pursue a career, which she tackled after their divorce. Today her fashion empire, backboned by the trademark wrap dress that has sold five million units, includes cosmetics, lingerie, jewelry, and a new perfume, Tatiana, named for her daughter who turns six tomorrow. "I believe in marrying fashion and function," she says. "Chic style and easy comfort, maximum impact, and minimum fuss."

# FEBRUARY 16 1977

Stark and dark David Mamet opens a tense thieves den, *American Buffalo*, on Broadway with Robert Duvall and John Savage starring. Teeming with intense characters and incisive, vulgar dialogue, the play wins the New York Drama Critics Circle award. Mamet keeps delivering a torrent of topical theatricals including *Glengarry Glen Ross*, a savage ensemble tragedy about shady real-estate salesmen peddling worthless parcels of land in Florida that wins a Pulitzer Prize, and later becomes a movie with Jack Lemmon and Al Pacino. "Always tell the truth," says Mamet. "It's the easiest thing to remember." Nearly two decades after Broadway theater buffs shuffle off to *American Buffalo*, a film version opens starring Dustin Hoffman and Dennis Franz.

# FEBRUARY 17 1972

Obscenity is in the eyes of the Supreme Court today as Ralph Ginzburg begins serving a three-year jail sentence. Convicted in 1963 of distributing the magazine *Eros*, he busted taboos and became embroiled in many legal run-ins. "'Obscenity' or 'pornography' is a crime without definition or victim," he says. "It is a bag of smoke used to conceal one's own dislikes with regard to aspects of sex." The Supreme Court rules not on *Eros*' content but its promotion, holding that if "the purveyor's sole emphasis is on the sexually provocative aspects of his publications," that could constitute obscenity. The Sexual Revolution gains a martyr, but Ginzburg ultimately becomes a pariah. "I have always felt that I might have become a major force in American publishing had it not been for my conviction," says Ginzburg, who later penned an autobiography, *Castrated: My Eight Months in Prison*. "Instead, I'm just a curious footnote."

# FEBRUARY 18 1973

No little feat, this. Led by idiosyncratic genius Lowell George, Little Feat releases its third album, the tasty *Dixie Chicken*. With George's seductive vocals and a backing boogie beat, the band tours incessantly, attracting an adoring but limited fan base. Breakout status eludes them. The band splits up, reforms, and after another critically acclaimed album, *Feats Don't Fail Me Now*, it finally takes off. Traveling in a Warner Bros. UK tour in early 1975, Little Feat blows away headliners the Doobie Brothers, Montrose, and Tower of Power. Their all-too-brief subsequent success ends when George, 34, dies of a heart attack on June 29, 1979. "Lowell George is the best singer, songwriter, and guitar player ever—hands down," says Bonnie Raitt, who performs at a fundraiser for his family that fall at the Forum in LA along with Jackson Browne, Emmylou Harris, and Linda Ronstadt.

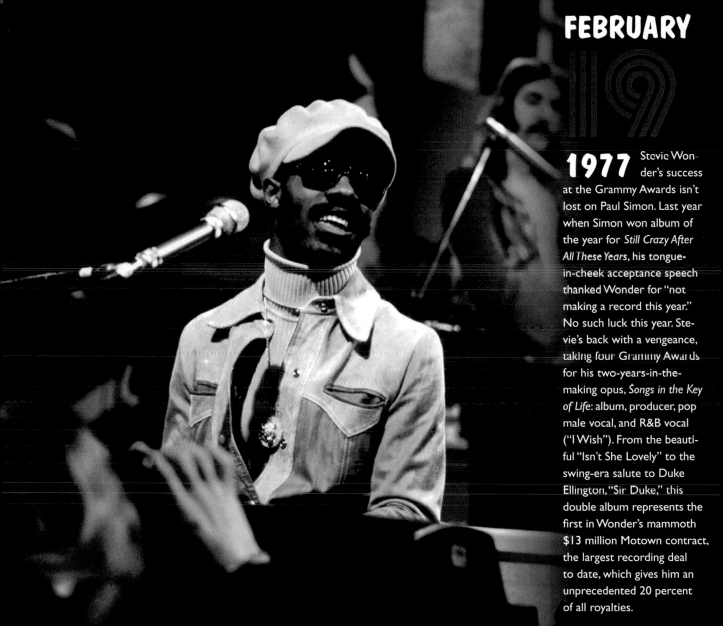

**1977** Stevie Wonder's success at the Grammy Awards isn't lost on Paul Simon. Last year when Simon won album of the year for *Still Crazy After All These Years*, his tongue-in-cheek acceptance speech thanked Wonder for "not making a record this year." No such luck this year. Stevie's back with a vengeance, taking four Grammy Awards for his two-years-in-the-making opus, *Songs in the Key of Life*: album, producer, pop male vocal, and R&B vocal ("I Wish"). From the beautiful "Isn't She Lovely" to the swing-era salute to Duke Ellington, "Sir Duke," this double album represents the first in Wonder's mammoth $13 million Motown contract, the largest recording deal to date, which gives him an unprecedented 20 percent of all royalties.

# FEBRUARY

# 20

## 1971

Saturday morning, 9:33: the AP and UPI wires read **"THIS IS AN EMERGENCY ACTION NOTIFICATION DIRECTED BY THE PRESIDENT. NORMAL BROADCASTING WILL CEASE IMMEDIATELY."** And for the next panicked forty minutes, many radio and TV stations do just that. The false alert triggers fears of an impending nuclear attack, and flashbacks to Pearl Harbor or the assassination of JFK. Turns out it's all due to human error, a plain old tape mix-up. Not tape as in videotape, but as in punched-paper strips transmitted on Teletype machines. Wrong tape, wrong message, big mistake. From the massive concrete bunker warning center deep in the mountains of Colorado, the fifteen-year veteran employee responsible later says, "I can't imagine how the hell I did it."

## FEBRUARY

**1971** It's a beauti ful day in the Treasure House. Captain Kangaroo has had lots of special guests on his show, from Pearl Bailey to Minnie Pearl to the Smothers Brothers. Today he welcomes his friendly competitor, Mister Rogers, after experts suggest that children's emotional security can be enhanced by seeing that their two favorites are friends. Captain Kangaroo (Bob Keeshan) had spread a little love around the neighborhood two weeks before by visiting Mister Rogers's show, and now the circle is complete. The idea's such a success that Mister Rogers later does a double dip with Big Bird, appearing on *Sesame Street* and inviting the big feathered fellow into his neighborhood, with a similar turn later on the animated series *Arthur*.

## FEBRUARY 21

**1970** Today straightforward rockers Creedence Clearwater Revival grace the cover of *Rolling Stone*, a deserved honor. In the past year alone they've scored three Top Ten albums and seven Top Ten songs, including two this week. Like many of their releases, one side's a slice of pure swamp rock ("Travelin' Band") while the other ("Who'll Stop the Rain?") is a protest song. "You want [people] to listen, especially if you're gonna say something that sort of reaches beyond normal entertainment," says band leader John Fogarty. "We've got enough goin' against us just because we have long hair." (Actually, every cover subject in *Rolling Stone* this year has long hair.) CCR later gets in a spot of trouble for "Travelin' Band" when copyright holders for Little Richard's library file a lawsuit claiming it's based on "Good Golly Miss Molly."

# FEBRUARY

## 23

**1971** Only fourteen minutes into its airing, CBS's explosive documentary *The Selling of the Pentagon* begins generating phone calls in protest. Narrated by Roger Mudd, its examination of Defense Department public relations campaigns to shape coverage of the military industrial complex exacerbates and escalates. Outraged congressmen attack its interview techniques that splice together disparate segments, claiming it shows bias. A landmark First Amendment case emerges as CBS president Frank Stanton refuses to back down, claiming "a duty to uphold the freedom of the broadcast press against congressional abridgment." The furor intensifies with the publishing of the Pentagon Papers by *The New York Times*, but contempt complaints against the controversial program eventually fail. Nevertheless, the press celebrates a decisive ruling against governmental interference.

# FEBRUARY

## 24

**1973** At the top of the charts today, Roberta Flack's "Killing Me Softly with His Song" is that rare instance of a #1 song inspired by another singer's #1. That tune? Don McLean's "American Pie," which singer Lori Lieberman had heard him play at LA's noted nightclub, the Troubadour. She jotted down the phrase "killing me softly," which a songwriting duo fleshed out into the song. Lieberman's version attracts little attention, but Flack hears it and records an ethereal, five-minute masterpiece that, like her first #1 ("The First Time Ever I Saw Your Face"), sounds like nothing else on the radio. "I've been told I sound like Nina Simone, Nancy Wilson, Odetta, Barbra Streisand, Dionne Warwick, even Mahalia Jackson," says Flack. "If everybody said I sounded like one person, I'd worry. But when they say I sound like them all, I know I've got my own style."

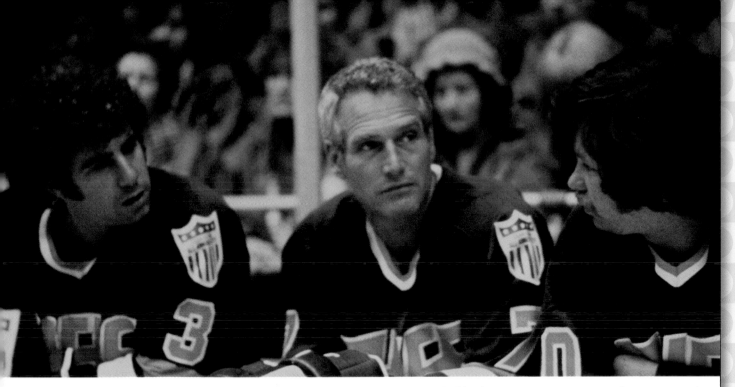

## FEBRUARY 25

**1977** Raw, raunchy, and rowdy, director George Roy Hill's *Slap Shot* shoots into theaters—and scooores! Paul Newman shines as an aging player coach of a minor league hockey team that's short on talent but long on fisticuffs. Their grueling, grinding season suddenly improves in direct proportion to their escalating level of violence, thanks largely to the arrival of the young'un Hanson Brothers (years before the adolescent band of the same name). Its blue language arouses instant media attention and notoriety, which even lingers for its lead. "There's a hangover from characters sometimes," says Newman. "There are things that stick. Since *Slap Shot*, my language is right out of the locker room." Which is exactly where screenwriter Nancy Dowd got a lot of the dialogue, learning from her brother, a former minor league hockey player and bit player in the film.

## FEBRUARY 26

**1970** Troubled times: Simon and Garfunkel's soothing "Bridge Over Troubled Water" soars today to #1 and holds that spot for six weeks, making it the year's biggest single. But ironically, behind the scenes the duo's tension-ridden professional relationship is crumbling. The recording sessions for the album of the same name prove rocky, as Art Garfunkel is often away filming his debut movie role in Mike Nichols's *Catch-22*. Paul Simon wrote the song (like virtually every S&G song), but later regrets allowing his partner to sing solo. It's the last studio album of new material they'll ever produce.

# FEBRUARY 27

**1977** Alarmed by what he sees as a proliferation of sex and violence on the small screen, conservative Mississippi clergyman Donald Wildmon launches "Turn the Television Off Week" with a national day of prayer. "Profit," says Wildmon, "that is what television is all about, and that's where we are aiming." Though he claims that thousands of churches and synagogues have agreed to join in, results appear nonexistent. One TV exec privately jokes that when the ratings are high enough, "sex and violence become love and adventure." But the religious right is just beginning to flex its muscles, and in 1979 an even more influential preacher, Jerry Falwell, founds the Moral Majority. "The idea that religion and politics don't mix," he says, "was invented by the devil to keep Christians from running their own country."

## MEANWHILE...

## THE WALKING WOUNDED

While the battles of cowboys and Indians are usually relegated to the distant past, a modern-day confrontation erupted in the 1970s. On February 27, 1973, the American Indian Movement (AIM) held protests in Wounded Knee, South Dakota. As most Americans knew from the 1970 book *Bury My Heart at Wounded Knee* by Dee Brown, the tiny town was the site of an 1890 massacre of three hundred Lakota Indians. Led by activist Russell Means, the protestors seized the town in an attempt to spotlight current Native American issues—poverty, poor health, substandard housing, and a longstanding federal policy marked by neglect, prejudice, and corruption. The tense standoff drew round-the-clock media coverage, and continued for seventy-one days. In the end two people were killed, twelve were wounded, and nearly twelve hundred were arrested.

# FEBRUARY 28

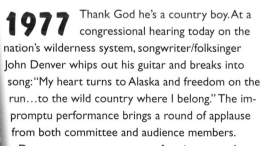

**1977** Thank God he's a country boy. At a congressional hearing today on the nation's wilderness system, songwriter/folksinger John Denver whips out his guitar and breaks into song: "My heart turns to Alaska and freedom on the run…to the wild country where I belong." The impromptu performance brings a round of applause from both committee and audience members. Denver, a strong supporter of environmental causes, had met briefly yesterday with President and Mrs. Carter at the White House. While his Top 10 days are over, he still exudes that grinning all-American image, and on tour draws packed houses for his gentle lyrics of peace and harmony on hits like "Rocky Mountain High" and "Annie's Song."

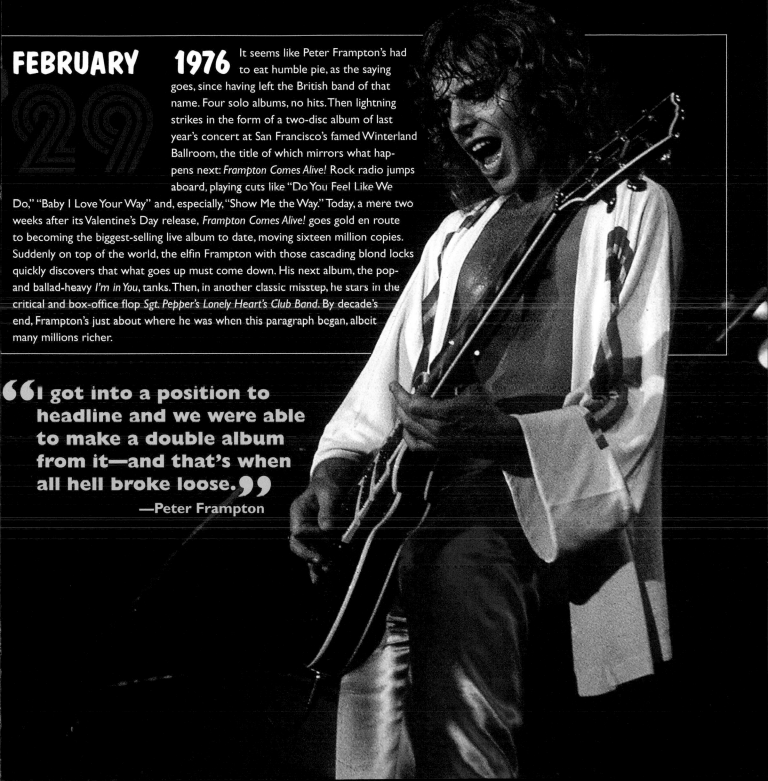

# FEBRUARY 1976

**29**

It seems like Peter Frampton's had to eat humble pie, as the saying goes, since having left the British band of that name. Four solo albums, no hits. Then lightning strikes in the form of a two-disc album of last year's concert at San Francisco's famed Winterland Ballroom, the title of which mirrors what happens next: *Frampton Comes Alive!* Rock radio jumps aboard, playing cuts like "Do You Feel Like We Do," "Baby I Love Your Way" and, especially, "Show Me the Way." Today, a mere two weeks after its Valentine's Day release, *Frampton Comes Alive!* goes gold en route to becoming the biggest-selling live album to date, moving sixteen million copies. Suddenly on top of the world, the elfin Frampton with those cascading blond locks quickly discovers that what goes up must come down. His next album, the pop- and ballad-heavy *I'm in You*, tanks. Then, in another classic misstep, he stars in the critical and box-office flop *Sgt. Pepper's Lonely Heart's Club Band.* By decade's end, Frampton's just about where he was when this paragraph began, albeit many millions richer.

**“I got into a position to headline and we were able to make a double album from it—and that's when all hell broke loose.”**
—Peter Frampton

# MARCH

## 1979

It's no contest as Stephen Sondheim's malevolently magnetic *Sweeney Todd* slaughters the competition on Broadway. From tonight's opening line—"Attend the tale of Sweeney Todd"—the production instantly transports theatergoers to nineteenth-century London, where the barbarous barber of Fleet Street (Len Cariou) does his grisly work. Director Harold Prince's musicalized stew of escapism and fantasy, sex and sexuality captivates as Todd's landlady/shop owner, Mrs. Lovett (Angela Lansbury), churns out tasty meat pies. Based on a blood-soaked tale first presented on the London stage in 1847, *Todd* goes on to sweep eight Tony Awards including best musical, actor (Cariou), actress (Lansbury), director, score, costume, and scenic design, plus nine Drama Desk Awards.

# MARCH

## 1978

In the early-morning hours, thieves commit a grave offense—snatching the body of Charlie Chaplin from a tiny Swiss cemetery. The film legend, who'd died last Christmas Day, had lived quietly with his family in a baronial estate overlooking Lake Geneva for the last quarter century. He'd departed the United States at the height of the Cold War, attacked for his outspoken leftist views. "I am appalled by this gruesome and sacrilegious act," says Britain's ambassador to Switzerland, while the actor's widow, Lady Oona Chaplin (daughter of playwright Eugene O'Neill), offers a different take: "Charlie would have thought it ridiculous." Several months later police recover the body in a cornfield ten miles away and arrest two Eastern European refugees who are later convicted of theft and extortion. The body is reburied under more than six feet of concrete.

# MARCH

## 1973

Looking back, Reginald Dwight probably doesn't regret not getting that King Crimson gig. A few years back he'd auditioned, unsuccessfully, for lead singer of Robert Fripp's band. Since then he's changed his name to Elton John ("Elton" borrowed from a former bandmate, "John" for British bluesman Long John Baldry), met lyricist Bernie Taupin, and has become an international superstar. Today *Don't Shoot Me, I'm Only the Piano Player* becomes the second of seven albums in three short years to reach #1 in America. It includes his first #1 single, "Crocodile Rock," as well as the ballad "Daniel," which just misses at #2. But Elton's just getting started. In May he forms Rocket Records, named for last year's hit, "Rocket Man." This fall, in the midst of a forty-two-date US tour, he headlines the Hollywood Bowl, where porn star Linda Lovelace emcees. Over the next three years he'll score five more #1's, and two of his studio albums—*Captain Fantastic and the Brown Dirt Cowboy* and *Rock of the Westies*—become the first in history to debut at the top of the US album chart.

# MARCH 4

**1974** Ready or not, here comes the wave of the future: celebrity-based quasi journalism. Today a heavily coiffed Mia Farrow, biting a string of pearls, graces the cover of the first *People* magazine. She's starring in the lavish Paramount remake of *The Great Gatsby* opposite Robert Redford. Dazzling star wattage, dim results. From venerable publishers Time, Inc., *People* bows with more features on Gloria Vanderbilt and Alexander Solzhenitsyn. "[We're] getting back to the people who are causing the news and who are caught up in it, or deserve to be in it," says managing editor Richard Stolley. "Our focus is on people, not issues." With deep pockets, a thirty-five–cent cover price, and a circulation base of one million, thanks to painstaking pre-launch research and marketing, *People* proves to be a smashing success that soon spawns puffy imitators. The bimonthly *Us*, from the New York Times Company, later sells to *Rolling Stone* publisher Jann Wenner, who foresees—too early—the importance of the youth market with his short-lived 1979 magazine, *Rolling Stone College Papers*.

# MARCH 5

**1971** Though it's not nearly as well remembered or documented, the night the laughter died precedes the day the music died (in Don McLean's "American Pie," see Dec. 4) by nearly a year. Tonight ABC's *The Odd Couple*, starring Tony Randall and Jack Klugman, airs without the canned laugh track both stars despise. The onetime experiment brings a flood of some fifty thousand letters that run overwhelming in favor of canning the added laughs permanently. So starting next season, the series shoots before a live audience with no studio "sweetening." Having arrived last year after previous Broadway and film incarnations, author Neil Simon's TV version has a strong five-year run, with messy nipping neat: Klugman wins two Emmys, Randall one.

## SONG WARNING

In a moment of righteous investiation, the Federal Communications Commission (FCC) issued a notice ordering radio stations to screen all songs for possible references to drug usage, in March 1971. Included in the notice was a list of twenty-two songs deemed to have "drug-oriented lyrics." Particularly suspected of—gasp!—youth corruption were some of the numbers below.

- "One Toke Over the Line," Brewer and Shipley
- "Puff the Magic Dragon," Peter, Paul and Mary
- "White Rabbit," Jefferson Airplane
- "Yellow Submarine," The Beatles
- "Magic Carpet Ride," Steppenwolf

# MARCH

**1974** The Watergate scandal continues to trigger shock waves. Today two major events occur on widely differing fronts. First, in Washington, DC, President Nixon finally admits that the Watergate burglars were paid hush money—edging him ever closer to the precipice from which he'll soon fall. Meanwhile, on the other coast Robert Redford pays $450,000 for the film rights to Carl Bernstein and Bob Woodward's Pulitzer Prize–winning *All the President's Men*. Adapted by veteran screenwriter William Goldman (*Marathon Man*), the film—featuring the potent pairing of Redford and Dustin Hoffman—comes out two years later and wins the Oscar for best screenplay as Americans flock to relive the only resignation of a president in US history. It makes huge box-office numbers, and is the second-highest-grossing movie of the year after *One Flew Over the Cuckoo's Nest*.

# MARCH

# 7

## 1970

Look! Up in the sky! It's not a bird, or a plane, it's not even Superman. It's the celestial spectacle of the century— a total eclipse of the sun. Millions look to the heavens, most without the eye protection recommended by scientists. Millions more watch the first complete eclipse televised round the world. One Mexican city hosts an especially large gathering of scientists and lay people since it offers maximum duration: three and a half minutes of darkness. "A great shadow fell upon the Pacific Ocean Saturday as the sun, moon, and earth, in the relentless march of the heavens, fell into step," writes the Associated Press. But dense clouds in Valdosta, Georgia, foil amateur astronomers. "This is exactly what we hoped would not happen," says a scientist coordinating the observation. He will get another chance— they come around every few years, but are visible from only certain parts of the globe.

# MARCH

**1971** Forget the hype and the hoopla—this is the real deal, and it lives up to its billing: the Fight of the Century. Madison Square Garden hosts the most anticipated bout since the Joe Louis v. Max Schmeling grudge rematch in 1938. Undefeated former heavyweight champion Muhammad Ali, 29, faces unbeaten current champ Joe Frazier, 27. The boxer versus the puncher. The brash, defiant ex-champ once stripped of his belt for refusing induction to the army against the relentless, hard-eyed blue-collar champ. A sold-out crowd of 20,455 buzzes, an estimated 300 million watch on closed-circuit TV, and even more listen to end-of-round radio reports. Celebs with connections abound, like Barbra Streisand, Bill Cosby, Sammy Davis, Jr., and Hugh Hefner. Tickets are so scarce that Frank Sinatra gets his by shooting photographs for *Life* magazine. The atmosphere is electric. And then the fight begins—a furious, toe-to-toe brawl that goes the fifteen-round distance. Frazier wins by unanimous decision, but Ali wins a rematch one year later, followed by the decisive Thrilla in Manila in 1975, where Frazier's trainer stopped the fight after the fourteenth round.

# MARCH

**1974** Strange bedfellows, indeed: sweet-sounding Little Eva and ear-splitting hard rockers Grand Funk. The latter act makes one of the most seemingly incongruous musical choices ever when it revives Eva's 1962 chart-topper "The Loco-Motion." Yet the song, hitting the charts today, moves around the floor and up the charts to the #1 spot too—only the second tune to hit the top by two different artists. "It's kind of weird hearing it done in a different way," says cowriter Gerry Goffin, "but you can still hear how it appeals to the kids." On their ensuing tour the band makes "The Loco-Motion" their crowd-pleasing finale, while a montage of train collisions projects on a screen behind. For the record, the first song to achieve two-fer #1 treatment? "Go Away, Little Girl" by Steve Lawrence and Donny Osmond.

# MARCH

**1979** Disco's never been hotter as it burns up seven of this week's Top 10 singles spots. At #1 is Gloria Gaynor's defiant "I Will Survive," a comeback for the "Queen of the Discos," as so dubbed by a group of deejays back in 1975. Since then she's relinquished the title to prolific hitmaker Donna Summer, whose "Heaven Knows" is #5 this week. For Gaynor "I Will Survive" becomes a disco classic, but, unfortunately, it's her career pinnacle. Summer, meanwhile, soon tops the charts with "Hot Stuff"—which her manager had suggested she pass along to Cher—and "Bad Girls," which critic Stephen Holden says "cheerfully evokes the trash-flash vitality of tawdry disco dolls cruising down the main drag on a Saturday night." Boston-born Summer took a circuitous path to fame, acting in road tours in Germany in musicals like *Hair* and *Godspell* before embracing music by singing orgasmicly on "Love to Love You Baby," her first hit. Summer later renounces her disco sex-goddess image for born-again Christianity.

# MARCH

**1970** And then there were four. By the time Crosby, Stills and Nash win a Grammy tonight for best new artist, they've already added a fourth bandmate: Neil Young. Their smoothly harmonizing, forthcoming album *Déjà Vu* features all four and captures the peace and love zeitgeist with songs like "Woodstock" and "Teach Your Children." They're an eclectic amalgam of bits of other bands—Graham Nash (Hollies), David Crosby (The Byrds), and Stephen Stills and Young (Buffalo Springfield)—that relies on the chemistry of their longtime relationships to spark new heights. One is reached barely two months later, when Neil Young pens "Ohio" in one night following the killings at Kent State. But personnel shifts persist, with members popping in and out while doing solo albums (Young's *After the Goldrush* and Stills's *Steven Stills*), which often include bandmates as backing musicians. An incestuous but pleasing bunch, the lot.

## MARCH 12

**1971** A dire US virus: a lethal disease, sinister science, and potential nuclear detonation combine as the highly contagious *The Andromeda Strain* opens. Veteran director Robert Wise (*The Sound of Music, West Side Story*) helms the medical techno-thriller, the first film based on a book by degreed doctor Michael Crichton from Harvard. "Crichton's narrative line is so strong, and his resources for sustaining it are so abundant," writes a book reviewer in *The New York Times*, "that *The Andromeda Strain* can't miss popular success." That quote also aptly describes Crichton's career, as he goes on to become a household name delivering print-slash-multimedia properties like *Jurassic Park* and *The Lost World*, and a little TV series called *ER*.

## MARCH 13

**1976** A few years ago minor soul singer Tyrone Davis scored big with "Turn Back the Hands of Time," and today the Four Seasons do just that. More than a decade earlier the band peaked with the piercing falsetto of Frankie Valli on hit after hit, like "Sherry," "Big Girls Don't Cry," "Walk Like a Man," and "Rag Doll," #1's, all. Today the boys from Jersey, with a few personnel changes, are back on top with "December, 1963 (Oh, What a Night)," a disco-fied tune whose lyrics had originally been about the repeal of Prohibition. But a comeback stalls, and out on his own Valli tops the charts again in 1978 with the title track from *Grease*. Billy Joel later sings the Valli-esque "Uptown Girl" that's right in the Four Seasons, doo-wop mode.

### TRENDSETTER

# PUTTING THE MADNESS INTO MARCH

March 1979 was a showdown for the ages between two college students: Larry Bird and Earvin "Magic" Johnson. Bird's undefeated Indiana State Sycamores and Johnson's Michigan State Spartans battled for the NCAA Championship crown, culminating with the two most electrifying players in college basketball meeting at last in Salt Lake City. Johnson prevailed with a score of Michigan 75, Indiana 64. "The Magic Man directed the show," acknowledged Michigan's coach, "and we got good basketball out of the rest of the team." And so it went into the pros—Larry, Magic, and a bunch of other guys. NCAA Player of the Year, Bird had already been drafted by the Boston Celtics and would win the NBA's Rookie of the Year in his first season. Underclassman Johnson also turned pro, signing with the LA Lakers and leading them to the world championship in his first season. Their rivalry transferred to the pro ranks for many thrilling years to come.

# MARCH 14

**1972** A King emerges: She'd already written four #1 hits alongside lyricist husband Gerry Goffin, including the Shirelles' "Will You Love Me Tomorrow" and Little Eva's "The Loco-Motion." After a divorce, Carole King decides to test out her pipes. Today she wins four Grammys: best female vocalist plus album (*Tapestry*), song ("You've Got a Friend"), and record of the year ("It's Too Late," with the flip side "I Feel the Earth Move"). From songwriter to song singer, King becomes the first musical superstar of the decade. Folks seemingly can't go anywhere without hearing her epochal album *Tapestry* playing, and it goes on to sell an estimated twenty-two million copies worldwide. "I want to connect with people," said King. "I want to make people think, 'Yeah, that's how I feel.' And if I can do that, that's an accomplishment."

# MARCH 15

**1977** Early on, *All in the Family* ran a hilarious episode in which Edith invites over a "swinging" couple, unaware of their sexual motives. The double entendres and sexual humor worked so well that that episode's writers melded the concept to a British comedy series called *Man About the House*. The result, premiering tonight, is ABC's *Three's Company*. John Ritter stars as a young man pretending to be gay in order to share an apartment with two sexy single gals (Suzanne Somers and Joyce DeWitt). It rockets into the top three for the next three seasons, but concurrently draws the wrath of religious leaders outraged by its sexual content and barely-there outfits. The show's meteoric run makes Somers a celebrity, but she exits in 1981 after unsuccessfully negotiating a sizable salary increase. Ritter, son of the late country singer Tex, sticks around and wins an Emmy for best actor. "I wish my dad were here tonight," he says at the ceremony, "so I could show off." Ritter gets off another good line at an earlier show when accepting an Emmy on behalf of no-show Marlon Brando, winner for a guest shot on *Roots*. "I'm sure if Marlon Brando were here, he would want to thank the Academy," says Ritter. "Perhaps not."

# MARCH 16

**1979** Into a world trembling with the nuclear shakes comes *The China Syndrome*. With a star-studded cast including Michael Douglas, Faye Dunaway, and Jack Lemmon, the topical, controversial film includes a scientist noting that a possible nuclear plant accident could "render an area the size of Pennsylvania" permanently uninhabitable. Twelve days later life shockingly imitates art when a reactor malfunction at the Three Mile Island power plant in Pennsylvania leads to a near-nuclear meltdown. The accident galvanizes interest in the film, which does boffo box office, and next month *Saturday Night Live* gets into the act with its now famous takeoff, "The Pepsi Syndrome," in which a spilled soft drink could bring about the end of the world as we know it. Janitor Garrett Morris is asked to go in and mop it up.

# MARCH 17

**1970** Bitter, bitchy, and biting, Matt Crowley's landmark gay play, *The Boys in the Band*, debuts in a movie version. Director William Friedkin, a few years before *The French Connection*, attracts the cast of the off-Broadway hit that ran for 1,001 nights after it opened two years ago. Coming less than a year after the Stonewall Riots, termed the "Boston Tea Party of the gay movement," it's the first mainstream play to approach homosexuality straight. Its stereotypical but often savagely funny view meets with mixed reviews. The *Los Angeles Times* sends mixed messages, praising it as "unquestionably a milestone" but refusing to run its ads. The *San Francisco Chronicle* calls it "bold and compassionate—a breakthrough play on a taboo subject." Through the prism of subsequent gay liberation post-Stonewall, it appears as a sort of gay minstrel show. Friedkin later feels the heat from gay activists outraged at his stereotypical portrayal of gay nightlife in *Cruising* with Al Pacino.

# MARCH 18

**1972** The coming of spring brings a *Harvest* of hits for sometimes soft, sometimes hard rockin' Neil Young. A mainstay of progressive FM radio, he has delivered back-to-back acclaimed albums *Everybody Knows This Is Nowhere* and *After the Goldrush*. Yet those albums' singles, like "Cinnamon Girl" and "Only Love Can Break Your Heart," have had little chart impact. Until today. His new album, *Harvest*, produces "Heart of Gold." Recorded in Nashville with background vocals from pals James Taylor and Linda Ronstadt, the song tops the singles charts for his first time. "This song put me in the middle of the road," says Young, formerly an erstwhile member of both Buffalo Springfield and Crosby, Stills, Nash and Young. "Traveling there soon became a bore so I headed for the ditch. A rougher ride, but I saw more interesting people there."

## MARCH

**1975** See them, feel them, now see them again on the big screen. It's pinball wizardry at the box office as The Who's energetic rock opera *Tommy* hits theaters today. The motion picture adaptation of the 1969 concept album stars the band's Roger Daltrey in the title role, along with standout performances by Ann-Margret as his mother, Tina Turner as the Acid Queen, and Elton John (replacing Rod Stewart, who later plays the part on the London stage) as the former pinball champ. Reviews may be mixed—not everyone gets Ann-Margret sloshing through baked beans, a Who tip-of-the-hat to their 1967 album *The Who Sell Out!*—but fans aren't saying "We're not gonna take it."

## MARCH

**1970** Looking to track down actor Steve McQueen? Then look no further than today's Grand Prix tune-up in Sebring, Florida, where Mario Andretti roars to victory in a Ferrari 512S. Twenty-two seconds behind charges the next team, racers Peter Revson and Mc-Queen in a Porsche 908. Until his movie career kicked into high gear a few years ago (with *The Thomas Crown Affair* and *Bullitt*), McQueen had been a regular fixture in sports-car racing. A little thing like a foot in a cast after a motorcycle accident doesn't stop him from today's race as he preps for his next film, *Le Mans*. That documentary will cover the famed twenty-four-hour race with extraordinary close-up camera work, and after that he races to *On Any Sunday*, a documentary by Bruce Brown that aims to do for motorcycles what his *Endless Summer* did for surfing.

## MARCH 21

**1976** Accompanied by Muhammad Ali, ex-boxer Rubin "Hurricane" Carter walks out of jail today after nearly a decade behind bars. Released on bail pending retrial, Carter has Bob Dylan to thank for his newfound freedom. Convinced of his innocence, Dylan released "Hurricane" a few months ago and helped focus a national spotlight on the murky case of a triple bar slaying in Paterson, New Jersey. "I'm going to a place where the trees are green, the sky is blue, and there are no bars on the windows," says Carter. He's later convicted in the second trial and returns to prison, but is released in 1988 after a successful federal appeal. In the same vein, author Norman Mailer later champions the cause of convicted murderer Jack Abbott. Mailer's high-profile support triggers his release in June 1981. Six weeks later, Abbott stabs a waiter to death when told the restaurant's restroom is for staff only.

## MARCH 22

**1978** Thar he goes: the world's most renowned high-wire performer, seventy-three-year-old patriarch Karl Wallenda, plunges to his death from a cable strung between two hotels in San Juan, Puerto Rico. Earlier this morning he dismissed questions about gusting winds, telling a circus coordinator that "the wind is stronger on the street than up there." Up there is where Wallenda felt most at home, though his ever-increasing and changing troupe, the Great Wallendas, had met tragedy several times before: the death of a nephew and son-in-law, the paralyzing of an adopted son in a human pyramid collapse in Detroit in 1962, the death of a son-in-law in West Virginia in 1972. "The rest of life," the elder Wallenda said after one funeral, "is just time to fill in between doing the next act."

## MARCH 23

**1973** High-society, well-coiffed, and accessorized ladies out on the town in—gasp!—ten-year-old outfits? *Quelle horreur!* Yet today no one minds as all pay tribute to late legendary Spanish designer Cristobal Balenciaga at the opening of an exhibit at New York's Metropolitan Museum of Art. "It's the height of fashion," enthuses Halston, "the most important statement of the century." But Calvin Klein isn't so sure: "Most of it looks out of date." Paintings by Goya, Picasso, and Velasquez adorn the walls to reinforce Balenciaga's Spanish heritage, but it's the clothing displayed on porcelain and steel mannequins that awe the assemblage: beaded velvet jackets to grand-entrance ball gowns, floating-lace baby-doll dresses to austere chemises. "Where have all the Balenciagas gone?" laments organizer and fashion mainstay Diana Vreeland, editor in chief of *Vogue*. Contributors include museums in Paris, Chicago, and Zürich and grande dames like the Baroness Philippe de Rothschild and the Marquesa de Villaverde.

## ROCKY'S RINGING ROOTS

No one gave ex-liquor salesman and security guard Chuck Wepner (a.k.a. the "Bayonne Bleeder") much of a shot on March 24, 1975, against Muhammad Ali. With vastly lesser skills, he entered the ring with a face the color of "well-worn pasty white burlap," wrote one reporter. The journeyman took a savage beating but gamely battled through, losing on a fifteenth-round TKO, but made the biggest payday of his life, $100,000 (to Ali's $1.5 million). Watching that night on closed circuit was a little-known, lightly regarded actor. But he was pumped! And within a week, he cranked out a rags-to-riches boxing screenplay. It was called *Rocky*, and the actor was, natch, Sylvester Stallone. After the movie debuted in 1976, it delivered the double Oscar shot of best picture and director, catapulted Stallone to star status, and spawned five sequels.

**"If not the Incredible, Stallone is at least the Improbable Hulk."**
—Russell Davies

# MARCH 24

**1973** Having departed the landmark Velvet Underground, Lou Reed transforms his career with the release of his gender-bending solo second album, *Transformer*. Coproduced in London by David Bowie, the seminal glam-rock release features the dirty ditty "Walk on the Wild Side" that's edited and/or banned in several countries. It's one of several tracks influenced or suggested by Andy Warhol and his bohemian coterie: "A hustle here and a hustle there, New York City's the place where they say, hey babe, take a walk on the wild side." Tonight at a concert in Buffalo a fan takes a bite on the wild side. He shrieks "leather!," leaps onstage, and bites Reed on the buttocks. The sore showman finishes the show and proceeds into his period of greatest commercial success. "Walk on the Wild Side" becomes his signature song and lone chart single.

# MARCH 25

**1973** Years ago a doo-wop group, the Capris, sang "there's a moon out tonight." Today that would be Pink Floyd's landmark *Dark Side of the Moon*. The progressive rockers' ode to life, death, time, money, and madness enters the charts for the first of what'll be a total of 741 weeks (that's more than fourteen *years*), unmatched in album chart history. It spawns the—ka-ching!—Top 15 single "Money," yet almost every other song becomes an FM staple, from the beautiful "Breathe" to the closing tour de force, "Brain Damage/Eclipse." Its use of sound effects to match the rhythm of each of Roger Waters's compositions, along with double-tracked vocals and seemingly quadraphonic sound, make it a benchmark recording. Indeed *Dark Side of the Moon* invariably rates high on listeners' and critics' all-time-best lists, like best album, best album cover, or, ahem, best album to make love to.

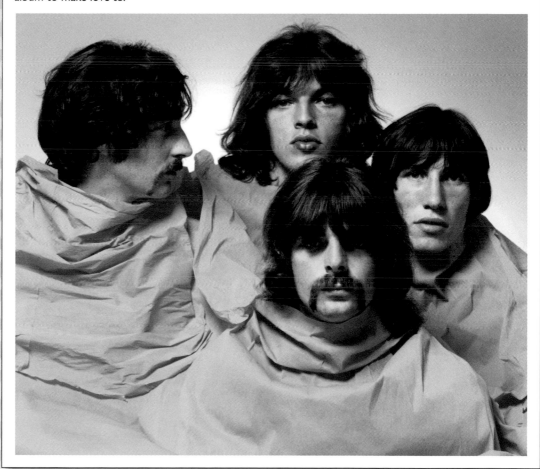

## 26

**1976** A nearby undertaker's not too keen about the name, but nevertheless The Body Shop opens its first shop today in Kensington Gardens, Brighton, UK. Founded by ex-hippie-turned-businesswoman and mother of two Anita Roddick, it sells fifteen beauty products in small, plain bottles. Customers are encouraged to bring in their own containers to refill, reflecting its bedrock support of recycling. Its other main focus is working with suppliers among indigenous people in developing countries, and the combination proves an international, principled phenomenon. From this first store with shelves painted emerald green, The Body Shop will expand over the next thirty years to 2,100 stores in fifty-five countries.

# MARCH 27

**1973** In *The Ten Commandments* Charlton Heston can part the Red Sea, but he's apparently not so gifted when it comes to doing the same for LA traffic. Tonight Clint Eastwood steps in on a moment's notice to cohost the Academy Awards ceremony when a traffic jam delays Heston. Despite the snarled traffic, better strap on your seatbelts—it's going to be a rocky night. *Cabaret* wins the most statues, eight, but Francis Ford Coppola's *The Godfather* wins three biggies: best picture, actor (Marlon Brando), and adapted screenplay (cowritten by novelist Mario Puzo and Coppola). Brando boycotts, sending an unknown Native American actress to read a statement decrying the industry's treatment of Indians (she's later discovered to be Mexican actress Maria Cruz). Eastwood is infuriated at having to follow her, as he announces the nominees for best picture.

# MARCH 28

**1978** Way, way beyond just "Stayin' Alive," the Bee Gees dominate the pop charts in a run that rivals The Beatles in their heyday. This week the Brothers Gibb account for four of the top five singles—that tune plus "Night Fever," brother Andy's "(Love Is) Thicker Than Water," and fellow Australian Samantha Sang's "Emotion," which goes gold today. And the hits just keep on comin'. Yvonne Elliman soon reaches the top spot with another Gibb song, "If I Can't Have You," and come summertime Frankie Valli joins the party with the Bee Gees–penned title track from the movie *Grease*. It's a long way (a decade, actually) from their chart debut, "New York Mining Disaster 1941," demonstrating vividly how the Bee Gees adapt to the changing times. Their next album, *Spirits Having Flown*, scores again, producing three more chart-topping hits: "Too Much Heaven," "Tragedy," and "Love You Inside Out." That's six #1's in a row, tying a mark set by the Fab Four.

# WE'VE GOT YOU COVERED

Even though Billy Joel's "New York State of Mind" wouldn't come out for another couple months, illustrator Saul Steinberg captured the essence in the last week of March 1976, in one of the most famous magazine covers of all time: the *New Yorker's* map of America. Its birds-eye view of Ninth Avenue to the Hudson River took up half the picture, with a narrow strip representing Jersey, then a short stretch of looming landmasses to LA and the Pacific Ocean beyond. His telescoped representation of how the average New Yorker views the world perhaps simultaneously captured non-natives' view of city residents' parochial views of their world. Three years later, the Village People would urge everyone to "Go West."

## MARCH

**1975** Just weeks after Mardi Gras, a New Orleans hooker shows it off as the star of the country's #1 song. "Lady Marmalade," LaBelle's naughty, bawdy, but irresistible dance smash represents a major comeback for the trio that had last scored in the early 1960s as Patti LaBelle and the Blue Belles. Performing their risqué hit on television, they're asked to change the suggestive chorus of "Voulez-vous coucher avec moi ce soir?" (originally a line from Blanche DuBois in *A Streetcar Named Desire*) to the inoffensive "Voulez-vous *danser*…," even though the rest of the song leaves no doubt as to its explicit sexual intent. More than a quarter-century later, that won't be a problem when it hits #1 again for a onetime grouping of four powerful female vocalists including Christina Aguilera and Pink. They not only sing the original lyrics but perform the song dressed like turn-of-the-century ladies of the evening. Yes they can can can.

## MARCH 30

**1978** Fresh from playing pub dates in their native Dublin, four high school mates audition for CBS Records. A couple weeks ago, they'd won a talent contest cosponsored by Guinness Harp Lager. The band— consisting of guitarist David Evans, bass player Adam Clayton, drummer Larry Mullen, Jr., and singer Paul Hewson—has gone by the name The Hype, but now call themselves U2. Hewson, spying a billboard advertising a hearing aid with the brand name Bono Vox, takes on a new performing name: Bono. Over the next year they sign with CBS and build a fan base in Ireland with radio play and record sales, but fail to stir any interest in England. At their first pub show in London in 1979, they're mistakenly introduced as "V2" to an audience of only nine people. Perhaps the 1980s will be better.

## MARCH 31

**1976** Headlines scream the news, stirring intense feelings on all sides. No single case has rocked America more than the sad, anguishing tale of Karen Ann Quinlan. After mixing alcohol and drugs at a party in April 1975, the twenty-one-year-old woman fell into a coma and suffered irreversible brain damage. Her Catholic family asked court permission to have her ventilator turned off, and was rebuffed. They appealed, and today the New Jersey Supreme Court gives its permission. So she's disconnected from the respirator. Yet even without assistance, she continues to breathe, fanning the flames on both sides of the right-to-die issue. Quinlan remains in a permanent vegetative state for the next nine years until she dies of pneumonia in 1985.

# APRIL

**1972** Hey ladies, Burt's in the buff. With director John Boorman's eagerly awaited *Deliverance* about to open, costar Burt Reynolds makes major waves as he appears nude in the centerfold of this month's *Cosmopolitan*. "What the hell, it's intended as a put-down for *Playboy*, which I hate," says the unabashed actor, who shows a touch of pubic hair. "Also, I'm thinking, 'I don't have any good publicity stills, so what can I lose? If something comes out good I can always crop it, right?'" What comes out especially good is Reynolds's performance as a macho bow and arrow wielding buddy whose weekend camping adventure with three pals (Ned Beatty and Ronny Cox, in their film debuts, plus Jon Voight) turns unexpectedly, lethally primal. In a career filled with questionable film choices, *Deliverance* remains one of Reynolds's smartest.

# APRIL

## 2

**1978** Deep drama in the heart of Texas: CBS goes drilling for ratings gold and hits a gusher with *Dallas*. The first successful primetime soap since *Peyton Place*, it catches the zeitgeist with over-the-top, big-budget melodrama. It oozes high fashion, high stakes, and high jinks galore. Featuring Larry Hagman as conniving patriarch J.R. Ewing ("a human oil slick," says *Time* magazine) and his large, ever-changing, oft promiscuous family including Victoria Principal, Barbara Bel Geddes, and Patrick Duffy, *Dallas* premieres tonight as a five-part miniseries. Most critics howl but fans flock to the glamorous, glitzy guilty pleasure. Within a year it's TV's top-rated show, and maintains that oily grip for four of the next five seasons. Its season-ending cliffhangers, like the "Who Shot J.R." quandary, become a national obsession.

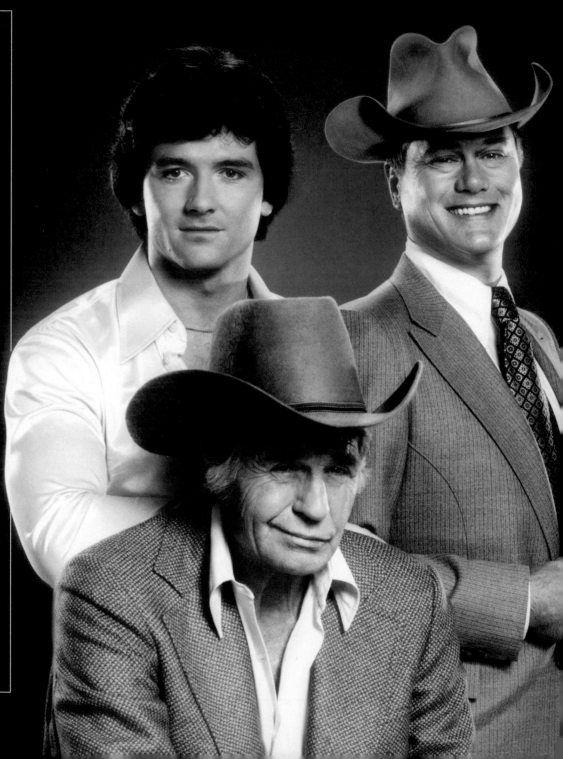

# OSCAR'S STREAK

Funny, we don't recall *Naked Came the Stranger* being nominated for an Oscar. As the 1974 Academy Awards ceremony neared its climactic close on April 2, debonair David Niven started to introduce Elizabeth Taylor (who would announce the nominees for best picture). Suddenly, from upstage appeared a naked, longhaired, mustachioed man who flashed a peace sign before dashing away. The ever-poised Niven deadpanned, "The only laugh that man will ever get in his life is by stripping and showing his shortcomings," as Henry Mancini's band struck up "Keep Your Sunny Side Up." The quick reactions led some to suggest that the event was staged—after all, this is Hollywood. The producers denied it, even though they let the streaker—Robert Opal, aged thirty-three—conduct interviews backstage (clothed). The next month singer Ray Stevens would hit #1 with "The Streak," but the fad—and Opal's fifteen minutes of fame—are short-lived. He would try stand-up comedy, streak at a party for composer Marvin Hamlisch and dancer Rudolf Nureyev, and move to San Francisco, where he was killed during a store robbery five years later.

## APRIL 3 — 1978

It's a rather strange night at the Oscars. When outspoken Palestinian rights activist Vanessa Redgrave wins best supporting actress for *Julia*, she peppers her acceptance speech with politics and her refusal "to be intimidated by the threats of a small bunch of Zionist hoodlums." The bewildered audience gasps, alternately booing or applauding. The tension in the room lightens considerably when perky Debby Boone sings "You Light Up My Life," the eventual winner for best song. Alongside her onstage are young students "associated" with a clinic for the deaf, who sign the lyrics. A sappy song, a syrupy sweet moment—the audience loves it. Turns out, though, that the kids aren't hearing-impaired—and their signing was gibberish. The Academy shame-facedly later admits that it recruited them from a local public school, but the longer-term brouhaha over Redgrave's outspoken activism still takes center stage.

## APRIL 4 — 1970

Long a stepchild to AM radio, FM broadcasters today show off a little bit o' soul (and rock and heavy metal and funk and jazz and country and...) at their first convention. Leading into the annual National Association of Broadcasters (NAB) convention in Chicago, the three-day confab attests to FM's growing prominence: 2,417 stations today versus 789 a decade ago. More are coming aboard every day, as album-oriented rock (AOR) supplants the three-minute single. Artists get more leeway, and more: higher quality sound, less static, interference, and hum than AM, and bandwidth for stereo transmission. As rock takes off, FM becomes an increasingly powerful force on the dial, with advertisers tuning its way.

# APRIL 5

## 1976

Come on up and see her sometime. Mae West's sultry, scandalous stardom has long since passed, but she does believe in keeping up appearances. Tonight the aged, painted dame enlivens CBS's *Dick Cavett's Backlot U.S.A.* special. Limping along with a visit to a Rin Tin Tin wannabe German shepherd and a blah interview with John Wayne, diminutive Cavett saves the best for last. He visits "a certain lady of Stage 14," and though the eighty-two-year-old blonde's trademark heavily made up appearance seems grotesque, West gamely chats it up and even sings two songs, "Frankie and Johnnie" and "After You've Gone." Her appearance revives her career, and next year she stars in her last feature, *Sextette.* Though it's pounded by critics, West endures, surrounded as always by hunky male escorts and ready with the quick quip: "I only like two kinds of men—domestic and imported."

# APRIL 6

## 1973

Mom may have always liked Dick best, but today the courts like each of the Smothers brothers equally. After a protracted breach of contract lawsuit, the Smothers Brothers emerge victorious. Today Tom and Dickie win a $776,300 judgment against CBS for canceling their show back in 1969. *The Smothers Brothers Comedy Hour* had been an irreverent hit with audiences but an irritant to network censors. They clashed frequently with the brothers over their anti–Vietnam War and civil rights stances, as well as the presidential parody campaign of Pat Paulsen. Legendarily tough CBS president William Paley abruptly canceled the series despite its solid ratings, triggering the case that's decided in the brothers' favor. An anti-Establishment win.

# APRIL 7

## 1972

An auction of biblical proportions rocks the usually quiet world of books as a rare, fifteenth-century Gutenberg bible sells for a record $2 million. That's nearly six times more than any book ever auctioned to date, surpassing an Audubon "Birds of America" folio that went for $360,000 at Christie's last November. Today the auction house sells the two-volume, leather-bound bible to a New York bookseller who quickly resells it to the West German state museum in Stuttgart. Of the original 185 bibles printed, around 1,450 on movable, metal type by Johan Gutenberg, only 48 are known to still exist. Only 21 of those are in their entirety. The last Gutenberg bible to be auctioned went for $26,000 to Yale University in 1926.

# HAMMERIN' HANK CONNECTS

The standing-room-only nighttime crowd tensed. With a 1-0 count, the batter swung and hit a towering drive to left center. All 53,775 fans at Atlanta-Fulton County Stadium erupted into cheers as the ball sailed into the home team's bullpen. On April 8, 1974, with his trademark graceful power, Atlanta Braves slugger Henry Aaron had hit home run number 715, overtaking one of the most storied records in baseball by surpassing Babe Ruth's legendary mark of 714. "I have never gone out on a ball field and given less than my level best," said Aaron. "When I hit it tonight, all I thought about was that I wanted to touch all the bases." Also going—not so happily—into the record books was LA Dodgers pitcher Al Downing, who gave up the gopher ball.

# APRIL

**1975** Networks, heal thyself. Responding to complaints from Congress and outside groups about increasingly violent and sexually suggestive fare, the National Association of Broadcasters (NAB) voluntarily agrees to institute a "family hour" from 8:00 to 9:00 p.m. next season. ABC announces plans to move cop show *The Rookies* and theatrical movies to 9:00 p.m. start times. But industry execs, fearing that kiddie-oriented shows won't appeal to its coveted 18-to-49 age demo, derisively dub the plan "Bambi hour." Cracks widen. "If this whole thing depends on [the networks'] reasonableness, their good faith," says one congressman, "that's like writing a letter to Santa Claus." The three major unions representing writers, actors, and directors sue the NAB and FCC, claiming censorship, and a year later a federal judge agrees.

# APRIL

**1979** Displaying true grit, superhawk (and very ill) John Wayne presents the Oscar for best picture to the harrowing antiwar film *The Deer Hunter*, which takes five including director and supporting actor (Christopher Walken). Another antiwar drama, *Coming Home*, also wins big with matching awards for best actress (Jane Fonda) and actor (John Voight), the latter winning over Laurence Olivier (*The Boys from Brazil*). Sir Laurence does pick up a special honoree Oscar, winning a warm ovation from the appreciative crowd. Olivier's nomination for playing a Nazi hunter represents a neat turnaround, since he was last nominated two years before as the scheming, torturous ex-Nazi in *Marathon Man*. "I don't think there's an actor here who doesn't acknowledge a great debt to the continuing legacy of Laurence Olivier," says a teary-eyed Voight, who bests him this night. Two months later Wayne, seventy-two, dies from stomach cancer. This fall, in New York, screen tough guy Walken asks two men to turn down their radio, triggering a fistfight that winds up breaking his nose and fracturing a finger.

# APRIL 10

**1970** On their most recent album, *Abbey Road*, The Beatles may have sung "Come Together," but the long-known truth is they're splitting apart. Today the dream is over when, in London, Paul McCartney announces he's leaving The Beatles for "personal differences, business differences, musical differences." It's not the top news story of the day, but for any kid listening to the radio, nothing else matters. Ironically, the #1 song is "Let It Be," which takes on added poignancy with their breakup. Days before, Ringo alone attended the final session for a Beatles recording, laying down drum tracks for three songs on the forthcoming *Let It Be* album, produced by Phil Spector. But it's clear that the foursome have already gone their separate ways. John has already embarked on a solo career with "Instant Karma" at #3 today, though he'll be the last Beatle to have a #1 US single. Solo albums from Paul and Ringo are only weeks away.

# APPRIL

||||  ||||

## 1971

Anyone for table tennis? Five days ago, the US team at a ping-pong tourney in Japan received a most unexpected invitation. Today Americans delight to the start of front-page coverage of their team's exploits in a country it's heard or seen little about—the People's Republic of China, now the PRC but then known as Red China. The team visits the Great Wall, Summer Palace, and other ancient sites, and loses all its matches, but gracefully. "You have opened a new chapter in the relations of the American and Chinese people," says Premier Chou En-lai at a banquet in the Great Hall of the People in Beijing. Then Glenn Cowan, a fast fan favorite here with flowing, dark D'Artagnan locks and infectious enthusiasm, asks the premier's opinion of the US hippie movement. "Youth wants to seek out the truth, and out of this search various forms of change are bound to come forth," says Chou diplomatically. "Thus this is a kind of transitional period." President Nixon's nascent rapprochement pays off, and several months later he announces his landmark 1972 visit to China.

# APRIL 12

## 1972

Based on a character created by underground comics legend R. Crumb, *Fritz the Cat* premieres in a storm of controversy. The first X-rated cartoon about a sex-drugs-rock 'n' roll hippie feline, once rejected by every studio in town, generates equally sizable grosses and headlines. "It's more twisted than my stuff," sniffs reclusive Crumb, who badmouths director Ralph Bakshi, to whom he'd signed the rights but later sues claiming he was duped. Business differences aside, the business buzz booms as *Fritz the Cat* becomes the first animated film to gross more than $100 million at the box office. Critics mostly approve, with Leonard Maltin calling it an "engaging, irreverent look at radical-hip lifestyles of the 1960s." *Time Out* sides more with Crumb, dismissing it as "a generally trivial exercise that never matches the punch of the original."

# APRIL 13

## 1970

"Houston, we've had a problem here." Two days into its journey to the moon, *Apollo 13* loses oxygen and electrical power when an oxygen tank explodes and damages the service module. For an instant, astronauts James Lovell and John Swigert think it's a prank by fellow astronaut Fred Haise, who has learned that he can scare them by actuating a lunar module relief valve, which makes a loud bang. But this explosion is real, a potentially catastrophic occurrence that will require extraordinary ingenuity under intense pressure, both in the capsule and back at mission control, to correct. The moon landing is aborted, and the craft eventually returns safely. Having taken off at 13:13 Houston time, and with the explosion on *Apollo 13* occurring on April 13, Lovell begins his post-flight press conference by saying, "I am not a superstitious person…"

# APRIL
# 14

**1979** Going "Minute by Minute" with the Doobie Brothers, fans enthusiastically dig their new funkier, R&B sound with the addition of Michael McDonald, ex-Steely Dan vocalist and keyboard player. "What a Fool Believes," cowritten by McDonald and Kenny Loggins, tops the charts today and later helps them win a slew of Grammy Awards (four) including Record of the Year. Through not minute by minute, the band has whirled through a good half-dozen personnel changes since forming in 1971. Early softer sounds like "Listen to the Music" and "China Grove" edge out their harder work "Black Water," their only previous #1.

# NO STATIC AT ALL

Once upon a time, AM was the cool setting for your radio, while FM was for your dentist's waiting room. In the '70s freeform, progressive, album rock—or whatever you want to call it—flipped the script. Here are some of the era's best in album-oriented FM from coast to coast.

- WNEW-FM (New York). During the day, gravel-voiced "Scottso" Muni played the newest "things from England," while at night Alison Steele ("The Nightbird") took listeners to new heights.

- KMPX and later KSAN (San Francisco). Home to Tom Donahue, one of the founding fathers of progressive radio, and, for a brief time, Howard Hesseman, who later played DJ Dr. Johnny Fever on TV's *WKRP in Cincinnati*.

- KPPC and later KMET (Los Angeles). Featured the thematic stylings of Jim Ladd; Top 40 convert B. Mitchel Reed; Dr. Demento (who dug way, way back); and comedy team The Credibility Gap, featuring future Spinal Tappers Harry Shearer and Michael McKean.

- WBCN (Boston). They were really rockin' in Boston, where the J. Geils Band's Peter Wolf came out to howl, Charles Laquidara nudged listeners awake on The Big Mattress, and Jerry "Duke of Madness" Goodwin ruled the overnights.

- WMMS (Cleveland). Proving Cleveland really does rock, "The Buzzard" gave acts like David Bowie, Rush, and Bruce Springsteen early exposure in America.

- WMMR (Philadelphia). The first spot on the dial to play artists like Yes and Billy Joel, thanks to Dave Herman's "Marconi Experiment" and Ed Sciaky's night show.

- WHFS (Baltimore). Home of the "never play a hit" policy, where personalities like the Weasel and Bob "Here" featured extra-long tracks from the likes of Frank Zappa, Genesis, and George Thorogood.

## APRIL 15

**1971** On Hollywood's starriest night, they throw a swanky party and almost no one—few winners, anyway—shows. The most famous no-show of the Oscar gala is cantankerous George C. Scott, who wins best actor for *Patton*. He'd already tried, unsuccessfully, to rescind his nomination, and on this night he's back in his apartment in New York, reportedly watching a hockey game on TV. Best actress winner Glenda Jackson (*Women in Love*) is home in London while Helen Hayes, winner for supporting actress (*Airport*), is doing a play in Washington, DC. Other notable no-shows include honorary awardee Orson Welles, *Patton* director Franklin J. Schaffner, screenwriter Francis Ford Coppola, and Ingmar Bergman, winner of the Thalberg Memorial Award.

## APRIL 16

**1972** Security's tight enough today in Washington, DC, for the arrival of a major foreign dignitary. But it's not one, it's two extra-special guests—pandas Hsing-Hsing and Ling-Ling. Gifts from the People's Republic of China, the young duo takes up residence in side-by-side pens at the National Zoo to national acclaim and attention. "Pandas can steal your heart away," says the zoo's director. They're here as a byproduct of President Nixon's historic rapprochement with China. Less publicized is the United States' animal gift to China— two musk oxen named Milton and Matilda. Their far more famous counterparts, Hsing-Hsing and Ling-Ling, attract millions of visitors during their twenty-year stay, but none of their eagerly anticipated five panda cubs live past a few days.

**APRIL 17 1975** A presidential precedent, tonight. Gerald Ford becomes the first sitting president to attend a performance at the Ford Theater since the 1865 assassination of President Lincoln. Breaking the 110-year standard, he gets a front-row seat amidst a specially invited audience of seven hundred for *Give 'em Hell, Harry*, a one-man play about President Harry Truman performed by actor James Whitmore. The actor later receives an Oscar nomination for his role in the film version that opens this fall. Ford sits about fifty feet from the box where John Wilkes Booth assassinated Lincoln. It remains empty, draped with a flag, bunting, and a portrait of George Washington—just like the last time Lincoln saw it.

**APRIL 18 1979** Presenting, palimony! It's a mixed bag for one of the most highly debated, highly watched celebrity court cases in a long while. A Los Angeles judge orders macho leading man Lee Marvin to pay $104,000 "for rehabilitation purposes" to his companion of six years, Michelle Triola Marvin. The money compensates her for time lost from her singing career, but his $3.6 million estate— of which she wanted half—is off limits. Both sides claim victory. "I am proud to have paved the way for unmarried women," she says, having also paved the way for her attorney Marvin Mitchelson's new (and booming) business. In legal circles, the potential ramifications reverberate. "This may open up the floodgates for future litigation," one lawyer warns—or is it welcomes? On the other side of the ledger this week, an NYC judge rules against Penelope McCall, who'd lived with rock singer Peter Frampton for six years. His estate's worth a bit more than Lee's—a cool $50 million.

**1977** Controversial material, a snake-bitten production. Seven weeks after a near-fatal heart attack, Martin Sheen returns to the Philippines to resume filming *Apocalypse Now*, Francis Ford Coppola's troubled take on the Vietnam War. A year before, Sheen had replaced Harvey Keitel two weeks into shooting, taking a role previously nixed by Steve McQueen, Gene Hackman, James Caan, et al. After crushing delays, nightmarish weather (it's monsoon season—hello?), and an overweight and recalcitrant Marlon Brando, Coppola later says, "We had access to too much money, too much equipment, and little by little we went insane." He later spends more than a year editing. When it finally opens in the summer of 1979, the film gets rave attention and does boffo box office. "My film isn't about Vietnam," says Coppola, "it is Vietnam."

# APRIL

## 20

**1977** Allen arrives with *Annie*: after a half dozen films Woody Allen delivers *Annie Hall,* his best to date (and some say best ever). Mixing his trademark riffs on life, death, sex, romantic angst, and neuroses, it does big box-office business and wins four Oscars: best actress (Diane Keaton), director (Allen), original screenplay (Allen and Marshall Brickman), and the top prize, best picture, over favored sci-fi smash *Star Wars.* Yet Woody's an Oscar no-show; he's off playing clarinet at Michael's Pub with the New Orleans Funeral and Ragtime Orchestra, his usual Monday night gig. "I couldn't let down the guys," he says. The film also leads an antistyle fashion trend, inspired by the ditzy title character's kooky look mixing men's clothes, grandma's clothes, and floppy hats that could've belonged to either.

# APRIL

## 21

**1977** *Annie Hall* yesterday, *Annie* today. The redheaded little orphan girl of funny pages fame transplants splendidly to the Great White Way, despite naysayers dubbing it "*Oliver* in drag." Opening tonight with Andrea McArdle ("a petite Merman with pipes of steel") in the title role, it quickly becomes Broadway's hottest ticket. Awards, like its most famous song, come out tomorrow: seven Tony Awards including best musical, score, book, and choreography, and seven Drama Desk Awards. Aided by Mike Nichols's uncredited creative advice, the musical extravaganza goes on to a long run and spurs tours. Not only is there a tomorrow for Annie on stage and on the big screen, but the original comic of *Little Orphan Annie,* discontinued in 1974, is brought back in 1979 for good, thanks to the success of the stage show.

## TRENDSETTER

# GIVE EARTH A CHANCE

Students in Oklahoma City buried a gasoline engine. In Washington, motorists in Tacoma shared the road with a procession of horseback riders, and a goat in Centralia wandered about bearing a sign: "I eat garbage, what are you doing for your community?" Welcome to the first Earth Day, April 22, 1970, when millions of Americans young and old united to make an unprecedented statement against pollution. Still, some saw subversion. "It's replacing the anti–Vietnam War movement as the thing to do," said one member of the Daughters of the American Revolution. Despite the handful of naysayers, the environmental movement only grew, getting an extra boost the next year with the formation of Greenpeace.

# APRIL

## 22

**1976** It's about time. It's about place. Today Barbara Walters does something no woman has ever done—cohosts a network evening newscast. ABC shells out more than a million dollars to lure the veteran reporter from NBC, where she's played a key role over the past fifteen years in the success of the *Today* show. There's just one catch: she must cohost with Harry Reasoner, who publicly disdains the new arrangement. With the press focusing on her contract and supposed "infotainment" style, the on-air partnership begins in October—and flops. The chemistry is definitely there, only it's the deadly kind. Within a couple years Walters is off to cohost ABC's newsmagazine *20/20,* and shapes a pretty darned good career thereafter.

# APRIL 23

## 1972

From uptown to downtown, tonight's Tony Awards gala sets a record when one producer, bustling Off Broadway's Joseph Papp, takes home the top prizes for best musical (*Two Gentlemen of Verona*) and play (*Sticks and Bones*). The former represents the night's most stunning upset, as previously *Follies* had taken home seven awards—with one reporter noting that its mega-producer, Hal Prince, collects Tonys "almost as easily as some men collect wide ties." *Sticks and Bones* playwright, David Rabe, expresses amazement at the success of his hard-hitting drama about a blinded Vietnam vet. "People didn't want to listen," says Rabe of his own 1966 homecoming after serving in Vietnam. "It was a kind of closed-mindedness that made you feel like you were talking to walls." Two standing ovations rock the house: for composing genius Richard Rodgers (*Oklahoma!* to *The Sound of Music*), and for Ethel Merman, who belts out standards "I Got Rhythm" and "Everything's Comin' Up Roses." In a neat touch of ethnicity, winner Vincent Gardenia (for *Prisoner of Second Avenue*) gives his acceptance speech in Italian.

# APRIL 24

## 1970

A fishnet see-through blouse—not exactly standard White House attire. But that's what Jefferson Airplane singer Grace Slick appears in today (along with a full-length skirt, boots, and leather jacket) for a tea for alumnae of Finch College, a New York girls school that both she and presidential daughter Tricia Nixon attended. Yet it's not her attire that throws the staff into a tizzy, but her escort: Chicago 7 member and yippie provocateur Abbie Hoffman. "I always have somebody with me," says Slick, "especially at the White House." The 375 elegantly dressed women kept waiting on the sidewalk are alternately amused or dismayed, as a steady rain causes hairdos to wilt and mascara to run. Perhaps the White House is worried about the silverware in light of Abbie's countercultural touchstone, *Steal This Book*, a manifesto of resistance. Eventually he's refused admittance, and as the couple departs he drapes a flag with a marijuana leaf over a White House fence. "We're coming back July Fourth," Abbie shouts, "with one hundred thousand people!"

# APRIL 25

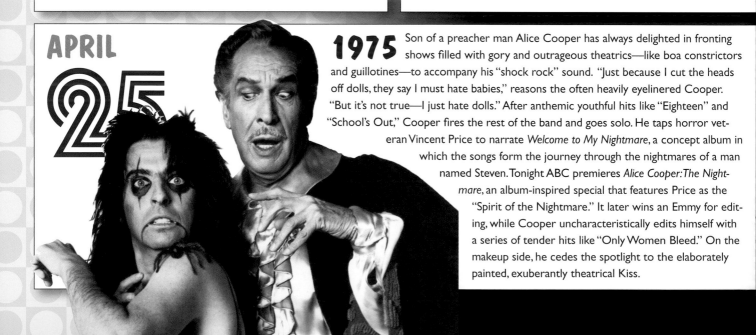

## 1975

Son of a preacher man Alice Cooper has always delighted in fronting shows filled with gory and outrageous theatrics—like boa constrictors and guillotines—to accompany his "shock rock" sound. "Just because I cut the heads off dolls, they say I must hate babies," reasons the often heavily eyelinered Cooper. "But it's not true—I just hate dolls." After anthemic youthful hits like "Eighteen" and "School's Out," Cooper fires the rest of the band and goes solo. He taps horror veteran Vincent Price to narrate *Welcome to My Nightmare*, a concept album in which the songs form the journey through the nightmares of a man named Steven. Tonight ABC premieres *Alice Cooper: The Nightmare*, an album-inspired special that features Price as the "Spirit of the Nightmare." It later wins an Emmy for editing, while Cooper uncharacteristically edits himself with a series of tender hits like "Only Women Bleed." On the makeup side, he cedes the spotlight to the elaborately painted, exuberantly theatrical Kiss.

**1978** Ringo Starr gets by with a little help from friends Art Carney, Carrie Fisher, John Ritter, and former bandmate George Harrison. In *Ringo*, an updated TV reworking of *The Prince and the Pauper*, the ex-Beatle swaps his pressure-packed pop-star lifestyle for that of a lowbrow seller of maps to the stars' homes. Intended to promote his upcoming album *Bad Boy*, the special includes newly recorded versions of "Act Naturally," "Yellow Submarine," and "You're Sixteen" (a duet with Fisher). Harrison narrates the comical tale/musical, while yet more friends drop by for cameos including Angie Dickinson, Mike Douglas, and Vincent Price. Despite the star wattage it's a ratings flop, and doesn't air in the UK for five years.

**MEANWHILE...**

## THE PARTY BEGINS

For over half a century, the midtown Manhattan property had variously housed opera, theater, radio shows, and TV productions. But none of the previous lives (or subsequent ones) of 254 West 54th Street could ever match the notoriety of Studio 54, which opened on April 26, 1977. No discotheque more embodied the hedonistic, heady days of the late '70s and early '80s than Studio 54, with its nonstop mix of sex, drugs, and alcohol—imbibed to a pulsating disco beat and dazzling light show. Run by flamboyant Steve Rubell and silent partner Ian Schrager, it famously attracted an A-list of celebrities, jetsetters, and glitterati ranging from dancer Alvin Ailey (whose troupe performed on opening night) to Andy Warhol. With a crowd crush and infamously demanding doormen, even chi-chi guests like Cher, Warren Beatty, and Frank Sinatra were denied admittance on opening night. Shortly thereafter, the club hosted a birthday soiree for Bianca Jagger, who entered atop a white horse—cementing the reputation of "The Studio" as the hottest club in town, and maybe on the planet.

# APRIL

# 27

**1971** Former all-star and Golden Glove winner Curt Flood retires from baseball today, a game he has changed forever. The ex–St. Louis Cardinals outfielder challenged baseball's decades-old reserve clause, arguing that it unfairly kept players beholden to the teams that originally signed them. He refused a trade, saying, "I do not feel I am a piece of property to be bought and sold irrespective of my wishes." The Supreme Court eventually rules in favor of baseball on a technicality. Targeted for his groundbreaking stance, Flood is vindicated in 1975 when the clause is struck down, leading to a new era of free agency. "At no time did he waver in his commitment and determination," said Marvin Miller, former head of the Major League Players Association. "He had experienced something that was inherently unfair and was determined to right the wrong."

**APRIL**

**1978** Today marks the battle of the bands. Make that the battle of the band *movies* as *FM* opens. The story of a maverick radio station bucking its corporate masters captures the times perfectly. It features the bravura film debut of Martin Mull as its craziest DJ, plus concert appearances by Jimmy Buffett, Tom Petty, REO Speedwagon, and Linda Ronstadt. Three weeks later, Casablanca Records unveils *Thank God, It's Friday,* a disco-fied answer to *Saturday Night Fever* that features the Commodores, Village People, and Donna Summer, who wins an Oscar for "Last Dance." Lastly comes *The Buddy Holly Story,* a biopic starring a mesmerizing Gary Busey as the bespectacled rock 'n' roll pioneer. Many of Holly's best ("That'll Be the Day," "Peggy Sue") fill the soundtrack, and the film also wins an Oscar for adapted score.

# 29

**1979** Born and raised in the heartland (Rockford, Illinois), Cheap Trick members can't catch a break in the United States. But for reasons unknown, the raucous rockers aren't only big in Japan— they're huge. Their first three albums go gold there while barely causing a ripple stateside. The band tours the United States, opening for bands like The Kinks, Boston, and Santana, but in Japan *they're* the stars. So they follow the money with a live recording in Tokyo, *Cheap Trick at Budokan*, that captures their hot pop performance and fan hysteria reminiscent of Beatlemania (The Beatles played the same hall in summer 1966). Today Cheap Trick releases a live version of "I Want You to Want Me," finally netting the band that elusive prize: a Top Ten hit in the States. Now their appeal turns not just Japanese but domestic.

# 30

**1976** At first it was chuckled about: a porn star going to jail. But after today, when Harry Reems is convicted in Memphis of obscenity for acting in the X-rated *Deep Throat*, people jump to attention. High-powered legal help like Harvard Law School professor Alan Dershowitz take the case, but the federal prosecutor remains adamant that the court's aiming for the throat: "We do not go after the projectionist or popcorn maker. That has no deterrent effect. We go after those who are profiteering." Invitation-only industry parties raise defense funds from a who's who of entertainment: Warren Beatty, Colleen Dewhurst, Jack Nicholson, Mike Nichols, Gregory Peck, Stephen Sondheim, and many more. Reems's conviction is overturned upon appeal the next year. He's granted a new trial, but charges are later dropped.

# MAY

## 1972

With a prized spot on President Nixon's "enemies list," muckraking columnist Jack Anderson adds another kind of prize today: a Pulitzer. He had exposed government secrets that showed the White House favoring Pakistan in a dispute with India during the formation of Bangladesh. He'd also published secret Watergate transcripts, the day's biggest story and sweet vindication for another Pulitzer winner, *The New York Times*, for its gutsy, groundbreaking running of the Pentagon Papers. "It is important to us today," says publisher Arthur Ochs Sulzberger, "and it will be important always." Anderson, a devout Mormon, avoids being eliminated by Nixon's political operatives and continues plying his craft as the president's ship goes down.

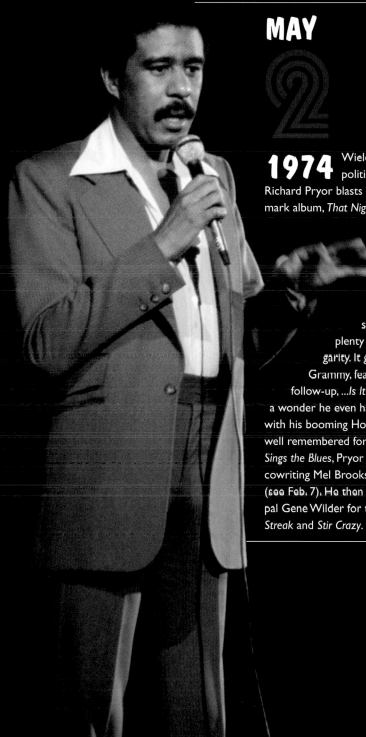

# MAY

## 1974

Wielding the eternally politically incorrect N-word, Richard Pryor blasts into fame with his landmark album, *That Nigger's Crazy*. Recorded live at Don Cornelius's *Soul Train* (see Oct. 2) nightclub, the manic funnyman delivers a topical stew of political, racial, and social commentary with plenty of wide-eyed, gleeful vulgarity. It goes platinum and wins a Grammy, feats Pryor repeats with his follow-up, *...Is It Something That I Said?* It's a wonder he even has time for records, what with his booming Hollywood career. Previously well remembered for his dramatic turn in *Lady Sings the Blues*, Pryor turns up the heat by cowriting Mel Brooks's riotous *Blazing Saddles* (see Feb. 7). He then teams memorably with pal Gene Wilder for two buddy classics, *Silver Streak* and *Stir Crazy*.

## MAY 3

### 1970

There's no sign of the yellow brick road, but today it's good-bye ruby slippers—and hundreds of thousands of other movie memorabilia. In the sweltering heat, three thousand people pack MGM's cavernous soundstage #27 on the first of the eighteen-day mega auction of forty-five years' worth of costumes and props. Sharp-eyed antiques dealers vie alongside self-styled entrepreneurs and even the occasional old-time movie fan. There's a marked absence of star power, though, except for sightings of a bubbly Debbie Reynolds buying scores of items for her proposed Hollywood hall of fame. Texas oil millionaire Lamar Hunt sails away with the Mississippi showboat from *Show Boat* for $15,000, the same amount a local collector pays for a pair of Dorothy's red slippers, one of several in existence. The wizard's suit goes for $650.

### MAY 1977

America has always liked second acts, and today it gets a big one. British interviewer David Frost goes from well-regarded bloke to giant slayer when he lands tonight's exclusive ninety-minute interview with former president Richard Nixon, the first of four. Trying to prove his innocence, or at least rehabilitate his image a bit, Nixon is overwhelmed by the evidence against him. In the parlance, it's "good television"—an out-of-the-park blast, the most-watched news interview in television history to date. The NYC station alone gets $7,500 for a thirty-second spot, five times the normal rate for the time slot's usual occupant, *The Merv Griffin Show*. Shown on an hour tape delay, the special allows Nixon a ten-minute timeout, stopping the taping so he can regain his composure. Over the years Frost snags five other presidents, six prime ministers, Muhammad Ali, and The Beatles…but Tricky Dick's always #1. But, remember, he's no crook.

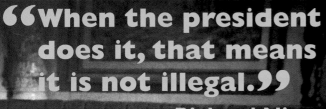

> **"When the president does it, that means it is not illegal."**
> —Richard Nixon

# DOES THIS LOINCLOTH MATCH THOSE SLIPPERS?

Though Dorothy's ruby slippers were the most-reported-on item for sale at the 1970 MGM auction, reporters looked on in wonder as thousands of items from the high-profile to the obscure were sold off. "In the end, the auction got to me also, of course," conceded one *New York Times* reporter who purchased two iron tubs for $40. "I wish I could say they will make darling planters, but they won't." Here are a few more items sold at the historic offering.

- Pantsuit worn by Lana Turner in *The Bad and the Beautiful* ($225)
- Four-piece salon set from *Marie Antoinette* ($1,200)
- Robby the Robot from the sci-fi hit *The Forbidden Planet* ($10,000)
- Chariot used in *Ben Hur* ($3,000)
- Crystal decanter from an unknown movie ($90)
- Brass bed from *The Unsinkable Molly Brown* ($3,000)
- Lion costume from *The Wizard of Oz* ($650)
- Time machine from *The Time Machine* ($10,000)
- Loincloth from *Tarzan* (price unknown)

## MAY 5

**1978** An ice cream dream: in a converted gas station at the corner of St. Paul and College Streets in Burlington, Vermont, Ben & Jerry's Homemade Ice Cream begins dishing it out. Scraping up $12,000, longtime pals Ben Cohen and Jerry Greenfield begin making their rich, dense ice cream with quirky names like Chunky Monkey and Dastardly Mash. Soon Ben is delivering pints to small grocers and restaurants in his old VW wagon; rabid demand necessitates a move to a pint-packing plant the next year. Nurtured with offbeat marketing, enormous growth propels the product to local and, later, national cult status. The original store goes under in 1982, but by then Ben & Jerry's is already a profitable force for social change and environmental responsibility.

## MAY 6

**1974** An electrical fire erupts at Samuel Goldwyn's Hollywood studio. As it spreads rapidly, a battalion chief of the LA fire department hurries over—from next door. (He's been consulting on the action/adventure spectacle, *The Towering Inferno*.) And with him comes Steve McQueen, the legendary tough and cool guy rehearsing for his role as the fire chief. He dons gear and joins firefighters, who are awed by their famous recruit. "My wife will never believe this," marvels one. Meanwhile, Steve's wife, Ali McGraw, looks on from a safe distance. "It's on-the-job training," she says. Released in November, *The Towering Inferno* does towering business, second only to *Jaws*. Reflecting major star wattage with Paul Newman, Faye Dunaway, William Holden, and Richard Chamberlain, plus a young O.J. Simpson, it wins Oscars for cinematography, editing, and song, "We May Never Love Like This Again" by Maureen McGovern. It's her second disaster-epic tune, her first, "The Morning After," was for *The Poseidon Adventure*.

# 7

**1978** They don't get no respect, and they're tired of it. The Eagles are arguably the hottest band in America with a string of #1 singles like "Best of My Love," "One of These Nights," and "Hotel California," plus multiplatinum albums, sold-out concert tours, and Grammy Awards galore. But they're miffed by what they perceive as short shrift from top rock rag *Rolling Stone*. So after the magazine takes especial pleasure in mentioning, several times, that The Eagles had lost a softball game to a team led by rock impresario Bill Graham (see June 27), the band challenges the scribes to a game. If The Eagles lose, they'll grant an interview. Intensely competitive publisher Jann Wenner puts his team through several weeks of rigorous practices, but to no avail: today the Eagles beat the Stones at USC. For the rock rag, it's gonna be a heartache tonight, but no interview.

# 8

**1971** She's not all that well known, yet. But with press like this, how long will it take? "That she doesn't appear here more often should be declared a crime against humanity," writes Mike Jahn in *The New York Times* about…Linda Ronstadt. Appearing tonight at the Fillmore East, the petite brunette is still singing mostly country and folk, with a rockin' backing band led by guitarist Glenn Frey (pre-Eagles). It takes a couple more years but Ronstadt catches on and catches fire. Aided by savvy song selection and copasetic producer Peter Asher (once half of the pop British singing duo Peter and Gordon), she delivers a string of much-praised albums like *Don't Cry Now*, *Heart Like A Wheel*, and *Living in the USA*, delivering rhythmic hits like the #1 "You're No Good," "When Will I Be Loved," and "Blue Bayou."

**1974** On this balmy spring evening in Cambridge, Massachusetts, a legend is born. Among a crowd attending a Bonnie Raitt concert at a sold-out Harvard Square Theatre is local rock critic Jon Landau, who's blown away by an opening act whose first two Columbia albums have generated lackluster sales. "I saw rock 'n' roll future, and its name is Bruce Springsteen," writes Landau of the songs performed from the then-unreleased album *Born to Run*. Landau eventually comes aboard to coproduce, and a year later the new album catapults Bruce Springsteen to fame. He soon becomes the only rock star to grace *Time* and *Newsweek* covers in the same week (see Aug. 13). The Boss's warm-up days are over.

## MAY

### 1970

The all-star defenseman collects a loose puck off the boards and feeds the center, who feeds him back as he breaks on goal. He's tripped, goes airborne, and sweeps the puck into the net—with forty seconds left in sudden-death overtime. The Boston Garden erupts as Bobby Orr leads the hometown Bruins to their first Stanley Cup title in twenty-nine years. The subsequent photo of Orr flying through the air, stick and arms raised, the puck already in and out of the goal becomes arguably the greatest hockey image of all time. In the 4-0 sweep of the St. Louis Blues, he shows peerless speed and acceleration, power, and pinpoint passing. He wins the Hart trophy as the league's MVP, Ross trophy (scoring leader), Norris trophy (best defenseman), and Conn Smythe as the playoff MVP. "He may be the greatest athlete who ever lived," says his coach Harry Sinden.

## MAY

### 1972

In a dubious attempt to shed his teenybopper image, clean-cut David Cassidy sheds his clothes for *Rolling Stone*. The risqué cover shot by Annie Leibovitz of a naked, stretched-out-in-the-grass Cassidy sends shockwaves through his legions of loyal fans. "Oh David, I know that you couldn't possibly have done this, because I know that you would have never posed nude for photographs," says Cassidy, facetiously mimicking the frantic fan letters that come pouring in. Between the covers he even shows a bit of pubic hair, and in the interview he tries to come across more like Keith Richards than Keith Partridge, his TV alter ego. He thinks he loves you, so what is he so afraid of? Clearly, not much.

## MAY 12

### 1971

So much for it being a secret. Paparazzi and reporters, as well as Beatles, Stones, and assorted friends and family engulf the tropical isle of Saint-Tropez for the wedding of Mick Jagger, twenty-seven, and Bianca Pérez-Mora Macias, twenty-six, a Nicaraguan beauty deemed "exotic" by the celebrity-crazed press. The Roman Catholic wedding, the first for both, ends in a collective all-star musical jam party that the bulging bride attends for only a few minutes (five months later, she gives birth in Paris to a daughter, Jade). The couple soon commence a two-week honeymoon at a secluded estate accessible only by boat. Among their ample wedding presents is a white bicycle-built-for-two from Stones' guitarist Mick Taylor. Mick (the other one) and Bianca divorce eight years later.

## MAY 13 1971

She's probably not "Pretty as You Feel": Grace Slick crashes her Mercedes near the Golden Gate Bridge in San Francisco, forcing the Jefferson Airplane to postpone a recording session. Slick, who'd given birth four months earlier to daughter China, is briefly hospitalized, but the band is in even worse shape. Since peaking in the late 1960s with "Somebody to Love" and "White Rabbit" and appearances at Woodstock and Altamont (the only other band to appear at both venues? Santana), they've been torn by disagreement and personnel changes. "Pretty as You Feel" soon becomes their last single to chart, though a later reformation as Jefferson Starship delivers more Top 10 entries, including "Miracles" and "Count On Me."

## MAY 14 1975

Ex-call girl turned madam Xaviera Hollander is getting plenty of exposure, but it's not all that flattering. A sanitized screen adaptation of her best-seller, *The Happy Hooker*, opens today with Lynn Redgrave in the title role. The middling reviews are far better than Hollander's own effort, a Canadian film entitled *My Pleasure Is My Business* that opened last year. "Hollander is so expressionless," says Leonard Maltin, "she can't even play herself well." Her version was made in Canada because that's where she's been deported after a bust for prostitution in New York. But regardless of her locale and legal restrictions, the proponent of the world's oldest profession continues to enjoy an onscreen presence. Last month, though, a judge ruled that the makers of a porn film, *The Life and Times of Xaviera Hollander*, couldn't use the *Mickey Mouse Club* theme song as background during an orgy scene.

# MAY

## 15

**1970** The Birmingham, England, musicians and schoolmates have been trying to find the right sound, not to mention the right name, for a while. Polka Tulk, leaning heavily on the blues, later becomes Earth, more of a jazz-blues fusion. But bassist Terence "Geezer" Butler's fascination with black magic and the macabre inspires him to write a song entitled "Black Sabbath." Voilá—the group now has a new name, image, and sound that'll inspire metal bands for decades to come. Today Black Sabbath's self-titled debut hits the stores, and while it does well on both sides of the Atlantic, it's their sophomore album, *Paranoid*, out by year's end, that truly defines the darker side of heavy metal: songs like "Iron Man," "War Pigs," and the title track, powered by Ozzy Osbourne's eerie vocals, prove to be timeless hard-rock classics.

# KOREAN KNOCKDOWN

Before the mega-successful sitcom came the original—Robert Altman's anarchic black comedy *M\*A\*S\*H*, which on May 16, 1970, won the grand prize at the Cannes Film Festival. Altman accepted, wearing a black arm-band in protest of the killing of student protestors at Kent State and the bombing of Cambodia. His freewheeling tale of an emergency medical unit commanded attention for its sharp take on the Korean War. After having long languished in development, the movie snagged an Oscar for adapted screenplay, became the year's second-highest grosser (just behind *Airport* and a nose ahead of *Patton*), and established Altman as a major iconoclastic force in film. It even survived being banned at Army and Air Force bases because it "reflected unfavorably" on the military.

## MAY 16

**1973** In the sharp-shooting vein, Prime Minister Charles de Gaulle winds up in the crosshairs of a wily assassin (Edward Fox) in the pulse-pounding movie *Day of the Jackal*, which opens today. Adapted from a best-seller by Frederick Forsythe, it's a crackling tale with masterful performances by Fox and Michel Lonsdale as his pressed and stressed pursuer, coolly directed by Austrian Fred Zinnemann (*High Noon*, *From Here to Eternity*). Since viewers know de Gaulle was not assassinated, it's the thrill of the chase that forms its centerpiece. The story twists and turns with handsome on-location shooting in England, France, and Italy, with the law always one step behind the calculating, cold-blooded killer who leaves a trail of bodies in his wake. Until he trains his gun-sight on the beloved World War II hero....

## MAY 17

**1975** Better late than.... Nineteen years ago he won an Oscar. Today he finally receives it. Blacklisted screenwriter Dalton Trumbo, sixty-nine, gets the trophy for *The Brave One*, awarded in 1957 to a pseudonymous "Robert Rich." He notes it's rather "like being presented with a bastard child—you're supposed to love it, but the emotion isn't there." After losing his career in the Red Scare of the early 1950s, he wound up serving ten months for contempt, moving to Mexico, and submitting scripts through third parties. It wasn't until 1960 that Trumbo again received a credit, for director Otto Preminger's *Exodus*. Then Kirk Douglas stepped up to reveal that Trumbo had also written the adventurous *Spartacus*. An ill Trumbo receives the Oscar at his Beverly Hills home, and dies the next year of congestive heart failure.

# "What did the president know, and when did he know it?"
## —Senator Howard Baker (R-Tennessee)

## HERE, HEARINGS

Less than a year earlier, Washington, DC, police had arrested five men for breaking into the offices of the Democratic National Committee. A firestorm quickly erupted and, on May 17, 1973, the sordid, once-covert affair burst onto live TV. An unprecedented 85 percent of Americans tuned in to at least part of the blockbuster coverage of the US Senate hearings on Watergate. They revealed an astonishing secret: the existence of a system that automatically taped everything said in the Oval Office. And so the dominoes began falling, culminating in President Nixon's resignation fifteen months later.

## MAY 18

**1976** The old lady turns eighty-five, and it's quite the party. New York's venerable Carnegie Hall hosts what some are calling the (benefit) concert of the century. Leonard Bernstein conducts the New York Philharmonic and plays harpsichord in a double-violin Bach concerto with Yehudi Menuhin and Isaac Stern. For the first time in thirty-five years, Vladimir Horowitz plays the piano in a Schumann composition. Corporations, foundations, financiers, and more snap up tickets, especially the coveted seats known as Sterns's "silver bullets," secured by what one reporter describes as "scores of the more assiduous music patrons endowed with some of the metropolitan area's most venerable eardrums." Backstage, Bernstein recalls his early days when he lived in a room above the hall, playing for dance classes. "I know every little rat's nest," he said.

## MAY 19

**1977** Wheeled and sealed: millionaire oil heiress and socialite Sandra West, thirty-seven, receives her final wish today. She's buried, as specified in her will, dressed in a lace nightgown and seated—at a comfortable reclining angle—in the driver's seat of her baby-blue 1964 Ferrari. Some three hundred mourners attend her burial in San Antonio, arranged by her brother-in-law, whose inheritance was tied to completing the unusual last request. Placed in a large crate, the car is lowered by crane into the ground. Trucks then pour in several loads of concrete to encase it. "Let's be frank," says the funeral home director. "We are concerned about vandalism."

## MAY 20

**1977** Seventeen minutes late, the famed *Orient Express* steams out of Paris' Gare de Lyon on her last journey: a three-day rail ride to Istanbul. But with only three day coaches and a single sleeper car, it's a far cry from the train's fabled heyday in the 1920s and '30s. Then, swells of royalty, celebrities, spies, and other exotic and pedestrian creatures enjoyed its opulent appointments, extravagant gourmet meals, and crackerjack wait staff. The stuff of mystery and intrigue, it began in 1883 and figured into classics like Agatha Christie's *Murder on the Orient Express*, James Bond's *From Russia with Love*, and in far-flung television episodes from *Star Trek: The Next Generation* to *Teenage Mutant Ninja Turtles*.

# MAY 21

**1975** All's awhirl for Peter Sellers as he reprises one of his most famous roles, bumbling French inspector Clouseau in Blake Edwards's *Return of the Pink Panther*. Arriving for the film's opening today with his current flame, model Tiki Wachtmeister (daughter of the Swedish ambassador to the United States for a time), he dresses and talks like Inspector Clouseau—and is named an honorary detective by the New York City Police Department. They're off the next day to London, then in July he's back in LA for *The Tonight Show Starring Johnny Carson*. After bypassing a recent, witless spinoff film, Sellers returns in this glorious throwback to *The Pink Panther* and *A Shot in the Dark*. Clouseau moves in ways most clumsy—completely unlike the graceful animated pink feline in its innovative and much-praised opening title sequence.

# MAY 22

**1973** Forerunner to the Internet, the Ethernet stirs to life today in a memo circulated by computer-science doctoral candidate Robert Metcalfe. A student at Harvard, he'd based his dissertation on a nascent networking project at MIT but had flunked. Today he writes about packet-switching data transmission at a new system at the University of Hawaii, making it the basis for his next (and accepted) dissertation about varying random access for improved transmission. A few months later, he and partner David Boggs create a working model of the system connecting computers in a local network. From small things, Mama, big things one day come.

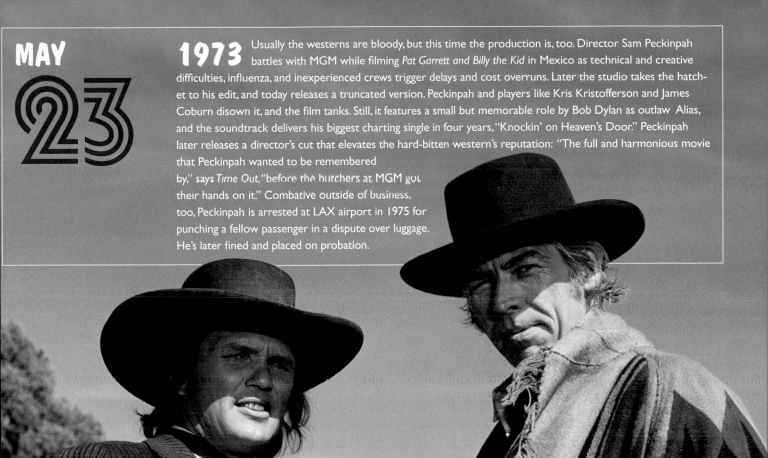

## MAY 23

**1973** Usually the westerns are bloody, but this time the production is, too. Director Sam Peckinpah battles with MGM while filming *Pat Garrett and Billy the Kid* in Mexico as technical and creative difficulties, influenza, and inexperienced crews trigger delays and cost overruns. Later the studio takes the hatchet to his edit, and today releases a truncated version. Peckinpah and players like Kris Kristofferson and James Coburn disown it, and the film tanks. Still, it features a small but memorable role by Bob Dylan as outlaw Alias, and the soundtrack delivers his biggest charting single in four years, "Knockin' on Heaven's Door." Peckinpah later releases a director's cut that elevates the hard-bitten western's reputation: "The full and harmonious movie that Peckinpah wanted to be remembered by," says *Time Out*, "before the butchers at MGM got their hands on it." Combative outside of business, too, Peckinpah is arrested at LAX airport in 1975 for punching a fellow passenger in a dispute over luggage. He's later fined and placed on probation.

## MAY 24

**1971** Turning the big three-oh, Bob Dylan visits the Wailing Wall today in Jerusalem with his wife, Sara. The spokesman of a generation is in a mellow space, having just recorded "Watching the River Flow" with Leon Russell on piano. His new surrealist book *Tarantula* has just come out, as is the documentary of his 1966 UK tour with the Hawks (later The Band), *Eat the Document*, which chronicles his transformation from folkie to rock 'n' roller. Originally commissioned for ABC, it has sat on the shelf for several years after the network was put off by its stream-of-consciousness flow. In August Dylan appears unannounced at George Harrison's Concert for Bangladesh (see Aug. 1), his only major appearance all year. This fall he records with David Bromberg, Allen Ginsberg, and friends, and joins The Band onstage at a New Year's Eve gig at the Academy of Music in Philadelphia. His marriage sours and is over in a few years, with the breakup edging through in the jarring *Blood on the Tracks*. Today, the Wailing Wall. By decade's end, born-again Christianity.

# MAY

## 1979

Intrepid Ellen Ripley battles an outer-space monster that's hard to stomach in director Ridley Scott's sci-fi churner *Alien*. Sigourney Weaver delivers a knockout performance in her first starring role, alongside fellow space travelers Yaphet Kotto, Tom Skeritt, Harry Dean Stanton, and John Hurt, the latter of whom meets an early demise when the alien living inside his chest suddenly exits, with shocking spewage. Transplanting the durable people-caught-in-a-haunted-house scenario to a spaceship, *Alien* soars to become the year's fourth-highest-grossing film. It also wins the Oscar for visual effects, with its horrific, shifting creature doing final battle with Ripley. Since she's the only one left alive, she returns for a few more dripping alien adventures, ignoring the original's visceral tagline: In space no one can hear you scream.

## MAY 26

**1973** They're really rockin' in Texas: it wouldn't be a Johnny Winter live show without the albino blues/rock guitarist turning the spotlight on younger brother Edgar. Night after night the multitalented keyboardist, drummer, saxophonist, and guitarist performs an extended instrumental composition that drives the crowds wild. So when Edgar goes into the studio, his bandmates and producer (and one-time "Hang On Sloopy" singer) Rick Derringer persuade him to record a shorter version of the showstopper. Through the magic of tape-splicing, Edgar and Rick trim the song to less than six minutes and slap it on the flip side of the first single from the album (*They Only Come Out at Night*), naming it "Frankenstein" as a nod to how it was created in the studio. When deejays turn it over and unearth "Frankenstein," they ask for an even shorter version. Realizing that it has indeed created a monster, CBS Records acquiesces. Today, "Frankenstein" is alive, alive at #1.

## MAY 27

**1975** Way up north it's way easier to get high. Today the Alaska Supreme Court shakes up the lower forty-eight states by legalizing marijuana for personal use in the privacy of your own home. In a case brought by the American Civil Liberties Union, pot possession becomes a civil crime punishable by a $100 fine. Debate rages, but the ruling withstands all challenges over the years. "It appears that effects of marijuana on the individual are not serious enough to justify widespread concern," writes the Court's chief justice, "at least as compared with the far more dangerous effects of alcohol, barbiturates and amphetamines." Last July tokers everywhere got to enjoy the first glossy national pop publication, *High Times* magazine.

## TRENDSETTER

# ACTION, THRILLS, AND SKY ADVENTURE

There are box-office hits, there are blockbusters, and then there's *Star Wars*. Released in May 1977, George Lucas's elaborate sci-fi saga catapulted into cinematic history. Jam-packed with villains, heroes, aliens, robots, and state-of-the-art special effects, *Star Wars* obliterated box-office records. The good-versus-evil interplanetary adventure wins instant, eternal fame, six Oscars, and spurred a franchise of epic proportions—all from a modest $13 million budget and a fertile imagination. Lucas matched that creativity with one of the savviest business decisions in Hollywood history: he took a reduced upfront fee in exchange for a larger percentage of merchandising rights, often previously considered "garbage rights." Over the next thirty years, the franchise would bring in merchandising revenue—from selling everything from action figures to underwear—topping $9 billion—almost $3 billion more than the worldwide box-office total. Apparently the creative genius was a business whiz, too.

# MAY 28

**1977** A thirty-foot reproduction of The Eagles's *Hotel California* album cover hovers aside the Oakland Coliseum stage. A sellout crowd of more than fifty thousand basks in the sun at promoter Bill Graham's morning-to-night "Day on the Green." It's California rock and lots more, with openers Atlanta Rhythm Section ("So in to You") and Foreigner ("Feels Like the First Time"), plus the Wilson sisters driving Heart ("Crazy On You"). As day turns into night the music heats up with the Steve Miller Band. Kicking off with three minutes of spacy synthesizer sounds before pounding into "Jet Airliner" and "The Stake," they deliver "the best paced and most fulfilling music of the day," says *The Oakland Tribune*, blowing away the headlining Eagles, who are arguably America's hottest band at the moment, with recent sold-out US and UK tours.

# MAY 29

**1977** Dealers in eye-shades watch over ten green-felt tables filling the back room of famed Hollywood eatery Chasen's. It's only 10 a.m. but a crowd has gathered for a fourteen-hour poker marathon to promote Universal's reissue of *The Sting,* the Robert Redford/Paul Newman con test and 1973's #1 movie. "The trouble with Hollywood is that everybody plays poker on Friday nights," says Richard Dreyfuss (*Jaws*), in rimless glasses and a rumpled denim shirt with rolled-up sleeves. "If I could only find a Monday or Tuesday night game." He's run out of this game early, along with cowboy-booted Ronny Cox, gentlemanly Greg Morris (*Mission: Impossible*), fastidious Ray Walston (*My Favorite Martian*), Elliot Gould, Milton Berle, and others. The prize? A beat-up bowling trophy bought at a local pawnshop. The winner? A TV reporter who showed up to interview the players.

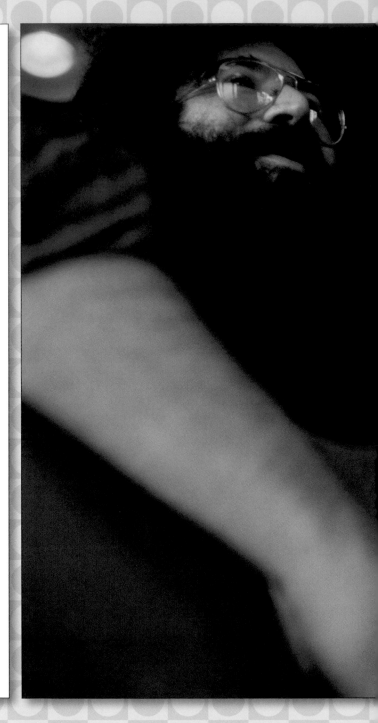

> **"Constantly choosing the lesser of two evils is still choosing evil."**
> —Jerry Garcia

## 1971

Many bands have fans. A few generate fanatics. But none have ever attracted a more loyal, devoted (some say crazed) following than the Grateful Dead. Today thirty-six deadheads at a concert in the Winterland Ballroom are treated after unwittingly drinking LSD-laced cider. "Our audience doesn't come to see theatrics," says driving force Jerry Garcia. "They realize we're not performers, that we're a group that's earnestly trying to accomplish something. And we don't quite know what that is." The acid rock/psychedelic pioneers began coalescing in San Francisco in 1965, producing a hybrid country-rock sound, legendarily long concerts, and a decidedly nonmainstream reputation. The band eschews singles and makes its name instead with albums like *Workingman's Dead* and *American Beauty*.

## 1975

"The record shows I took the blows, and did it my way!" From Frank Sinatra's lips to Evel Knievel's life, the death-defying daredevil simultaneously amazes and horrifies America. Today the red, white, and blue–spangled Knievel takes his act global, hurdling fifteen double-decker buses at London's Wembley Stadium before ninety thousand fans. The crash landing breaks his pelvis, just another mishap in his ever extravagant, elaborate stunts, like last year's attempt to soar sixteen hundred feet across Idaho's Snake River Canyon in a rocket-powered contraption. Over the years Knievel's stunts produce countless shattered bikes and bones, with his body eventually having so many aluminum plates and pins that subsequent accidents even break some of the metal inserts. Still, the ex-Army paratrooper, hockey player, card shark, and petty thief motors on.

JUNE

# JUNE

## 1975

When people talk about "tripping," it usually has to do with dropping acid, man. But for poor President Ford, it's taking on a far more literal meaning. Arriving today in Salzburg for talks with Egyptian president Anwar el-Sadat, he trips and falls down the last few rain-slicked stairs exiting *Air Force One* alongside wife Betty. He falls several more times during the conference, blaming an old "trick knee" football injury. Yet over the next year come more occasions: hitting his head on the side of a pool, bumping his head while climbing into a helicopter, and jumping into a campaign crowd after getting spooked by an exploding flashbulb. The president isn't the only one falling down on the job: in just a few months, comedian Chevy Chase will make a cottage industry out of Ford's clumsiness on the first season of *Saturday Night Live*.

## CAN'T HELP FALLING

While President Ford built his career on his military service and negotiation skills, Chevy Chase built his on falling down. Here are his most memorable pratfalls while playing the thirty-eighth president.

- The president delivers a speech to "Saturday Night Live with Harvey Cosell" (a rip on the identically named Howard Cosell show), then hits his head on the podium, falls over some folding chairs, and announces, "Live from New York, it's Saturday night!"
- After attempting to get Anwar el-Sadat and Henry Kissinger to speak by holding two phones up to each diplomat, Ford shows the audience some polling figures, only to drop the placard over his desk. He tumbles right behind it.
- President Ford performs a free-association test with a psychiatrist (Dan Akroyd), where he gives the answer "apple" to "apple," and "house" to "house." The doctor explains the test again, and continues. Apple: "cider." Rug: "trip." Carpet: "spill." Head: "bump." Primary: "lose." Reagan: "hair dye." When the next word is "China," the president excuses himself, only to get up on the wrong side of the couch and crash through the wall of the set.

## JUNE 2

## 1979

One way or another, new wave-ish Blondie is determined to follow up their smash debut single, "Heart of Glass." It happens today with, you guessed it, "One Way or Another," the second single from their album *Parallel Lines*, which goes platinum (one million units) by week's end. Fronted by striking blonde Debbie Harry, rock's latest and hottest sex symbol, Blondie delivers a crisp pop/punk/rock sound, though the band takes some heat for the commercially disco-tinged "Heart of Glass." "I don't think being commercial is totally derogatory," says Harry. Good thing, because for the next couple years Blondie reigns as one of rock's top bands, touring nonstop and delivering strong albums and three more #1s: "Call Me" (from *American Gigolo*), "The Tide Is High," and "Rapture."

## JUNE 3

**1972** Let me take you where? Born in the Mississippi Delta, Roebuck "Pop" Staples followed a long hard road. Moving to Chicago, he worked in a steel mill by day while singing gospel at night with his fast-growing family. The Staple Singers became one of the country's leading gospel groups in the 1950s, but crossing

over from gospel to secular music is a treacherous road on which many have fallen. Signing with the legendary Stax Records, the band smartly elevates the spirit-lifting voice of daughter Mavis to lead. Songs like "Express Yourself" bring the group newfound prominence, nationally and internationally. They tour the United States, Europe, and Japan, earning a spot opening for the high-flying Bee Gees. Crossover audiences take to their inspiring, uplifting material, so much so that today, the gospel according to Pop is the #1 song in the country, "I'll Take You There."

## JUNE 4

**1972** The Rolling Stones' latest single, "Tumbling Dice," might also apply to its first North American concert tour since the Altamont debacle (four dead) in 1969: it's a gamble. But opening the US portion tonight in Seattle, the Stones still clearly have what it takes, mixing old numbers with fresh material from their new double album, *Exile on Main Street*. Opening act Stevie Wonder, now 22, is a smart choice, too. Still, the tour has some rocky moments. A bomb in Montreal destroys their equipment, but a resourceful local band manager quickly secures replacement gear. In Boston, bad weather diverts their flight to Rhode Island, where Keith Richards punches a pushy photographer. Boston mayor Kevin White intervenes, and Wonder covers with a two-hour opening set 'til the Stones arrive, a tiresomely fashionable, five hours late. The band—and the mayor—get a standing ovation from the sold-out Boston Garden crowd. Three years later Major White goes from great to goat when he cancels a Led Zeppelin concert after fans riot while waiting to buy tickets.

# JUNE
# 5

**1974** One hit single does not a series star make, as the "Ode to Billie Joe" singer proves with tonight's debut of CBS musical variety series *The Bobbie Gentry Show* (a.k.a. *Bobbie Gentry's Happiness*). It's gone in less than a month, just like whatever Billie Joe McAllister threw off the Tallahatchee Bridge. Back in 1967 that story line sparked overnight success. The "B" side turned hit generated airplay, controversy, and sales. It topped the charts, helping Gentry win three Grammys en route to duets with Glen Campbell and headlining in Las Vegas. Though this series flops, she's still got some gas in the tank. In two years her signature song inspires *Ode to Billy Joe*, with movie posters promising, "What the song didn't tell you, the movie will." Robby Benson stars as Billy Joe, tormented by his possible homosexuality.

**1973** It turns out that even by himself, Curtis Mayfield makes impressions. Three years after leaving the group of that name, where he'd been the driving force behind hits like "It's All Right," "Keep on Pushin'," and "People Get Ready," the smooth soul singer has two solo albums certified gold today. On his 1970 solo debut *Curtis*, Mayfield experiments with longer jams, including the now classic "Move On Up." On his latest, *Back to the World*, he takes a tip from Marvin Gaye's "What's Going On" and focuses on socially conscious funk like "Future Shock." Still, his biggest success comes with his soundtrack to the blaxploitation classic, *Superfly,* which generates his only two Top 10 hits: the title track and "Freddie's Dead." That's what I said.

# JUNE

## 1971
Gracing the cover of *The New York Times Magazine*, glowing health food enthusiast and entrepreneur Jerome Rodale, seventy-two, tapes an appearance on *The Dick Cavett Show*. Known as the guru of organic food, he runs a successful publishing house and claims he'll "live to a hundred unless I'm run down by some sugar-crazed taxi driver." After his interview, as Cavett talks with journalist Pete Hamill, Rodale appears to nod off. "Are we boring you?" quips the host. But Rodale isn't asleep. He's dead, killed by a heart attack. The show never airs, though Cavett marvels in later years about the people who constantly tell him they watched it. "Hey Dick," he recalls people say, "I'll never forget the look on your face when that guy died on your show." But unless they were in the studio audience, they never saw it.

# JUNE
## 8

## 1974
Lights and lasers flash. Clouds of dry-ice vapors rise. Synthesizers and symphonic sounds swirl. Welcome to the bombastic, fantastic world of Yes. The arrival of classically trained keyboardist Rick Wakeman in 1972 brings the British band its most commercial success, the album *Fragile* (featuring matching cover art by illustrator Roger Dean) and the Top 20 hit "Roundabout." Today, a couple months after they packed Madison Square Garden for two sold-out nights, Wakeman announces his departure. His debut solo album, *Journey to the Center of the Earth*, soon soars to #1 in the UK and #3 stateside. Wakeman's lush run continues with *The Six Wives of Henry VIII*, though he does wind up reuniting with Yes from time to time over the years.

# JUNE 9

**1973** One, two, three wins he's in! Secretariat blazes to a record 31-length victory in the 105th annual Belmont Stakes, becoming only the ninth horse ever to win racing's Triple Crown. Like he did in the Kentucky Derby and Preakness Stakes previously, jockey Ron Turcotte leads "Big Red" to victory. "Secretariat has opened a twenty-two–length lead," cries CBS sportscaster (and later Belmont track announcer) Chic Anderson. "He is going to be the Triple Crown winner!

Here comes Secretariat to the wire. An unbelievable, an amazing performance!" The first Triple Crown winner in twenty-five years since Citation in 1948, Secretariat leads the way for two other Triple Crown winners in the 1970s: Seattle Slew in 1977, and Affirmed in 1978. Secretariat also posts the highest non-human ranking on ESPN's Top 100 Athletes of the Twentieth Century list, coming in at #35 just ahead of basketball's Big O, Oscar Robertson.

# JUNE 10

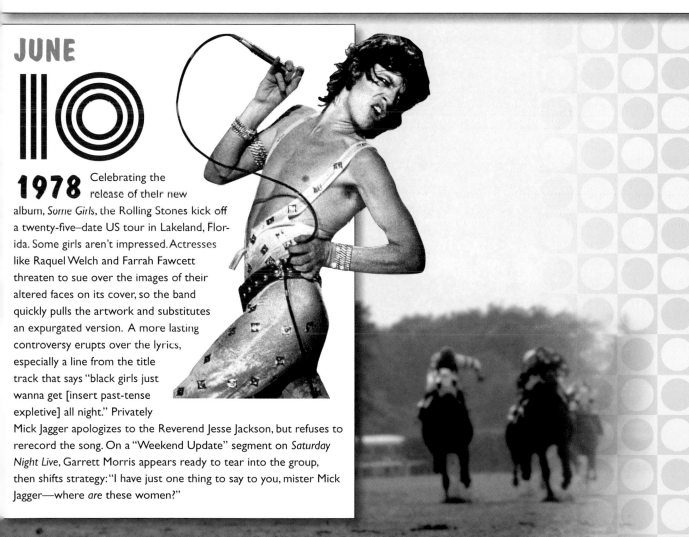

**1978** Celebrating the release of their new album, *Some Girls*, the Rolling Stones kick off a twenty-five–date US tour in Lakeland, Florida. Some girls aren't impressed. Actresses like Raquel Welch and Farrah Fawcett threaten to sue over the images of their altered faces on its cover, so the band quickly pulls the artwork and substitutes an expurgated version. A more lasting controversy erupts over the lyrics, especially a line from the title track that says "black girls just wanna get [insert past-tense expletive] all night." Privately Mick Jagger apologizes to the Reverend Jesse Jackson, but refuses to rerecord the song. On a "Weekend Update" segment on *Saturday Night Live*, Garrett Morris appears ready to tear into the group, then shifts strategy: "I have just one thing to say to you, mister Mick Jagger—where *are* these women?"

# JUNE

|| ||

**1970** Soon to become famous for her celebrity shots, Annie Leibovitz enjoys her first *Rolling Stone* cover: a shot of young anti–Vietnam War protestors for the lead story, "On America 1970: A Pitiful Helpless Giant." (But it's not all bad news—another story, "George Harrison in New York," recounts the ex-Beatle producing a Billy Preston album and jamming with Bob Dylan.) Within six months publisher Jann Wenner has splashed his covers with Leibovitz photos of Janis Joplin, Rod Stewart, and the coup de grâce: a pensive John Lennon, followed by John and Yoko. Her year's primo run continues apace with some of rock's biggest names: Elton John, Ian Anderson ("Jethro Tull Might Do Something Weird"), Jefferson Airplane, The Beach Boys, Ike and Tina Turner. The list—and Leibovitz's career—go on and on.

## ALTMAN'S OPUS

Conventional film wisdom of the '70s was that American audiences preferred a single protagonist and a straightforward story line...until iconoclastic producer/director Robert Altman tossed conventional wisdom overboard and fashioned *Nashville*. The film, which premiered on June 11, 1975, was a multilayered tableau of competing country-music stars, their families, wannabes, and assorted hangers-on in a cutthroat company town. Joan Tewkesbury's inspired script intertwined music with politics and dreamers with doers, and featured improvised dialogue by a stellar ensemble cast including (where to start?) Lily Tomlin, Ned Beatty, Allen Garfield, Henry Gibson, Shelley Duvall, Keith Carradine, and Karen Black. Its toe-tapping original soundtrack drove a nuanced, cinematic tour de force whose power remains undiminished.

## JUNE 12 1973

Late at night, Marlon Brando and Dick Cavett take a stroll through New York's Chinatown. Brando earlier gave his first interview, on *The Dick Cavett Show,* since his infamous snubbing of the Oscar for *The Godfather* at the awards ceremony last March. They're trailed by notorious paparazzi photographer Ron Galella, a Brooklyn-born ex-GI, who asks Brando to remove his sunglasses. Then things get a little out of hand—or fist. "Bang, out of the blue—one punch," says Galella. "I didn't even see it coming." The punch breaks his jaw and requires nine stitches to close a cut lower lip. "Brando's upset about the mistreatment of Indians. What about the mistreatment of photographers?" But there's little public sympathy for Galella, who was recently ordered by a judge to keep a distance from Jacqueline Kennedy Onassis and her children after he "relentlessly invaded" their privacy. His tricks included bribing her maid for information, donning disguises and even scuba diving off the Greek island of Skorpios in search of photo ops.

## JUNE 13 1978

Hey kids, wanna get into the Guinness World Book of Records? Several thousand middle schoolers and their teachers try to do just that in a large-scale tug-of-war today in Harrisburg, Pennsylvania. But when the long, industrial-quality braided nylon rope snaps under the pressure of more than four thousand straining hands, bloody hell breaks loose. More than two hundred are injured, the most serious being a half-dozen students who lose fingers or parts of fingers. Plus there's plenty of cuts, heavy-duty rope burns, and broken limbs. Guinness later discontinues the category, and families file a lawsuit naming the school district, principal, teacher who conceived the idea, and Pennsylvania Power and Light, which supplied the rope.

## JUNE 14 1974

With an estimated four thousand people dying in the United States every year from choking on food, surgeon Henry M. Heimlich has an idea. Today he gives a public demonstration of his simple, life-saving, arm-wrapping maneuver that dislodges items trapped in the windpipe. "We are hoping this will lead to a first aid method for café coronary," says Heimlich, referring to the term used to describe an emergency in which a diner cannot talk or breath and appears to be having a heart attack. An unassisted victim will die within four minutes. Within days Heimlich's method is saving lives. Soon to become famous forever, the busy doctor gladly promotes his better mousetrap to whoever will listen. Ever inquisitive, he has a letter published several days later in the *New York Times* on a totally unrelated matter, nuclear power in the Mideast.

## JUNE 15

**1972** Dubbed the "Christian Woodstock," a weeklong evangelical conference and rally in Dallas, Texas, attracts eighty thousand people from seventy-five countries. Training to spread the fervor globally, they hear Reverend Billy Graham tonight at a huge outdoor rally, one of six all week. Having just published *The Jesus Revolution*, Graham rejoices in his perceived spiritual awakening of the nation. He describes seeing a group of demonstrating hippies and wanting to "shave them, cut their hair, bathe them, and then preach to them." In a Chicago crusade later this summer, his Jesus warriors surround demonstrators and chant Jesus' name to drown them out. "Without the welcoming arms of Billy Graham," says Christian historian Larry Eskridge, "and other evangelical leaders, there would have been no bridge back for thousands of refugees from the counterculture—just another disillusioning hassle and prolonged battle with another facet of the Establishment."

## JUNE 16

**1970** Soon the top song on everyone's mind won't be a song, but a movie. Today Chicago Bears running back Brian Piccolo, twenty-six, dies of cancer. ABC's *Brian's Song* retells the story with James Caan as Piccolo and Billy Dee Williams as NFL star Gale Sayers. A top college player but undrafted because of his small size, Piccolo had signed with the Bears and worked up from the practice squad to special teams to starting halfback after Sayers hurt his knee. Returning from surgery, Sayers won an award for courage in 1969. "Brian is the one who should get this award—he is the one who knows about courage," says Sayers, who delivers him the trophy the next day at the hospital. After Piccolo's death today at Chicago's Memorial Hospital for Cancer and Allied Diseases, longtime Bears owner George Halas, Sr., says: "Ah, he was a tough one."

## JUNE 17

**1972** The song may go "Sunrise, Sunset," but the sun has yet to set for *Fiddler on the Roof.* Today marks the musical's 3,225th performance, making it the longest-running show on Broadway to date. When the curtain rose in 1964, Zero Mostel brought author Sholem Aleichem's Tevye to life with a Tony award-winning turn as the humble dairyman attempting to maintain "Tradition" even as his daughters marry and the czar threatens the villagers with eviction. A pre-*Maude* Bea Arthur costars as Yente, the matchmaker, and the traditional, touching show sweeps nine Tony Awards including best musical, choreography, and direction (Jerome Robbins). A 1971 movie version from director Norman Jewison also does big business. Though *Fiddler* soon ends its seventeen-year Broadway run, revivals continue for years to come, echoing one of its famous numbers: "To Life."

## JUNE 18

**1977** Who needs *As the World Turns* when you've got Fleetwood Mac? Songs on the group's latest album, conveniently titled *Rumours*, hint at the incestuous romantic woes of its members: the separation of bassist/founder John McVie and wife/keyboardist Christine, the impending breakup of guitarist Lindsey Buckingham and singer Stevie Nicks, and the divorce of drummer Mick Fleetwood and wife (who, oddly enough, is not in the band). Luckily, the album fares far better than the interpersonal relationships, spending thirty-one weeks at #1, a run unsurpassed by any album since. It also produces four Top 10 singles, including the group's only #1, "Dreams." Today both album and single top their respective charts. During a *Rolling Stone* shoot at the peak of the *Rumours* success, the members poke fun at their relationship troubles by posing in the same bed. "Tales of flamboyant infidelity and dementia circulated like polluted air," says Mick Fleetwood. "So rampant were the rumors that we sometimes heard them fifth-hand."

# JUNE 19

## 1973

It's a family affair today in Houston as hockey legend Gordie Howe skates out of retirement to sign with the World Hockey Association's Houston Aeros. His primary motivation, beside the money, is to play alongside sons Mark and Marty, but even wife Colleen gets a job as an amateur hockey consultant. Struggling for recognition, fans, and box-office dollars, the Aeros sign the NHL's most prolific scorer to a four-year, $1 million contract. In a last ditch effort to keep him from jumping rinks, the NHL offers a half-million dollar contract as a roving public relations ambassador, but he's lacing up the skates. The WHA also pays a million to sign Bobby Hull, blazing shooter of the Chicago Blackhawks. The rejuvenated Howe, forty-five, plays for another seven years and eventually retires with a record 1,071 goals and 1,518 assists.

MEANWHILE...

## HARK! A SHARK

At the time, the young director had only one feature film to his credit, the modestly successful *Sugarland Express*. But on June 20, 1975, Steven Spielberg's newest film steered his career straight into the fast lane and on into the sea. *Jaws* successfully tapped into one of man's primal fears—what's lurking beneath the surface of the ocean? Aided by a gigantic marketing push, the film also tapped into popular culture, and became the quintessential summertime blockbuster—not to mention the highest-grossing movie of all time (until *Star Wars* in 1977). This being Hollywood, lesser sequels soon surfaced, but Spielberg was on to far more momentous fare: *Close Encounters of the Third Kind*, *Raiders of the Lost Ark*, and *E.T.: The Extra-Terrestrial*.

# JUNE 20

**1974** A stark film noir in color, *Chinatown* evokes shades of Dashiell Hammett and Raymond Chandler. The convoluted 1930s detective yarn spins along with star turns by Jack Nicholson as the hard-pressed, hard-luck PI, femme fatale Faye Dunaway, and John Huston as the omnipotent villain. It's the last film shot stateside by director Roman Polanski, who later flees to France after his conviction on a charge of statutory rape. A box-office and critical winner, it receives a whopping eleven Oscar nominations but comes home with a lone win: Robert Towne for original screenplay. In the intensely competed lead actor category, Nicholson faces Al Pacino (*The Godfather Part II*) and Dustin Hoffman (*Lenny*)—but the surprise winner is veteran Art Carney for *Harry and Tonto*. Still, the steamy, smoky *Chinatown* weathers on to lasting acclaim. "Undoubtedly," says *Time Out*, "one of the great films of the '70s."

# JUNE 21

## 1977

All the president's men weren't as lucky as Richard Nixon, who was pardoned by successor Gerald Ford one month after Ford assumed office. Today Nixon's former chief of staff, buzz cut H.R. Haldeman, convicted of obstruction of justice and perjury in the Watergate scandal and cover-up, begins serving an eighteen-month term at the Lompoc federal pen in California. Tomorrow once-imperious John Mitchell, the only US attorney general ever to have been convicted and imprisoned, begins a sentence for conspiracy, obstruction of justice, and perjury at a military prison in Alabama. He's paroled for medical reasons after serving only nineteen months. The pugnacious Mitchell delivered one of the most famous threats in the history of American journalism: "Katie Graham [publisher of the *Washington Post*]," he warned reporter Carl Bernstein in 1972, "is gonna get her tit caught in a big fat wringer if that's published."

# JUNE 22

## 1979

It's taken two decades, but the Muppets have finally made it to the big screen. Puppeteer—make that Muppeteer—Jim Henson's cast of wondrous characters has grown larger as they've gone from a local five-minute show in Henson's native DC, and starring in coffee commercials, to appearances on *The Ed Sullivan Show*, *Sesame Street*, and the internationally seen *Muppet Show*. The popularity of characters introduced there—including Fozzie and Miss Piggy—suggests a transition to movies. Today *The Muppet Movie*—"More Entertaining Than Humanly Possible!"—opens to glowing reviews en route to big box office. Musically, Kermit the Frog's big number, "Rainbow Connection," snags an Oscar nomination and rises to #25, the only frog-sung number in chart history. (Henson's only other hit? Ernie's "Rubber Duckie" in 1970.) More Muppet movies follow, though Henson's next film project involves helping to create a character for the *Star Wars* sequel *The Empire Strikes Back*. Enter Yoda.

## 23

**1971** What a complicated life she leads...two of them, actually. Onscreen Jane Fonda today undergoes a remarkable transformation from the sci-fi sex kitten of *Barbarella* to a modern, practical call girl in *Klute*. In a role nixed by Barbra Strei-sand, she gets strong reviews. Director Alan Pakula's complex psychological thriller also features Donald Sutherland and Roy Scheider. Fonda takes the Oscar for best actress, but offscreen she's generating even more heat with her vocal anti-Vietnam War stance (see July 14). She and costar Sutherland cofound a troupe that travels the college circuit protesting the war. Life later imitates art when Fonda wins her second best actress Oscar in 1978 as an anti-war wife in *Coming Home*. Offscreen, meanwhile, she finds another way to get back onscreen, with her workout videos (and books) making Fonda the celebrity queen of fitness. Work it, girl.

# JUNE

**1970** Quintessential bad boy Dennis Hopper sues pal Peter Fonda today for a profit percentage from *Easy Rider,* their epochal anti-Establishment road movie slash late-1960s time capsule. Hopper wants a bigger share for his contribution to the screenplay, which is awash with sex, drugs, rock 'n' roll, adrenaline, and casual violence. A pretty fair description of his offscreen life too, some say, as mammoth drug and alcohol intake have made him industry enemies galore. "The man is an idiot," says Peter's papa, Henry Fonda. "He's a total freak-out, stoned out of his mind all the time." Off the success of *Easy Rider,* Universal bankrolls Hopper to write and star in *The Last Movie,* an alternately dazzling and chaotic film that tanks at the box office. On Halloween 1971 he and Michelle Phillips (from The Mamas & the Papas), both recently divorced, marry. Their blissful union lasts eight days. But Hopper's a survivor who eventually revives and thrives with later hits like the twisted *Blue Velvet.*

# JUNE

# 25

**1973** Trailer. Parked. Today a smash new opening comes to Broadway: a white trailer selling half-price tickets from a tri-cornered island in Times Square. Abounding with drugs, robberies, and prostitution, the Midtown area's desperate for resuscitation. So Mayor Lindsay and the Office of Midtown Planning and Development approach the Theatre Development Fund (TDF), a young not-for-profit performing arts service organization, to sell same-day, half-price tickets to Broadway shows. It's an overnight and lasting success, and soon the trailer is replaced by a white-piped structure lashed to four concrete anchors so it won't blow away. With twin lines wrapping around each side, the booth serves memorably and admirably until a major rehab in the early twenty-first century.

## JUNE

**1972** A shopper hands a cashier a ten-pack of Wrigley's chewing gum at the Marsh Supermarket in Troy, Ohio, and the earth moves. The Universal Product Code (UPC) scanner reads its first barcode and records its first transaction. Long in development by engineer George Laurer at IBM, the scanner instantly becomes embedded in commerce and life. IBM's fixed-length, all-numeric system identifies both the product and manufacturer. It simultaneously captures valuable consumer info and inventory data. Initially there's an unintended side effect: consumers gripe that products no longer have prices on them with purple ink stamps or little paper stickers. But the father of the UPC never looks back, creating and collecting more than twenty-five patents until he retires in 1987. Today? That first barcode reads sixty-seven cents.

## JUNE

**1971** The times they are a'changing, and not for the better according to rock impresario Bill Graham. Disillusioned by the increasing commercialization of rock and greedy musicians who'd rather play twenty thousand-seat arenas than smaller, more intimate clubs, he's shuttering the Fillmores East and West, musical birthplaces of many of the nation's top bands. Tonight's invitation-only closing party at New York's Fillmore East, featuring the Allman Brothers, Albert King, J. Geils Band, Mountain, and Country Joe McDonald, is broadcast live on WNEW. "It's a strange feeling," says Graham of the closing night's mixed vibes. "If I can just put it into little jars and put it on my shelf, I will be very happy." A week later there's a similar lively end at San Francisco's Fillmore West to the sounds of Creedence Clearwater Revival, Santana, and Tower of Power, whose biggest single sadly sums up the night: "So Very Hard to Go."

# JUNE 28

## 1976

As the commercial goes, there's something about an Aqua Velva man. In this case it's something rather bizarre, as the aftershave's most recent pitchman is Detroit Tigers rookie pitcher Mark "The Bird" Fidrych. With his frizzy blond curls and wild on-field antics, he brings a welcome, entertaining aspect to the grand old game—talking to both himself and the ball between pitches, grooming the mound on his hands and knees, shaking the hands of infielders after good plays. Tonight an announcer calls him "the most interesting player since Dizzy Dean," and "The Bird" is the word from coast to coast. Voted AL Rookie of the Year, he shares a cover of *Sports Illustrated* with *Sesame Street*'s Big Bird and becomes the first athlete to grace the cover of *Rolling Stone* ("America's Hottest Baseball Card"). Unfortunately this Bird flies off too quickly, as a torn rotator cuff and wildness ends Fidrych's too-brief career in 1980.

## LOTS OF SPOTS: FAMOUS COMMERCIALS

Aqua Velva men weren't the only spokesmen on TV in the '70s. Here's a sampling of some of the decade's most memorable advertising moments.

- **Keep America Beautiful:** Cherokee Indian Iron Eyes Cody paddles his canoe past smokestacks and debris-infested waters, a single tear rolling down his weathered face. (1970)
- **Alka-Seltzer:** An inmate (George Raft), disgusted by the lousy chow, pounds his cup and leads his fellow mess hall prisoners in a thunderous chant of, "Al-ka Selt-zer, Al-ka Selt-zer!" (1970)
- **Coca-Cola:** Young folks of all colors and creeds gather on a sunny mountainside to sing the praises of the soft drink, to the bubbly tune of "I'd Like to Teach the World to Sing." (1971)
- **Quaker Oats:** Two young brothers suspiciously eye a box of Life cereal, refusing to try it 'til they test it out on their chubby-cheeked, picky three-year-old brother: "He likes it! Hey, Mikey!" (1972)
- **Crest:** Talking teeth lament the departure of fellow member Harold, felled by the owner's excessive "caramels, jaw breakers, pizza pies…. If only we'd been brushed." (1972)

- **Xerox:** After a rotund Franciscan monk painstakingly hand-letters a parchment sheet, his superior asks for five hundred more. The monk buses to his local copy shop, and upon returning with the goods his superior exclaims, "It's a miracle!" (1975)
- **Dannon yogurt:** A choir of old men sings as scenes pass of weathered Russians smiling and dancing, closing on one who's eating. A voice-over tells the audience, "Temur Vanachu thought Dannon was really fine yogurt. He ought to know. He's been eating yogurt for 105 years." (1976)
- **Polaroid:** Sparring lightly with Mariette Hartley, actor James Garner lauds a camera "so simple to operate, even a woman can use it." (1977)
- **BASF cassette tapes:** An unlucky soldier receives a tape from home with bad news: his girl's found another, his brother. As he sits stunned, a sergeant snaps, "Play it again, John." (1979)
- **Coca-Cola:** Glowering Pittsburgh Steelers' lineman Mean Joe Greene chugs the soda bottle offered by a young lad, to whom he gratefully tosses his jersey. (1979)

# JUNE 29

**1972** Off the success of *Butch Cassidy and the Sundance Kid*, Robert Redford combines his matinee good looks with solid performances in a string of successful films. Today he opens as an idealistic but opportunistic underdog running for the US Senate in *The Candidate*. Written by a former speechwriter for failed presidential candidate Eugene McCarthy, the film features cameos by politicos like Hubert Humphrey and George McGovern, and an uncredited cameo by Groucho Marx in his last film. Redford invests some earnings in a Colorado ski resort and renames it Sundance. A few years later an independent film festival debuts in Salt Lake City with films like *Midnight Cowboy* and *Mean Streets*. Intrigued, Redford soon provides backing and so begins the Sundance Film Festival, an offshoot of his Sundance Institute.

# JUNE 30

**1971** Rockin' the boat for the vote: spurred on by the raging Vietnam War, state legislatures rush to ratify the Twenty-sixth Amendment that will lower the voting age from twenty-one to eighteen. Today passage in Alabama and Ohio brings ratification to the brink, and tomorrow North Carolina and Oklahoma put it over the top—a fast five-month march representing the quickest ratification of any constitutional amendment in US history. "An injustice in the voting rights has stood too long uncorrected, an injustice against over ten million citizens," says this book's coauthor Harvey Solomon at a 1970 Rotary Club meeting in Rhode Island. "Let's take a step that will be a vote of confidence toward America's youth, tomorrow's leaders."

# JULY

## 11

**1971** As a follow-up to his shocking and successful *Midnight Cowboy,* the only X-rated Oscar winner for best picture in history, John Schlesinger (who also took home the directing trophy) tries an even more sensationalistic slant—full frontal male nudity. *Sunday Bloody Sunday,* opening today, features a frank and graphic triangular love affair among Peter Finch, Glenda Jackson, and Murray Head. Finch got the role only after first choice Alan Bates was unavailable (he was filming the *Go-Between*), and the original actor was fired for too much timidity in playing the role of a homosexual Jewish doctor involved with bisexual designer Head. Finch nets an Oscar nomination for his work, considered quite brave at a time when playing gay is perceived as a career-killer. He wins the trophy five years later, posthumously, for his role as an unhinged anchorman in *Network* (see Nov. 27).

# JULY

## 2

**1971** When *Shaft* first calls, the big, buff, broad-shouldered black singer Isaac Hayes hopes it's for the lead role. That winds up going to Richard Roundtree, so Hayes instead does what he does best. His soundtrack does double duty, winning a Grammy for best score and an Oscar for best song ("Theme from Shaft"). Released today, the first mainstream, commercially successful movie about a black private eye kicks off the blaxploitation genre with a hot mix of sex, drugs, and hot buttered soul. Hayes catapults to fame, assuming the nickname of his next album, *Black Moses.* He tours internationally with a crowning gig at London's Royal Albert Hall and mixes easily on primetime TV with everyone from Jack Benny to the Osmonds. Next year *Shaft*'s producer's son, Gordon Parks, Jr., delivers *Superfly* in the same vein. Its soundtrack, by Curtis Mayfield, delivers two breakout hits: "Superfly" and "Freddie's Dead."

## JULY 3

### 1974

Starting tonight, you can tie a yellow ribbon 'round the ole tee vee. For CBS, it's the dawn of a new day, or rather the day of a new dawn, i.e., Tony Orlando and Dawn. On the strength of chart hits like the #1 "Tie a Yellow Ribbon ('Round the Ole Oak Tree)," they get the time slot vacated by *The Sonny and Cher Comedy Hour*, doomed by the couple's divorce. The bubbly trio had a most unusual beginning: working for a music publisher, Orlando recorded their first song ("Candida") as a favor to his boss. It was only after recording their second, "Knock Three Times," that he even met bandmates Telma Hopkins and Joyce Vincent Wilson, who recorded their backing vocals in California. Their music-and-skits format clicks, and the summertime show winds up returning for two more seasons. After Dawn the sun shines brightest for Telma, who costars with Tom Hanks on *Bosom Buddies* and goes toe-to-toe with Urkel on *Family Matters*.

---

**TRENDSETTER**

## BORN TO BE WILD

Doors' front man Jim Morrison led a turbulent life. Two years after forming in 1965, his LA-based band topped the singles charts with "Light My Fire" and "Hello, I Love You." But more than just strong albums cemented his reputation as a fiery, anti-Establishment warrior. Morrison had several high-profile arrests, including one for exposing himself and simulating masturbation at a gig in Miami, and one for disorderly conduct on an airplane. Evading the legal system, Morrison bolted for Paris, where he wrote poetry, released a book, and, on July 3, 1971, died a mysterious death in his bathtub. Conspiracy theories still abound: Forty-five years later, a former nightclub manager wrote in a book that Morrison actually overdosed on heroin in a club's toilet, and drug dealers carted his body back to his apartment. No matter what the cause, his Paris gravesite, near those of Oscar Wilde, Edith Piaf, and Frederic Chopin, has forever become a shrine.

> **"I'm interested in anything about revolt, disorder, chaos, especially activity that appears to have no meaning. It seems to me to be the road toward freedom."**
>
> —Jim Morrison

## JULY

**1970** Long live the King! On July Fourth, rising blues legend B.B. King plays the three-day Atlanta Pop Festival alongside rock acts like Jimi Hendrix, Jethro Tull, the Allman Brothers, and Johnny Winter. The summertime event in tiny Byron, Georgia, gets far less attention than Woodstock the summer before, but draws up to half a million people—at $11 a ticket. "There were so darn many of them," says the police chief, "that they ran the alligators and water moccasins right out of the creek." King has run off a string of R&B hits since the 1950s, but is now finally crossing over to tasty mainstream success with "The Thrill Is Gone," a strings-enhanced slice of blues rock. King begins a long reign with his trusty Gibson guitar Lucille, so named after an early performance in an Arkansas bar when a fight erupted and forced an evacuation. He dashed back in to rescue his guitar, later learning that the fight had broken out over a girl named Lucille.

## JULY

# 5

**1978** The third time's a charm, but he won't stop there. Today strapping Swedish tennis champion Bjorn Borg dismantles Jimmy Connors in straight sets to claim his third straight Wimbledon title. Since becoming the All England Club's youngest winner ever two years ago at age twenty when he beat Romanian Ilie Nastase, Borg has dominated men's tennis. His steady baseline game features his trademark, whip-fast two-handed backhand and looping, topspin forehand. This year he's improved his serve "from a rifle to a cannon," says one sportswriter. "The bigger the challenge, the better he responds has become the essence of Borg." He'll go on to win here the next two years, too, for an unprecedented five consecutive Wimbledon titles, a record that stands for a quarter century until it's matched by Switzerland's Roger Federer.

# JULY 6

## 1974

Candy may be leaving a rather bitter taste in people's mouths these days. Sugar prices have more than tripled in the last year, squeezing the manufacturers of candy and soft drinks. Life Savers enlarges its candy's holes and boosts its price from ten to fifteen cents, though a twenty-one-year-old Australian still sucks one for a record four hours and forty minutes on the same day in 1979 as A Taste of Honey wins the Grammy for best new artist. Necco Wafers reduces their diameter from 1¼" to ⅞", and so-called nickel candy bars are now fifteen cents. Today a Hershey's Milk Chocolate bar weighs 1.4-oz.; by 1977 it'll be a 1.2-oz. bar going for twenty cents. Smaller sweets for the sweet.

# JULY 7

## 1977

The furor has died down, but not the action. Roger Moore stars for the third time as British secret agent James Bond in *The Spy Who Loved Me*, and no one's thinking much about the departed Sean Connery. A royal premiere today in London even attracts Princess Anne, as if Moore needed the help. The rip-roaring film's got a smart, sexy, stylish Bond girl, Barbara Bach; a steely (and steel-toothed) henchman, 7'2" Richard Kiel; an array of neat gadgetry like a Lotus Esprit that runs both on land and underwater; a Marvin Hamlisch score featuring one of the franchise's most memorable tunes, Carly Simon's "Nobody Does It Better"; exotic locales like the Bahamas, Egypt, Sardinia, Scotland, and Switzerland, plus spectacular stunts and special effects. Good thing it also has the biggest budget ($13.5 million) of any Bond film to date.

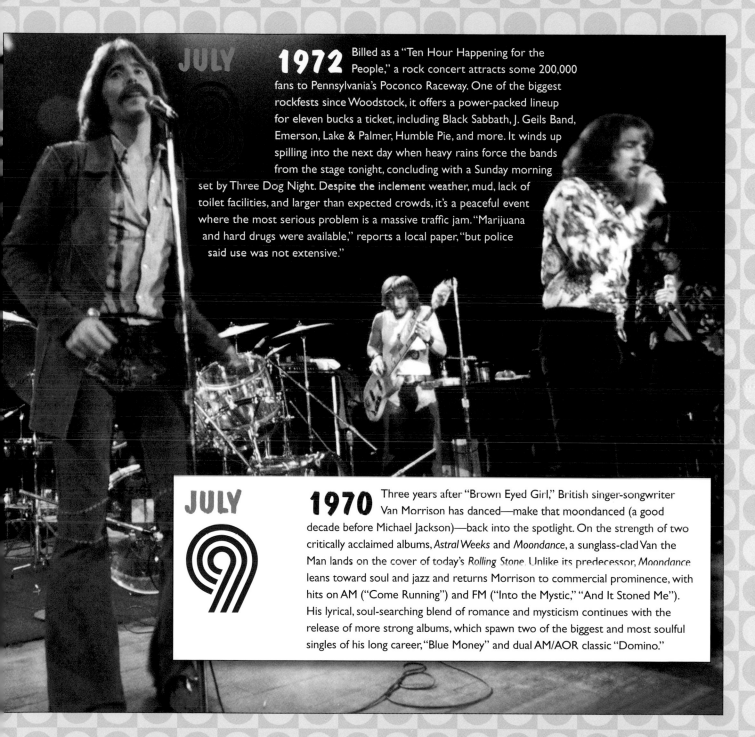

**JULY 8 1972** Billed as a "Ten Hour Happening for the People," a rock concert attracts some 200,000 fans to Pennsylvania's Poconco Raceway. One of the biggest rockfests since Woodstock, it offers a power-packed lineup for eleven bucks a ticket, including Black Sabbath, J. Geils Band, Emerson, Lake & Palmer, Humble Pie, and more. It winds up spilling into the next day when heavy rains force the bands from the stage tonight, concluding with a Sunday morning set by Three Dog Night. Despite the inclement weather, mud, lack of toilet facilities, and larger than expected crowds, it's a peaceful event where the most serious problem is a massive traffic jam. "Marijuana and hard drugs were available," reports a local paper, "but police said use was not extensive."

**JULY 9 1970** Three years after "Brown Eyed Girl," British singer-songwriter Van Morrison has danced—make that moondanced (a good decade before Michael Jackson)—back into the spotlight. On the strength of two critically acclaimed albums, *Astral Weeks* and *Moondance*, a sunglass-clad Van the Man lands on the cover of today's *Rolling Stone*. Unlike its predecessor, *Moondance* leans toward soul and jazz and returns Morrison to commercial prominence, with hits on AM ("Come Running") and FM ("Into the Mystic," "And It Stoned Me"). His lyrical, soul-searching blend of romance and mysticism continues with the release of more strong albums, which spawn two of the biggest and most soulful singles of his long career, "Blue Money" and dual AM/AOR classic "Domino."

# JULY

## 1976

While disco's mostly ruled by divas, funky white boy Harry Wayne Casey gets in his licks too. Today the band that the former Florida record store clerk formed, KC and the Sunshine Band, shakes up the charts with "(Shake Shake Shake) Shake Your Booty." It'll soon be their third chart topper, after "Get Down Tonight" and "That's the Way (I Like It)." Their high-energy, funky R&B-ish sound, backboned by Casey's cowriting and producing skills, makes his mostly black band a dynamic disco force. Much of their success stems from Casey's retail roots, as he recalled many store customers who could never quite remember a song's title, just the melody. So repetition becomes a prime ingredient, like today's entry that repeats the word "shake" four times in its title alone, a record for a #1 (ABBA's "I Do, I Do, I Do, I Do, I Do" stalled at #15). Early next year KC's back on top with "I'm Your Boogie Man," which segues into "Keep It Comin' Love," which just misses at #2.

# JULY III

## 1979

The Skylab is falling! The Skylab is falling! After six years in orbit, the Skylab space station is coming back to earth—though where it'll land, nobody knows. The demise triggers an international media event, with *The San Francisco Examiner* offering $10,000 for the first piece delivered to its offices. Tonight pieces fall over a remote stretch of Australia. Shaggy-haired seventeen-year-old Stan Thornton, a trucker's helper, scoops some up and jets to San Francisco courtesy of a local radio station. Rushing to the newspaper's offices, he describes watching as "big balls of fire turning into little balls of fire" rained down on his tiny hometown. Then Stan waits an agonizing week until NASA authenticates his charred chunks. His parents and fiancée arrive shortly, and they tour the Bay Area before returning home and living happily ever after.

# JULY I2

## 1976

The family that plays together...may just win $5,000 together. Welcome to *Family Feud*, the latest TV creation of quizmasters Mark Goodson and Bill Todman (*Password, The Match Game*), debuting this afternoon on ABC. The real fun of *Feud* stems less from the game itself and more from the rapport between the players and host Richard Dawson. Late of *Hogan's Heroes* and *Rowan and Martin's Laugh-In*, Dawson brings a congenial, comedic flair. He spends almost as much time kibitzing with—and kissing—family members as actually conducting the game. *Family Feud*'s success later lands a plum primetime time slot, too. Dawson has become so identified as a game show host that he's tapped to play one in Arnold Schwarzenegger's futuristic thriller, *The Running Man*. He ditches his nice-guy persona to play a smarmy host of the movie's do-or-die gladiator-style series.

## BURN BABY BURN

A literal disco inferno erupted on July 12, 1979, at Comiskey Park on Chicago's South Side. Scorned by his former station firing him when they switched to an all-disco format, disc jockey Steve Dahl, along with Mike Veeck (son of White Sox owner and legendary promoter Bill Veeck), planned a promotional stunt to take place during a Sox-Tigers doubleheader. Any fan who brought a disco record would gain admittance for 98 cents (the station's position on the dial), and between the games Dahl would set fire to them on the field. As advertised, Dahl detonated a huge crate filled with the disks. But mayhem ensues as the crowd—which had already been tossing the records around like Frisbees—rushes the field. In addition to the huge hole made by the explosion in the infield grass, parts of the field are dug up and set fire to in small-scale riots. Chicago police finally restore order, but Tigers' manager Sparky Anderson pulls his team for its own safety, and the White Sox are forced to forfeit. Internationally, the story makes headline news. Nationally, the stunt comes to signify the disco backlash. Locally, managers grouse about the lousy field conditions for the rest of the season.

## JULY

# 13

## 1979

Racing to a feverish finish, the unpretentious sleeper *Breaking Away* breaks out unexpectedly at the box office, too. Four townie

pals—Dennis Christopher, Dennis Quaid, Daniel Stern, and Jackie Earle Haley—enter a bicycle race patterned after the real-life Little 500 race at Indiana University. The conflict builds between these steadfast working-class kids, dubbed "cutters" (after workers in the nearby limestone quarries), and the privileged college chaps personified by Hart Bochner. Unsentimentally optimistic, the film nets a surprising five Oscar nominations including best picture, and wins one for its script. It later inspires a short-lived sitcom that attracts several cast members including Oscar nominee Barbara Barrie.

## JULY 14

**1972** Smack dab in the midst of the Vietnam War, activist actress Jane Fonda makes an incredible, incendiary visit to North Vietnam. Over two weeks she tours villages, hospitals, schools, and factories, and poses with soldiers around an anti-aircraft gun. Today she makes a broadcast over Radio Hanoi in which she calls American political and military leaders war criminals. Though her trip gathers middle media attention now, it later personifies and solidifies the undying enmity that many Americans carry forever toward "Hanoi Jane," a derisive nickname patterned after World War II propagandists Tokyo Rose and Axis Sally. But the Nixon administration, already reeling from the unpopular war, declines to press any giving-aid-and-comfort-to-the-enemy charges for fear of creating a martyr. Years later Fonda offers repeated, yet qualified, statements. "I will go to my grave regretting the photograph of me in the anti-aircraft carrier," she says, but she resolutely refuses to apologize for the trip itself. Not that that would have changed any minds.

## JULY 15

**1974** Sarasota public affairs reporter Chris Chubbuck introduces a segment on her show about a local restaurant shooting the day before. The tape jams and won't run. "In keeping with Channel 40's policy of bringing you the latest in blood and guts," she says, "and in living color, you are going to see another first—an attempted suicide." Drawing a .38-caliber pistol from a bag, the depressed twenty-nine-year-old virgin with a lackluster social life shoots herself behind the right ear. Chubbuck pitches forward violently as a camerawoman, incensed at what she thinks is a prank, rushes over and sees the twitching body. Chubbuck dies at a local hospital fourteen hours later. "We suffer at our sense of loss," says a speaker at her funeral. "We are frightened by her rage. We are hurt by her choice of isolation, and we are confused by her message."

JULY **1973** On a hot summer night a line snakes down Boylston Street in downtown Boston. "Who're you seeing?" calls out a passerby. "The Wailers," answers a fan. "The gah-den's thataway," the passerby replies facetiously, referring to the Boston Garden and the NHL's Hartford Whalers. The masses haven't yet heard of the dreadlocked Jamaican reggae band and its superstar, Bob Marley, but the cognoscenti have. Fans pack five sold-out shows all week long at Boston's small, legendary club Paul's Mall. Amid a thick backstage smell of ganja and the sweet backing harmonics of the I-Threes (Judy Mowatt, Marcia Griffiths, and Bob's wife, Rita), the Wailers tear up the joint with their rock and reggae beat—one that the world's soon to discover and embrace.

JULY **17** **1973** Contestants vie to identify mystery personalities as NBC premieres a new daytime game show, *The Wizard of Odds*. A dapper Canadian, making his American debut, hosts. It lasts but one season, though its replacement, *High Rollers*, hosted by the same gentleman, runs for six. The host hits the jackpot some years later with a new syndicated version of *Jeopardy!*, the long-running network game show, originally hosted by Art Fleming, which had been stupidly canceled by NBC. Producer Merv Griffin steers the strip into a powerhouse franchise, entering the lexicon of pop-culture phenomena alongside its equally famous companion, Griffin's *Wheel of Fortune*. "When Merv Griffin created *Jeopardy!*," says distributor Roger King of King World, "I think he created a format that will be around for a hundred years." The name of that host who started on *The Wizard of Odds*, in the form of a question, please: Who is Alex Trebek?

**1976** A perfect ten. While people will give stunning Bo Derek that label in a few years, today the world celebrates a perfect, petite ten—Romanian gymnast Nadia Comaneci. At the Summer Olympics in Montreal, the 4'11", eighty-six-pound dynamo becomes the first Olympic athlete to ever earn a perfect score of ten for a routine on the uneven bars. Electrifying the sport and the world, she'll collect an unprecedented seven perfect scores by the time these Olympics end. "She can block out the whole world—it's just her and the apparatus," says Rod Hill, manager of the American women's gymnastics team. "She's the epitome of perfection." Dubbed by one reporter a "Barbie doll with bangs," Comaneci actually collects dolls, with her collection now including dolls from more than sixty countries. Discovered as a six-year-old kindergarten student in her Russian hometown, Comaneci has always shown the aptitude. Today she matches that with an extraordinary performance done with seemingly effortless ease.

**1978** With its stated mission "to defend and preserve the individual rights and liberties guaranteed to every person in this country by the Constitution and laws of the United States," the American Civil Liberties Union (ACLU) takes on some very weighty First Amendment cases. And sometimes it makes for pretty strange bedfellows, like last year's suit against Skokie, Illinois, that defends the rights of Neo-Nazis to demonstrate and express their racial slurs publicly. The ACLU wins, as a judge later reaffirms the ruling: "It is better to allow those who preach racial hatred to expend their venom in rhetoric rather than to be panicked into embarking on the dangerous course of permitting the government to decide what its citizens may say and hear."

# EXIT THE DRAGON

On July 20, 1973, just six days before the premiere of his first Hollywood film, *Enter the Dragon*, martial arts wonder and cultural icon Bruce Lee passed away in Hong Kong. Lee had parlayed his martial arts skills—honed by exhaustive training—along with his good looks and a charismatic personality, to the brink of stardom before his untimely death a the age of thirty-two. According to Lee researcher John Little, here are some of the amazing physical feats performed by the always-humble master.

- Doing push-ups while supporting himself with only the index finger and thumb of one hand
- Throwing a grain of rice in the air, then catching it with chopsticks
- Holding a 125-pound dumbbell with his arms extended straight out in front of him
- Kicking Kareem Abdul-Jabbar (who was 19 inches taller than him) in the chin in the never-completed film *Game of Death*
- Sending opponents flying 15 feet with a punch delivered from 1 inch away
- Kicking out a light bulb by jumping 8 feet in the air
- Thrusting his fingers through steel cans of Coca-Cola

> **"Showing off is the fool's idea of glory."**
> —**Bruce Lee**

## JULY 20

**1970** Burgers, fries, and a prize? Maybe not. Today the Federal Trade Commission (FTC) accuses McDonald's of distributing only $13,000 in winnings from a contest that had promised $500,000 in prizes. Promoted in *Reader's Digest*, the sweepstakes offered 15,610 items, but awarded only 227. Next year McDonald's agrees to discontinue that kind of contest and ensures that all future promotions award every prize and specify its exact nature and odds of winning. Today the FTC also comes down on three detergent makers for inflated claims of their products' effectiveness in removing stains like blood, rust, and grease. "In our judgment, no useful purpose can be served by prolonging a controversy about the interpretation of this advertising," says a Procter & Gamble spokesman who can't admit defeat. "We are confident that housewives have not been misled by this advertising."

## JULY 21

**1973** Curly-haired Jim Croce, sporting a Fu Manchu moustache, had kicked around a lot of odd jobs—day laborer, radio ad salesman, truck driver—while nursing his musical dreams. In one stint as a telephone lineman, he'd encountered a belligerent coworker who became the inspiration for "Bad, Bad Leroy Brown," which today hits #1 and ignites his career. "I'm a kind of music psychologist, or a musical bouncer, or a live jukebox," says Croce. "It depends on the audience." The years of struggle have paid off, finally, and amid a heavy touring schedule he soon releases his third album, *I Got a Name*. Late in September, following a college concert in Louisiana, he boards a private plane that crashes upon takeoff. Croce was thirty. "Time in a Bottle," rushed out as a single, tops the charts at year's end.

## JULY 22

**1976** With thousands of conventions held every year, the larger world barely noticed when a gathering of American Legionnaires began yesterday at the Bellevue Stratford Hotel in Philadelphia. Today a handful of attendees at its US Bicentennial celebration begin to feel unwell. Within a week the story's front-page news worldwide as 29 people have died and more than 150 are hospitalized with headaches, chest pains, high fever, and respiratory problems. Authorities, as baffled as the public, descend upon the hotel en masse and race to discover the cause. It's not until January of next year that the Centers for Disease Control and Prevention in Atlanta identifies a bacterium that had bred in the hotel's air-conditioning system. Though they determine that it had existed previously, the illness forever bears the name Legionnaires' disease.

# JULY
# 23

**1970** In the title of the Carpenters' first hit—and today their first #1, "(They Long to Be) Close to You"—the keyword is "close." For over the past few years, harmonizing siblings Karen and Richard Carpenter have come tantalizingly close to making it big. Originally The Carpenter Trio, a jazz ensemble including a third member on tuba, they won a Battle of the Bands at the Hollywood Bowl and signed with RCA Records, only to be later dropped. A second attempt resulted in rejection letters from every record label in town. The third time's almost the charm as the duo signs with Herb Alpert's A&M Records. Their first single, a remake of the Beatles' "Ticket to Ride," can't crack the Top 50. Finally the follow-up, "Close to You"—a Burt Bacharach/Hal David song Alpert himself had turned down—zooms to #1. A long run of hits ("Rainy Days and Mondays," "Top of the World") follows before Karen's illness (anorexia nervosa) and death in 1983.

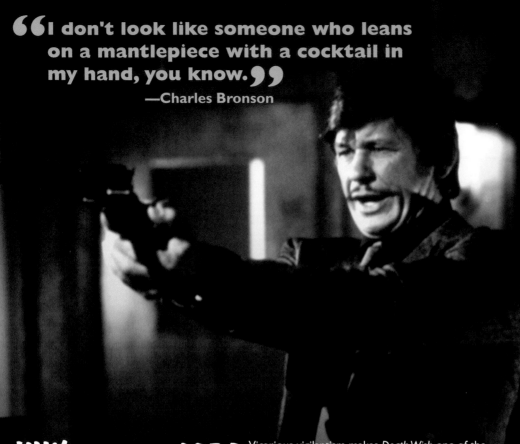

> **"I don't look like someone who leans on a mantlepiece with a cocktail in my hand, you know."**
> —Charles Bronson

**1975** Moving from the periphery directly to center stage, *A Chorus Line* opens tonight and enthralls Broadway with its high-stepping, high-voltage production. No glitz, little glamor, minimal sets, utilitarian costumes—but plenty of heart, craft, and intelligence. Creator-director-choreographer Michael Bennett draws inspiration from hundreds of hours of interviews he'd taped with chorus dancers, the theater's unsung "gypsies." Blending this raw source material with fresh musical interpretation, his magnum opus goes on to sweep nine Tony Awards and win a Pulitzer Prize, a rare accomplishment for a musical. The landmark play becomes a legend, one of the longest-running musicals of all time.

**JULY**

**1974** Vicarious vigilantism makes *Death Wish* one of the year's biggest box-office hits, turning taciturn Charles Bronson into a star. Packing a powerful punch (and later, firepower), it delivers a simplistic, manipulative take on one man taking the law into his own hands after attackers kill his wife and maim his traumatized daughter for life. (Jeff Goldblum makes his film debut as one of the murdering, raping thugs.) Many critics rage, but moviegoers—especially city dwellers fearful of the escalating urban violence—root on the merciless avenger who's pursued by a dogged police chief (Vincent Gardenia) with a cold that won't quit. Brian Garfield, whose book inspired the movie, lambastes director Michael Winner for making the protagonist "who was supposed to be evil [into] a knight on a white horse." Five years later onscreen violence encourages real-life carnage when screenings of Walter Hill's *The Warriors*, about NYC street gangs, triggers vandalism, riots, and at least three deaths.

**1971** Hold your applause: pay attention, 'cause it gets a bit confusing here. Anne Baxter played the title role in the 1950 movie *All About Eve*, a scheming understudy to aging actress Margo Channing, a role immortalized by Bette Davis ("fasten your seatbelts, it's going to be a bumpy night"). Baxter and Davis each won Oscar nominations for best actress, and the theatrical blockbuster won six Oscars including picture, director (Joseph L. Mankiewicz), and screenplay. Today Baxter steps into that lead role of Channing in the Broadway musical adaptation retitled *Applause*. She replaces Lauren Bacall, who'd won a Tony in the role.

**1972** What a difference four years make: the FBI, unable to unearth any substantial evidence despite multiple undercover investigations, generates a confidential internal memo today: "[John] Lennon is reportedly a 'heavy user of narcotics' known as 'downers'....If Lennon were to be arrested in the US for possession of narcotics he would become more likely to be immediately deportable." Privately the Nixon administration directs the investigation, publicly it denies any particular interest. The ACLU later cites this memo as proof that the FBI has been engaged in an "abuse of its authority in order to neutralize dissent." Exactly four years later, on July 27, 1976, the politically motivated plot to deport Lennon ends when he wins formal permission to remain in the United States as a permanent resident. At today's hearing Norman Mailer, Geraldo Rivera, and Gloria Swanson testify on his behalf. "It's great to be legal again," says Lennon.

# JULY

 **28**

## 1978

What *Mad* magazine was to the 1960s, *National Lampoon* is to the '70s—a clever, irreverent magazine that delivers a monthly humor fix to millions of addicted young Americans. After adding albums, a weekly radio show, high school yearbook, and Sunday newspaper parodies into the mix, the franchise makes its first foray today into feature films— and comedy's never the same. The road-tripping, prank-pulling, beer-swilling, toga-partying frat brothers of *National Lampoon's Animal House*, led by Tim Matheson and *Saturday Night Live* not-ready-for-primetimer John Belushi, offer a sophomoric, slapstick spoof of college life in the 1960s. The year's third-highest-grossing film, it spawns a spate of raunchy, inferior imitations and a deservedly short-lived ABC sitcom, *Delta House*, notable only for the debut of a comely coed known as The Bombshell—a young Michelle Pfeiffer in her acting debut.

# JULY

 **29**

## 1970

Shock proof: good drama thrives on a strong hero and villain, but in Alvin Toffler's eagerly awaited book *Future Shock*, both parts are played by the same thing: technology. He predicts "shattering stress and disorientation" will rock Americans reeling from the rapid pace of technological and societal change. "Change is avalanching upon our heads," says Toffler, "and most people are grotesquely unprepared to cope with it." Random House publishes the book today, and it gains instant status as a selection of three book clubs with a lengthy adaptation in *New York* magazine. Widely hailed as an influential social thinker, Toffler follows up his examination of the process of change in each successive decade with *The Third Wave* (1980), which explores the directions of change, and *Powershift* (1990), an examination of the control of changes still to come. But his first book makes the biggest bang.

# JULY
# 30

**1975** He's impatient. He's annoyed. He's been stood up for lunch. And he's been known to have a temper. A little after 2 p.m. in a restaurant parking lot in Bloomfield Township, Michigan, he telephones his wife from a pay phone. He's a stocky man, wearing a dark-blue short-sleeve shirt, blue trousers, white socks, and black Gucci loafers. Sometime later a maroon sedan pulls in and in he gets. No one ever sees Jimmy Hoffa again. The ex-Teamsters boss had gone to prison for jury tampering, conspiracy, and mail and wire fraud. Now he was out, after receiving clemency from President Nixon, and he wanted back in. Hence today's scheduled meeting with a Detroit mobster and a New Jersey labor leader. Alibis and clues come and go, but the mystery—and any trace of the body—remains unsolved.

# JULY
# 31

**1971** Longhaired, handsome James Taylor stares out pensively from the cover of his debut Warner Bros. album, *Sweet Baby James*. But his angelic look belies an inner turmoil: heroin addiction, rehab, and the suicide of a friend that he taps into to make his first breakout single, "Fire and Rain." "I'm probably genetically predisposed to substance abuse, so I didn't stand a chance," says Taylor. "It felt like it solved all kinds of problems for me." Today J.T. tops the charts with "You've Got a Friend," written by his friend Carole King, and his life turns around: TV appearances, the cover of *Time* magazine, sold-out tours, and a chance backstage introduction to fellow singer-songwriter Carly Simon, whom he marries the following year.

AUGUST

# AUGUST 11

## 1971

Their chart-topping days as a duet may be over, but Sonny and Cher still share a magical chemistry onstage. So after years of successful nightclub and concert appearances, CBS tonight premieres *The Sonny and Cher Comedy Hour.* The campy act who many call "money and hair" meshes perfectly: straight-man Sonny opposite Cher's sexy, sassy persona, with little daughter Chastity often brought in for a rousing finale of "I Got You Babe." Offscreen, though, it's a different story. He's boss and one shrewd operator, and they're having marital woes. After breaking up each tries solo TV efforts—Sonny on ABC, followed by Cher on CBS—but each flops. A professional reconciliation is arranged, though Cher is now married to rock singer Gregg Allman. But the magic's gone and so, too, is the show by summer's end in 1977.

( MEANWHILE... )

## BIRTH OF THE CELEBRITY FUNDRAISER

On August 1, 1971, modern-day Robin Hood George Harrison didn't steal from the rich—he just tapped his wealthy pals to contribute their talents for free. The needy in this instance were refugees in East Pakistan, and Harrison assembled a stellar lineup for his Concert for Bangladesh. The stars performing at Madison Square Garden included Badfinger, Eric Clapton, Billy Preston, Leon Russell, Ravi Shankar, and Bob Dylan, who showed up unannounced to play his first concert in two years. The most prominent no-show? John Lennon, who'd agreed to play solo as Harrison had asked—until Yoko found out she wasn't invited. Uh-oh. The event provided UNICEF with an immediate $250,000 relief check, with more coming from future record sales.

> ❝It really made the show... Bob [Dylan] just gave it that extra bit of clout.❞
> —George Harrison

# AUGUST 2

## 1978

Love gone bad: designed as a dream community in the late 1890s, little Love Canal, New York, turns out to be the exact opposite: a terrifying nightmare. Today mass evacuations begin in a neighborhood exposed as having been built on the former site of a massive toxic-waste dump. Hundreds of tons of chemicals, buried under a layer of dirt by the area's former owner, the Hooker Chemical Company, have leaked and leached, causing untold catastrophic illnesses, stillbirths, miscarriages, and birth defects. Five days later President Carter designates it a federal disaster area. "The profound and devastating effects of the Love Canal tragedy," says the New York health commissioner, "in terms of human health and suffering and environmental damage, cannot and probably will never be fully measured."

# AUGUST 4

**1975** Vacationing on the Greek isle of Rhodes, Robert Plant of Led Zeppelin and his wife, Maureen, are badly hurt today in a car accident. Fitted with casts, they fly to England for further treatment. But when additional time there will mean paying full income taxes, ex-UK native Plant returns to New Jersey, where his injuries take more than a year to heal, and spurs a respite from the band's relentless touring and recording. Since tearing onto the charts with "Whole Lotta Love" in late 1969, Led Zeppelin has released a series of million-selling albums that make them one of rock's biggest (and loudest) international acts. Their incomparable "Stairway to Heaven" reigns as the most requested cut in rock history. They form their own label, Swan Song, and release *Physical Graffiti*, which boasts "Kashmir."

# AUGUST 3

**1970** Among all else The Beatles had become major film stars with *A Hard Days Night* and *Help!,* and John Lennon even dabbled in non-band roles in films like *Oh! What a Lovely War*. So when cinematographer Nicolas Roeg, who'd worked on popular films like *A Funny Thing Happened on the Way to the Forum* and *Far from the Madding Crowd*, proposed a project with the Rolling Stones' Mick Jagger, Warner Bros. smelled box-office excitement and flashed the green light. But Roeg's original light tone turned ominously dark, and *Performance* remained unreleased for two years. Until today. Most critics savage the violent, intense film starring Jagger as (what else?) a fading rock star, James Fox as a complex killer on the lam, and Mick's then real-life girlfriend, Anita Pallenberg. Richard Schickel calls it "the most completely worthless film I have seen since I began reviewing." The violence turns off many, but in future years its reputation is rehabilitated, validating one lonely critic's early description of *Performance* as a "perfectly poisonous, cinematic flower." Either way, Jagger draws kudos for his solo soundtrack song, "Memo from Turner."

## AUGUST

**1979** Twenty, twenty, twenty-four hours ago, the Ramones make their mighty movie debut in *Rock 'n' Roll High School*. The film's heroine (P.J. Soles, married to Dennis Quaid) will do anything to get a ticket to a concert of her favorite band after a new hard-nosed principal (Mary Woronov) confiscates her last one. She incites the student body after the principal ignites a pile of rock records, and in the resulting mayhem who should appear but Joey, Johnny, Dee Dee, and Tommy, the Queens, New York–based quartet that took their name from a pseudonym (Paul Ramon) that Paul McCartney occasionally used. The oldies-laden soundtrack includes vintage Ramones numbers ("I Wanna Be Sedated" and "Sheena Is a Punk Rocker") plus classics like Alice Cooper's "School's Out" and Brownsville Station's "Smokin' in the Boy's Room."

## AUGUST

**1970** See? I *told* you you'd spoil it for everyone! Today when three hundred hippies gather for a ragtag rally at Disneyland's make-believe City Hall, everybody gets sent home early. Unfurling Viet Cong and marijuana banners, the vocal, longhaired hooligans even tear down the red, white, and blue bunting. Imagine! More than one hundred baton-wielding police appear, dispersing the unruly mob and arresting eighteen for disturbing the peace. The park sends home its other thirty thousand visitors five hours early—only the second time in its history (the first was for JFK's assassination) that Disneyland shuts down. One thirteen-year-old girl, a frequent visitor with her parents whose happy day is cut short, despairs. "If the hippies are allowed into Disneyland to do their dirty work, next thing you know they'll start in at nursery schools preaching pot and LSD," she writes in a letter to a local paper.

# AUGUST 7

**1974** The wide worlds of rock and film draw a little bit closer today with the Beverly Hills marriage of Peter Wolf and Faye Dunaway. It's the first wedding for both. Having shot to prominence in 1967 in *Bonnie and Clyde*, Dunaway has re-emerged with a vengeance after a dry spell in *Chinatown*, gracing countless magazine covers and drawing rave reviews (and an Oscar nomination) as sultry femme fatale Bonnie Parker. Wolf, lead singer of the raunchy, blues rockin' Boston-based J. Geils Band, seems to have found the answer to the band's first Top 40 single, "Looking for a Love." In concert he's described as maintaining a "still seedy left-bank image—beret, dark glasses, and close-cropped beard." His high-wattage bride, formerly linked romantically with actors Marcello Mastroianni and Harris Yulin, offers an enigmatic opinion of her marriage. "It puts a definition on a relationship," she says. "A door has been closed." The door reopens five years later, and Dunaway later has a son by and marries fashion photographer Terry O'Neill.

## SHORTLIST
## CELEBRITY COUPLINGS

The marriage of Peter Wolf and Faye Dunaway was just one of the many celebrity nuptials in the '70s. Here's a list of the decade's most famous (and infamous) Hollywood marriages.

- Michelle Phillips and Dennis Hopper (1970) (lasts only eight days)
- Carly Simon and James Taylor (1972)
- Natalie Wood and Robert Wagner (second time) (1972)
- Indian actress Shakira Baksh and Michael Caine (1973)
- Jane Fonda and activist Tom Hayden (1973)
- Sissy Spacek and art director Jack Fisk (1974)
- Tuesday Weld and Dudley Moore (1975)
- Cher and Gregg Allman (1975)
- Elizabeth Taylor and Richard Burton (second time) (1975)
- Melanie Griffith and Don Johnson (1976)

# AUGUST 8

**1977** A little boy is dying of cancer, so an obliging pro player phones him and promises to try to hit a home run that night... then hits two! It should have all the ingredients of a heartwarming story, but this one has a nightmare ending. Bedridden Scott Crull, age twelve, of Calumet City, Illinois, is dying of cancer and has been given less than two months to live. Today he's elated when he gets to talk with his favorite baseball player, Bobby Murcer of the Chicago Cubs. After Murcer's home-run feat, a team official slips a note to the *Monday Night Baseball* broadcast booth about the story, and ABC announcer Keith Jackson—without knowing the boy's parents haven't told him he is dying—tells the world that Murcer has just fulfilled a young boy's last wish. Upon hearing the news about his life expectancy on TV, Scott has to be placed under sedation, and he dies two weeks later. A newspaper editorialist mourns for him, and Jackson as well: "He deserves to know that we understand his feeling of grief, of shame, and of innocence."

"Guess what?
I might be the
first hippie
pinup girl."
—Janis Joplin

**1970** She lived fast, drank hard, sang unforgettably, and died relatively young. Janis Joplin buys that woman a tombstone at her gravesite in suburban Philadelphia, according to news reports today. She was big blues singer Bessie Smith, the "Empress of the Blues," who died in a car crash in 1937. Her funeral attracted seven thousand mourners, but the grave never got a stone. Reports suggest that her husband, from whom she had been separated, absconded with the funds raised. So thirty-three unmarked years later, Joplin splits the $500 cost of a headstone with Juanita Green, a registered nurse who met Bessie back in the 1930s. "The Greatest Blues Singer in the World Will Never Stop Singing" reads the newly chiseled gray and black stone.

# AUGUST

## 10

**1975** Interviewed tonight on CBS's *60 Minutes*, First Lady Betty Ford makes some candid comments that cause quite a stir. She says that she believes all her children have tried marijuana, and that the Supreme Court made a "great decision" in legalizing abortion. Trying to tamp down the controversy, President Ford's press secretary comments the next

day: "The president has long ceased to be perturbed or surprised by his wife's remarks." But the loudest condemnation comes not from her remarks about drugs or abortion, but premarital sex. After saying she wouldn't be surprised to discover that her eighteen-year-old daughter

Susan was having an affair, Ford suggests that premarital relations might help lower the divorce rate. "We deplore the deterioration of morality around the world," cries Mormon elder Gordon B. Hinckley. "Chastity is to be observed before marriage, and fidelity after marriage."

---

**TRENDSETTER**

## WHAT IT IS IS WHAT IT WAS

Question: What became of the boys with the DA haircuts and the girls in the poodle skirts who lived for sock hops, cruisin', and hanging out at the drive-in? Answer: They grew up. But they never forgot those times, and in the '70s, everything from the 1950s (and early '60s) is back. Seeds were sown as the decade began with rock 'n' roll revival shows featuring real '50s groups along with made-up bands like Sha Na Na that aped the genre. *Grease* re-created the era on stage, and later in film. On the radio,

comebacks for '50s icons like Elvis Presley ("Burning Love") and Rick Nelson ("Garden Party") were followed by new hits with an old sound like Elton John's "Crocodile Rock" and Loggins and Messina's "Your Mama Don't Dance." On August 11, 1973, George Lucas released his major motion picture period piece, *American Graffiti*, which was perhaps the most influential pop cultural homage to the decade...until the premiere of a certain sitcom six months later (see Jan. 15).

# AUGUST

▌▌▌ ▌▌▌

## 1972

It's not nice to fool Mother Nature. Dressing her up may not be such a great idea either, as celebrated big-canvas artist Christo discovers today. Twenty-eight hours after hanging a four-hundred-foot, six-ton, quarter-mile-long orange parachute-cloth curtain across Rifle Gap in Colorado, high winds tear it to shreds. But the failure of the $700,000 project, condemned by environmentalists, doesn't deter Christo and his wife, Jean-Claude, who'd previously wrapped part of the Australian coast to international acclaim and delight. Soon they're winning new fans with more large-scale outdoor wrappings of the Reichstag in Berlin and the Pont Neuf bridge in Paris. "Our work," says Christo, "is a scream of freedom."

## AUGUST 12

### 1978

When you're a teenager, eight minutes can seem like an eternity—especially when they're spent in the back seat of a parked car with that gal or guy for whom you're hot hot hot. For all eight-plus minutes of Meat Loaf's operatic "Paradise by the Dashboard Light"—which lands on the charts today—the sexual tension builds, peaks, and explodes "like a tidal wave." Writer/arranger Jim Steinman and producer Todd Rundgren tap New York Yankees announcer Phil Rizzuto to deliver a scintillating play-by-play of Meat Loaf's cruising to an entirely different first, second, and third base. Intertwining his churning, yearning vocals with those of is-she, isn't-she-willing Ellen Foley, the song generates plenty of heat, airplay, and sales. Bat Out of Hell, the debut solo album from Meat Loaf (born Marvin Lee Aday) that had been rejected by many major labels, bursts out with other mini-epics like "Two Out of Three Ain't Bad." Out of the gate, several million copies sold triggers an incredible eighty-two-week chart, success that makes both its hefty lead singer (who'd played Eddie in the Rocky Horror Picture Show) and Steinman hot properties.

# AUGUST
# 13

**1975** Time's running out. Hailed as the next Bob Dylan back in 1972, it's been three years and two marginally selling albums since. Is the Boss worried? Don't count on it. From the wailing sax of Clarence Clemons kicking into "Tenth Avenue Freeze-Out," Bruce Springsteen has 'em right where he wants 'em. Tonight's show at the Bottom Line, a cramped Greenwich Village club, scorches the place with "Thunder Road" and more from new LP *Born to Run*. It's the first of ten sold-out shows here that bode well for Springsteen and the future of rock. Though with nearly one thousand of the four thousand tickets reserved for the media, some grouse about Columbia Records' over-the-top PR campaign. Springsteen simultaneously graces the covers of both *Time* and *Newsweek* the week of October 27. "It was our coming-out party," says Springsteen.

# AUGUST 14

## 1975

After a successful stage run of several years in London, the musical inspired a movie version. Okay, nothing so unusual about that—but then all madness broke loose, and hasn't stopped since. The sci-fi-comedy-musical-horror hyphenate that is the *Rocky Horror Picture Show* opens in movie theaters in the UK and United States, and quickly becomes a pop-culture phenomenon and cult-movie classic extraordinaire. Midnight screenings attract fans, dressed as their favorite characters, who bring appropriate props, shout out lines, and generally cavort and carouse. They affectionately refer to themselves as sluts, as opposed to virgins (who've never seen the movie). Who's bringing the rice!

> **"And what charming underclothes you both have."**
> —Tim Curry as Dr. Frank-N-Furter

# AUGUST 15

## 1979

The wait is over. Almost five years after his last film, *The Godfather: Part II*, Francis Ford Coppola unleashes *Apocalypse Now*, his famously tempestuous and troubled take on the Vietnam War. Shooting in the Philippines ran twice as long as projected, and costs more than tripled to $31 million, but no one quibbles with the results: a visually stunning masterpiece crammed with surrealistic and symbolic sequences that depict the confusion, fear, and horror of war. The increasingly unpredictable journey of a conflicted assassin (Martin Sheen), sent to eliminate an ex-colonel turned warlord (Marlon Brando), serves as a metaphor for what engulfed the United States in Vietnam.

# AUGUST 16

## 1977

Two weeks after the tell-all book *Elvis: What Happened?*, written by former members of the Presley camp, hits stores, Elvis's girlfriend discovers him unconscious at Graceland, his Memphis mansion. Hours later he's pronounced dead at age forty-two. Nearly 100,000 fans flock to Memphis over the next two days to pay respects to the King. President Carter calls Elvis "unique and irreplaceable." If this isn't enough heartbreak, the day after Elvis's funeral the world loses another king of entertainment, Groucho Marx. With his trademark greasepainted moustache, bushy eyebrows, ever-present cigar, and rapier wit, Groucho duck-walked through more than a dozen classic comedies along with brothers Chico and Harpo. He later made the transition to TV as host of *You Bet Your Life*. Unlike Elvis, Groucho was no rocker, but in his final years did number rock stars like Alice Cooper and Elton John as friends. The story goes that one time when Groucho pointed his index fingers like guns at Elton, he responded, "Don't shoot me, I'm only the piano player"—which later became the title of Elton's 1973 album.

**1973** Want to learn about sweet harmony that cuts across just about every style of music? Allow us to give you a few pointers. Ruth, Anita, Bonnie, and June Pointer, to be exact: daughters of minister parents from Oakland, California, raised on gospel but longing to sing anything but. After doing backup for the likes of the Elvin Bishop Band, Taj Mahal, and Boz Scaggs, the quartet decides to go it on their own, opting for a retro 1940s, thrift-store look and a bebop style mixed with the occasional modern-day funk. So can the Pointer Sisters and their debut single, entering the charts to-day, deliver the goods? Yes they can can as the infectious "Yes We Can Can" catches on and sparks enthusiastic public and critical response. "Their entire act is a musical cloudburst, exuding joy, limitless energy [and] a natural sense of har-mony," writes the *Los Angeles Times*.

# AUGUST
17

**1974** A simple phrase first appeared scrawled on the wall of a London tube station in the mid-1960s: "Clapton is God." That graffiti spreads worldwide as Eric Clapton, one of the most celebrated hired hands in rock 'n' roll, plays heavenly guitar licks for bands like the Yardbirds, John Mayall's Bluesbreakers, Cream, Blind Faith, Derek and the Dominoes (see Sept. 6), and Delaney & Bonnie. He even finds time to record a solo album that generates radio hits "After Midnight" and "Let It Rain." In 1971, though, heroin addiction sidelines Clapton. Nearly three years later, having finally won the battle with his demons, he enters a Miami studio, address 461 Ocean Boulevard. He lays down tracks for a second solo outing, including a slowed-down, shuffle-over cover of Bob Marley's reggae "I Shot the Sheriff." Today Clapton's comeback album, *461 Ocean Boulevard,* moves to an even better address: #1. A few weeks later there's a new "Sheriff" in town and on the charts as both Clapton and Marley claim their only #1 song in the United States as recording artist and writer, respectively.

## AUGUST 19

**1978** Makin' the world safe for funk! That's visionary showman extraordinaire George Clinton, melding soul, rhythm and blues, jazz, gospel, and psychedelic rock into an outrageous new funky sound. Today "One Nation Under a Groove," his rousing community anthem, enters the R&B charts en route to his career-defining peak with aggregate Parliament/Funkadelic P-Funk. "I am intent on making the word 'funk' as legitimate as jazz and rock 'n' roll," says Clinton. That materializes with more than a dash of flash, like his adventurous concerts in the UK this winter that feature, among all else, a life-size flying saucer. Clinton's sounds prefigure the rise of rap, hip-hop, and techno.

## AUGUST 20

**1977** Cue the choir: The Prophet of Love's preaching, and today his sermon's entitled "It's Ecstasy When You Lay Down Next to Me." Yes, three-hundred-pound Barry White has a surefire formula: his rich baritone, steamy lyrics, and the lush forty-piece Love Unlimited Orchestra. What springs forth is gold record after gold record, like "Never, Never Gonna Give Ya Up," "Can't Get Enough of Your Love, Babe," and "I'm Gonna Love You Just a Little More, Baby." He's come a long way from early days as a juvenile delinquent in LA who was once jailed for stealing three hundred tires. He paid his dues, producing "Harlem Shuffle" for the duo Bob and Earl, creating the sexy female trio Love Unlimited, and writing them a million-seller. His lovin' style makes him a winner on both sides of the Atlantic, with countless cool nicknames bestowed upon him, like the Love Guru and the Walrus of Love.

## AUGUST 22

**1972** As bank robberies go, it won't go down in history as one of the most successful, but it surely qualifies as the most surreal. Today small-time crook John Wojtowicz enters a Chase Manhattan bank in Brooklyn to steal money to fund his boyfriend's sex change operation. Police get called, and an ensuing hostage situation plays out before a crush of cameras and a growing crowd. This strange scenario gets a superb cinematic retelling three years later in director Sidney Lumet's *Dog Day Afternoon*, with Al Pacino as the put-upon wannabe thief and the late John Cazale (best remembered as Fredo in *The Godfather*) as his befuddled partner in crime. Frank Pierson's richly detailed script wins the Oscar, studded with unforgettable moments like Pacino's inciting of the crowd with his cries of "Attica! Attica!" invoking memories of the bloody 1971 prison uprising.

## AUGUST 21

**1979** In the battle between good and evil, the devil always plays second fiddle. That's the lesson of the Charlie Daniels Band's part-country, part-rock 'n' roll stomper "The Devil Went Down to Georgia," their biggest single ever. After years of steady session work, most notably on Dylan's *Nashville Skyline*, North Carolina singer/guitarist/fiddler Daniels steps up as part of the burgeoning Southern rock invasion. Also waving the Confederate flag are Texas trio ZZ Top, South Carolina's Marshall Tucker Band, Arkansas' (surprise!) Black Oak Arkansas, and the pride of Florida, Lynyrd Skynyrd, who generate geographical confusion with their Top 10 debut, "Sweet Home Alabama." Today Daniels's "Devil" goes gold, an especially fitting tribute since the prize in the song to fast-fingered Johnny is the devil's solid-gold fiddle. But the instrument heard on the record is actually an electric viola.

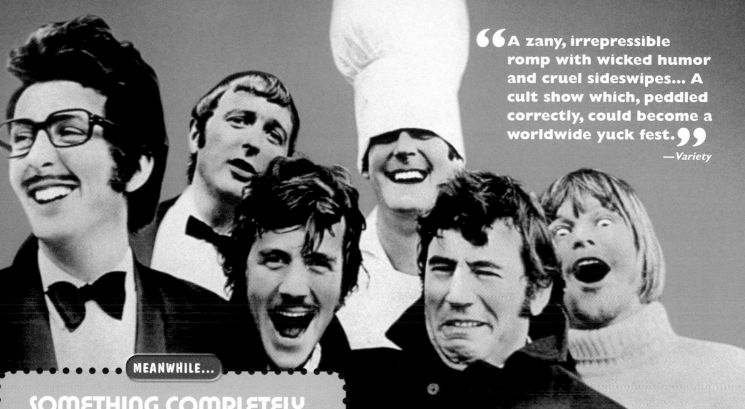

> **"A zany, irrepressible romp with wicked humor and cruel sideswipes... A cult show which, peddled correctly, could become a worldwide yuck fest."**
> —*Variety*

· · · ▶ MEANWHILE...

## SOMETHING COMPLETELY DIFFERENT

They had unleashed their anarchic humor—a mix of outrageous skits and graphics—three years earlier in the UK. For their stateside debut, the Monty Python comedy troupe stitched together some legs—no, wait, that was the Piranha Brothers. The Pythons stitched together favorites from their first two TV seasons—like the dead parrot sketch, the lumberjack song, and the underworld exploits of Doug and Dinsdale Piranha—into a film, *And Now for Something Completely Different*. Released on August 22, 1972, it garnered reasonable reviews but a meager audience unaccustomed to the atypical across-the-pond sense of humor. All that would change in a couple years, when PBS stations began airing the original BBC episodes, and a rabid American fan base formed.

**AUGUST 23**

**1976** In his hallmark white suit, pioneering journalist Tom Wolfe forever defines a generation. Today's *New York* magazine cover story dubs the overly self-involved 1970s the me decade. "The old alchemical dream was changing base metals into gold," says Wolfe. "The new alchemical dream is changing one's personality, remaking, remodeling, elevating, and polishing one's very self…and observing, studying, and doting on it. (Me!)" Recent fads include Rolfing, EST, yoga, primal therapy, and "finding your inner child." The "me decade" broadens into the "me generation" of the 1980s, when selfishness and greed drive baby boomers to new levels of affluence and authority in Ronald Reagan's America. Wolfe then reaches into his bag for a new chic term, and finds it: the "splurge generation."

# AUGUST

## 24

**1979** You take the good, you take the bad, you take Mrs. Garrett from *Diff'rent Strokes* and there you have *The Facts of Life*. Mired in third place, NBC has but one series in the Top 20, the fading *Little House on the Prairie*. But last year *Diff'rent Strokes* arrived, delivering a much-needed hit due largely to pint-size, wisecracking Gary Coleman ("What you talkin' bout, Willis?"). The Peacock Network quickly relocates Charlotte Rae's character, benevolent housekeeper Edna Garrett, into *The Facts of Life*, which premieres tonight. It goes on to a strong nine-year run, with the boarding school housemother guiding the girls in her care: rich girl Blair, streetwise Jo, impressionable Natalie, and ever-in-love-with-Michael-Jackson Tootie. Together they really do face the good and bad, with both the spin-off and original dealing with mature issues like death, divorce, and sexual awakening in what are billed as "very special episodes." *Diff'rent Strokes* even snags a very special guest for an anti-drug program: First Lady Nancy Reagan.

# AUGUST

## 25

**1972** Up with John Lennon, down with Alfred Hitchcock! At a rowdy rally today in New York City, the National Organization for Women (NOW) doles out cheers and jeers on the fifty-second anniversary of women's suffrage. Lennon and Yoko Ono share a "Positive Image of Women" award for "Woman Is the Nigger of the World," but otherwise it's mostly thumbs down for people like Hitchcock, for *Frenzy*; author David Rubin, for *Any Woman Can*; and *New York* magazine drama critic John Simon, for "continual reference to the physical attributes of actresses rather than to their acting abilities." When an analysis of TV ads shows women mostly doing household chores or serving as sex objects, NOW facetiously comments that women's "extraordinary incompetence is exceeded only by their monumental stupidity."

# AUGUST

## 26

**1973** Watch out, Roman Civ. Giving new meaning to the term "gut classes," the University of Texas at Arlington becomes the first accredited college in the United States to offer a belly dancing class for credit. There's no word on how well or well-attended the class turns out, but none other than social arbiter "Dear Abby" soon devotes a column to the dance, to overwhelmingly positive response. One reader notes that since belly dancing originated in the Middle East during biblical times, it's entirely appropriate to teach it in the Bible Belt. "People put belly dancing in the same category as stripping," says one instructor. "It isn't. Stripping is artless and vulgar. Belly dancing is an ancient, respected art form." One middle-aged reader offers a more modern, still less prurient take: "Anyone watching us sweat it out would hardly get aroused…"

# AUGUST

## 27

**1976** Pro tennis, usually an also-ran in American sports coverage, makes front-page headlines today, but it's not about some scintillating five-set match. No, the news trumpets the case of transsexual Dr. Renee Richards's banning from New York's prestigious US Open for refusing to take its just-instituted chromosome test. The former Richard Raskind, after having undergone gender reassignment surgery, had competed in several California tournaments before a journalist reported her story. "I heard from blacks, convicts, Chicanos, hippies, homosexuals, people with physical handicaps, and, of course, transsexuals," says Richards. "My God, the whole world seemed to be looking for me to be their Joan of Arc." Richards's stakes are high, but she sues and wins a landmark case. The next year she competes at the Open, losing in the women's doubles finals.

# AUGUST

# 28

**1975** Me, Tarzan.
You.... Tarzan?!
Today four former screen men
of the jungle gather in Los
Angeles to commemorate the
one-hundredth anniversary of
the birth of their character's
creator, Edgar Rice Burroughs.
Of the four, the most famous
is Johnny Weismuller, the
former Olympic swimming
champion who taught Bur-
roughs's children how to swim.
The others are Buster Crabbe,
Jock Mahoney, and James
Pierce, and the quartet gamely
does the famous jungle call
in unison. While the fortunes
of the ape man created sixty-
three years before have swung
up and down, Tarzan's current-
ly on the upswing with books,
comics, and comic strips in
addition to many film, serial
and television adaptations.
The lively crowd also includes
thirty-five enthusiastic busi-
nessmen who have licensed
the Tarzan name and image,
and three former screen Janes
show up, too.

# AUGUST

## 29

**1974** Castle Rock: A "happening" happening at a park on a royal estate west of London thumbs its collective countercultural snoot at the Royal Family and, essentially, the Establishment. Devoid of big band names, the Windsor Free Festival has drawn overflow hippie, Woodstock-ish crowds to its free countryside concerts for the last three years. Today, in the midst of what's supposed to be a ten-day event, police swoop in on the campsite of two thousand fans. In a pitched eight-hour battle, 220 are arrested, dozens are injured, and 15 are transported to hospital. "I don't know why the police got so violent," says one twenty-two-year-old Sussex youth. "People were being thrown into police vans for no reason." Authorities cite drug use and neighbor complaints for the melee, but the Home Secretary demands a special report by the local chief constable that quickly draws a harsh reply from organizers: "It would be grotesque to see junior officers who overstepped the mark at Windsor being dealt with at formal disciplinary proceedings by a man ultimately far more culpable than themselves."

# AUGUST

## 30

**1974** They've got the zeitgeist by the tale, it's plain to see. Wholesome, well-scrubbed kids + wise, tolerant parents = lots of gosh-o-golly good clean fun. *The Brady Bunch*, a throwback to 1950s middle-class family sitcoms like *Ozzie & Harriet* and *Leave It to Beaver*, ends its

five-year run on ABC tonight. Never rating in the Top 25 or winning any awards, it has nevertheless crossed the elusive Rubicon to achieve enduring status as a lifelong inductee into the American pop-culture hall of fame. Fans old and new show their undying loyalty to fresh Brady incarnations like sequels, specials, made-for-TV movies, theatricals, and even a touring stage show.

# AUGUST

## 31

**1974** Emerging director Francis Ford Coppola. Silent-film star Gloria Swanson. Controversial German documentarian Leni Riefenstahl. A formidable trio, indeed, and all are present tonight in the mountains of Colorado as the first Telluride Film Festival opens in a restored opera house. Organized by James Card, head of the motion picture collection of the George Eastman House, the indie event draws an intimate crowd of 350 to a smattering of screenings, easy contact, intense discussion, and heady mountain air. "There [are] no Belgian starlets showing a bit of leg any place," writes the *Los Angeles Times*, "no black tie champagne fetes or honking taxi cabs or dazzling leading men emerging from sleek limousines." There are, however, stars—not quite as numerous as the skies above, but dazzling nonetheless: Pedro Almodovar, Julie Christie, Catherine Deneuve, Clint Eastwood, David Lynch, Peter O'Toole, and Meryl Streep.

SEPTEMBER

# SEPTEMBER

## 11

### 1972

A geopolitical glow: all eyes of the world turn to tiny Reykjavik, Iceland, for a Cold War battle redux—eccentric American challenger Bobby Fischer, twenty-nine, versus Soviet champ Borris Spassky. From its opening last April, when Fischer didn't even show, the World Chess Championships have been part chess, part circus: a British financier kicking in $125,000 at the last minute to keep a balky Fischer; whispered phone calls to Fischer from Henry Kissinger; Fischer threatening to ban television cameras. On the boards, he's down 2-0 when he beats Spassky for the first time—ever. And from then on he's an inexorable force until today, when Spassky phones it in—his resignation from the final adjourned game. Ending twenty-four years of Soviet dominance, Fischer becomes the first native-born American chess champion.

## SEPTEMBER

### 1979

Hi ho, Silver! The Lone Ranger lives to ride again, even though today the law turns against him. An LA judge rules that actor Clayton Moore can no longer wear the trademark mask of the character he portrayed in hundreds of TV episodes and at personal appearances for decades. "It's our mask," says a lawyer for the Wrather Corporation, which is planning a new movie with a younger lead. "We own the Lone Ranger." Legally, they're right, but in the court of public opinion they're big-time losers. Their 1981 movie flops, while Moore's back in the saddle within a month after the decision, promoting baseball's Texas Rangers with wraparound sunglasses in lieu of the missing mask. "I have no animosity toward the Wrather people," he says. "I just hope and pray that they live up to the moral code of Clayton Moore for the last thirty years." Moore later countersues, wins, and resumes his costumed character appearances for many years until his death three days before Y2K.

# SEPTEMBER 3

**1971** Don't cry for her, Argentina—she never wanted to leave you, and now she has been found. Nearly twenty years after her death, larger than life Eva Perón makes headline news. Today her embalmed body, missing for the last sixteen years, is returned from an unknown site in Italy to the Madrid home of her exiled husband Juan Perón. The body had disappeared in 1955 after Juan was overthrown. Perónists, who unsuccessfully petitioned the Vatican to make Eva a saint, had made the return of her body a rallying cry ever since. One of the world's most powerful and charismatic leaders, she died of cancer at age thirty-three. Juan Perón returns to power in Argentina in 1973, and after he dies the next year Eva's body is returned to her native land.

## TRENDSETTER

# FASHIONABLE FOOD

Before supermarkets found their way into the city, corner grocers, butchers, bakers, and other specialty shops provided the staples of life to countless generations of New Yorkers. But things were stirred up in September 1977, when Joel Dean and Giorgio DeLuca made culinary history with their upscale market, Dean & DeLuca. Dean, a former history teacher turned cheese-shop owner, and DeLuca, a publishing employee and son of a food broker, designed the 2,500-square-foot food emporium with loftlike white space surrounding an ambitious array of delectable foodstuffs from around the globe—plus classy kitchen accessories. It soon became a New York institution, helping to revitalize its neighborhood and usher in a new era of fine food offerings nationwide.

# SEPTEMBER 4

**1972** Mark Spitz strikes gold for a record seventh time tonight in Munich, the most ever for an Olympic athlete—and all his times were world records. Winning four individual and three relay races, the mustachioed swimmer not only lives up to but also surpasses all the pre-summer games hype. He later receives a hero's welcome, signing as a spokesperson for Adidas, Schick, Speedo, the California Milk Advisory Board, and more. His medal-laden poster will make him the hottest pin-up since Betty Grable. But back here in Munich, a few hours after Spitz's seventh gold-clinching race, the 400-meter medley relay, tragedy strikes.

# SEPTEMBER

# 5

**1972** At dawn, eight Black September terrorists in tracksuits invade an Olympic dorm in Munich where they kill two and seize nine Israeli athletes. Instantly, happy thoughts of the games evaporate as footage of the tense standoff with gun-wielding terrorists beams live globally. The world waits, apprehensively. And tomorrow, its worst fears are realized when a battle erupts at the military airport to which authorities had ferried captives and captors by helicopter. All hostages die, as do five terrorists. Three are captured but released several months later after two Palestinians hijack a Lufthansa plane in Beirut and demand their release. The West German government immediately agrees, and they are flown to Libya and a thunderous heroes' welcome. After a day of mourning and a memorial service attended by 80,000, the games continue. Mark Spitz, who is Jewish, flies home before the closing ceremonies as a precaution.

**"We had no choice. We had to make them stop, and there was no other way... we are not very proud about it. But it was a question of sheer necessity. "**

**—General Aharon Yariv, on the Israeli response to the Munich massacre**

# SEPTEMBER

**1970** For the record: Derek and the Dominoes finish sessions for the seminal double-disc *Layla and Other Assorted Love Songs*, as notable for what's happening behind the scenes as on the record. Eric Clapton's title track is inspired by his affair with Pattie Boyd, wife of pal George Harrison. It features a spirited guitar duel between him and Duane Allman alongside sterling sidemen: keyboardist Bobby Whitlock, drummer Jim Gordon, and bassist Carl Radle. "Forget any indulgences and filler—it's one hell of an album," writes Ed Leimbacher in *Rolling Stone*. "The Dominoes together do make for an hour or so of heaven. Maybe the critics, audience and musicians can agree, just this once." Released in December, it features other telling tracks like "Have You Ever Loved a Woman" and "It's Too Late."

# SEPTEMBER

# 7

## 1979

As a former play-by-play broadcaster for the Hartford Whalers, Bill Rasmussen had a dream. He envisioned, along with his son Scott, a local sports network that would carry University of Connecticut games via satellite. But when he discovered that it would cost the same to transmit them nationally, that's just what he did. Today Rasmussen launches Entertainment & Sports Programming Network (later shortened to ESPN), on an acre of land he buys in an industrial park in Bristol, Connecticut, for $9,000. Within a year, Getty Oil recognizes the potential and invests $100 million.

## THE SKY'S THE LIMIT

A gold rush for cable franchises in urban and suburban America sends the number of cable homes skyrocketing, paving the way for the introduction of many new programming services. Beginning with HBO in 1972 (see Nov. 8), here are some of the earliest satellite-delivered channels:

- In 1977 the Madison Square Garden Sports Network was launched, and would change its name to the USA Network in 1980.
- The Christian Broadcasting Network, formed by Pat Robertson, premiered in 1977. It was re-named The Family Channel twelve years later.
- Filling the need for a political feed, the cable industry funded C-SPAN, which went live on March 19, 1979, to 3.5 million households with a speech by Congressman Al Gore. The nonprofit network soon expanded its gavel-to-gavel coverage with Senate hearings, news conferences, speeches, and more.
- Nickelodeon had been broadcast in Columbus, Ohio, for a few years, but went national on April 1, 1979. Used as a noncommercial goodwill tool to win cable franchises and subscribers, its only original series was *Pinwheel*, which interspersed puppets and actors with acquired cartoons.
- After HBO's success, movie channels abounded. The Star Channel, which had been distributing videotapes of movies to cable affiliates since 1973, was relaunched as The Movie Channel in 1979. In the early '80s it would be bought by Showtime, which launched in 1976.
- In 1979 the Ted Turner—owned WTCG, a broadcast station in Atlanta, goes national as WTBS.

# SEPTEMBER

**1979** Oh, Carol! Versatile entertainer Carol Burnett ends her popular CBS variety show tonight. In its sketches she's assumed many diverse personas, aided by the masterful hand and mind of designer Bob Mackie. For all the series' eleven years he's provided just the right clothes and accessories to enhance Burnett's many characters. Another of Mackie's clients also hosts a variety show on CBS but prefers over-the-top outlandishness: the bejeweled, bedazzling Cher. Her trademark look brings him nicknames like the Sultan of Sequins and the Rajah of Rhinestones. His eclectic, star-studded clientele ranges from Marlene Dietrich to RuPaul, with even a dash of designer Barbie.

# SEPTEMBER

**1973** The sun that rises in the East sets on China's all-powerful leader as Mao Tse-Tung passes away peacefully in his sleep at age eighty-two. News of the death of the iron-fisted ruler of the world's most populous nation trumps all else as politicians publicly mouth platitudes. "Chairman Mao was a remarkable and a very great man," says President Ford, praising his "great ability and skill and vision and foresight." Privately, they and everyone else ponder what news and/or upheaval might emanate next from Peking (the re-jiggered pinyin phonetic spelling of "Beijing" for Peking and "Zedong" for Tse-Tung won't happen for awhile). For now pageantry tops pragmatics, with millions of Chinese streaming by his body lying in state in Peking's Great Hall of the People. Later, inevitable power struggles prove remarkably bloodless.

## SEPTEMBER 10

**1975** One sings, the other doesn't. Right there Dave Starsky and Ken Hutchinson aren't your typical plainclothes cops. But then again ABC's *Starsky & Hutch*, bowing tonight, isn't your typical TV cop show. Don't let the Lalo Schifrin (*Mission: Impossible*) theme song or the fact that it's an Aaron Spelling production fool you. Paul Michael Glaser and David Soul may not be as hip as ABC's original trio of rockin' undercovers, *The Mod Squad*, but they've got hot wheels (a fire-red Ford Torino, even though a green-and-white Chevy Camaro was the producers' first choice) and the coolest of informants in the sartorially challenged Huggy Bear (Antonio Fargas). Facing lots of primetime cop competition, the show lasts a respectable four seasons. Soul even goes pop as his recording of "Don't Give Up on Us" hits #1 with several bullets—after all, this is a tough neighborhood, partner.

# JACKED UP

Wiseass Jack Nicholson got good grades in school, but was always a troublemaker. Those innate traits served him well in his Hollywood career, beginning with Roger Corman B-movies like *The Little Shop of Horrors*. In the '60s Nicholson did lots of TV—acting in such shows as *Dr. Kildare* and *The Andy Griffith Show*—and wrote several screenplays including *Head* for the Monkees. His big break may have come in 1969's *Easy Rider* (where he famously assumed the role of hard-drinking lawyer George Hanson, originally intended for Rip Torn), but his leading-man debut came on September 11, 1970, when Bob Rafelson's *Five Easy Pieces* was released. Nicholson starred as conflicted oil rigger/piano virtuoso Robert Dupea, who attempts to reconcile his perceived failures by feigning ambivalence. More great films and multiple Oscar wins (including one for 1975's *One Flew Over the Cuckoo's Nest*) followed, but even in a career filled with innumerable memorable performances and dozens of quotable lines, it's hard to top Dupea's attempt to order off-menu at a roadside diner.

**66 OK, I'll make it as easy for you as I can. I'd like an omelet, plain, and a chicken salad sandwich on wheat toast—no mayonnaise, no butter, no lettuce. All you have to do is hold the chicken, bring me the toast, give me a check for the chicken salad sandwich, and you haven't broken any rules. 99**

—Jack Nicholson as Robert Dupea

## SEPTEMBER

**1974** One of the most popular TV shows of the 1970s takes place in the 1870s. *Little House on the Prairie*, a heartwarming family drama based on the books by Laura Ingalls Wilder, dawns onscreen tonight. A year after the end of *Bonanza*, Michael "Little Joe" Landon changes locales if not eras, going from Nevada's Ponderosa to a Minnesota farm. No doubt it's inspired by CBS's *The Waltons*, even though that's set sixty years later during the Depression. The parallels between the two hit series could fill this page: leading men (Landon and Richard Thomas) with big families and family values, struggling to make ends meet amid natural disasters, disease, and economic crisis. And love—read no sex and no violence—always prevails, affording each nine fruitful seasons.

## SEPTEMBER

**1978** Here's a tip, buddy: tonight, for a one-way trip to laughs, catch this *Taxi*. The ensemble sitcom—created by four alums of the Emmy-winning *Mary Tyler Moore Show*—premieres with a cab ride from New York City all the way to Miami. When cabbie-for-life Alex (Judd Hirsch) discovers the daughter he left behind fifteen years ago is changing flights there, it means a road trip with fellow hack Tony (as in Danza) as well as mechanic Latka (*Saturday Night Live*'s Andy Kaufman). With Napoleonic dispatcher Louie (Danny DeVito), spaceshot driver "Reverend Jim" (Christopher Lloyd), and girl-in-a-roomful-of-men Elaine (Marilu Henner) also along for the ride during *Taxi*'s five seasons, it's easy to see why reviews are better than "just fare" and why it wins the Emmy for best sitcom in its first season, displacing *All in the Family*.

# SEPTEMBER 13

## 1974

The small screen's awash with private investigators like tubby Frank Cannon (William Conrad), folksy Barnaby Jones (Buddy Ebsen), and tough guy Joe Mannix (Mike Connors). Tonight, into the mix strides a kinder, gentler fellow, ex-con Jim Rockford. James Garner charms as the knockabout, beach-abiding private detective in Stephen Cannell's *The Rockford Files*. Unlike those other shows, it's less about crime and detection than character and relationships, especially with his prickly yet loving pop (Noah Beery, Jr.), wily and wild ex-cellmate (Stuart Margolin), and ever-reliable girlfriend/attorney (Gretchen Corbett). Keeping the tone light, with strong anti-authoritarian touches on political, corruption, and bureaucratic matters, *The Rockford Files* becomes a perennial Emmy nominee, and wins in 1978. It ends prematurely in 1980 when Garner retires.

# SEPTEMBER 14

## 1978

Tonight a UFO—that's Unidentified Funny Object—lands on ABC in the form of Mork from the planet Ork. In *Mork & Mindy*, Robin Williams, late of NBC's failed attempt to revive *Laugh-In* last year, stars as the alien whose jokes and impressions come faster than the speed of light. It's actually a spinoff of an episode from *Happy Days*, when Mork landed in 1950s Milwaukee to kidnap Richie Cunningham. Clearly Orkan spaceships can travel through time, as Mork now finds himself in 1970s Boulder, Colorado, and rooming with human-as-Gidget Mindy. During this first season its ratings go into outer space, but then ABC and show producers mess with the formula: new characters, more serious themes, and eventually having Mork and Mindy marry and give birth to baby Mearth (Jonathan Winters). If it ain't broke, don't fix it. Viewers bid Mork a fond "na-nu-na-nu" (good-bye), and ratings quickly fall back to earth before it's abandoned four years later.

# SEPTEMBER 15 1971

Uh, there's just one more thing….Appearances can be deceiving. Just ask any of the clever, cocky murderers eventually caught by the rumpled detective (Peter Falk) in *Columbo*. Inverting the standard whodunnit, the ninety-minute movies (despite network begging, Falk never did it as a weekly series) follow the seemingly bumbling title character relentlessly stalking his prey. In the end, in time-honored Perry Mason fashion, the crook confesses in the face of the incontrovertible evidence Columbo has amassed. Tonight's premiere pits Columbo against a mystery writer (Jack Cassidy, David and Shaun's papa) who's knocked off his writing partner. A panoply of juicy guest villains appear over its long run, from Eddie Albert to Oskar Werner.

# SEPTEMBER 1972

Go out Saturday night? What, and miss great TV? CBS rules Saturday prime-time with three rock-solid shows: *All in the Family*, *The Mary Tyler Moore Show*, and *Mission: Impossible*. Tonight two new sitcoms join the night, including *The Bob Newhart Show*. It settles in for a comfy six-year run, a big improvement over the first *Newhart* show, a one and out NBC variety series a decade earlier. The doctor is in, the patients are out, way out, but nothing fazes mild-mannered therapist Bob Hartley (Newhart). Plugging along with sardonic wife Emily (Suzanne Pleshette) and/or uninvited guest Howard (Bill Daily), he somehow never loses his cool no matter how ridiculous things get. What's really ridiculous is that for its entire run, *The Bob Newhart Show* never wins an Emmy. Perhaps if Academy members had, like college students at the time, started tossing down an alcoholic beverage any time anyone in the show said "Hi, Bob," things may have gone differently.

## M*A*S*H IT UP AGAIN

Many movies spawn TV series that quickly (and usually thankfully) disappear. But on September 17, 1972, a rare spinoff premiered. M*A*S*H, a sitcom based on the popular Robert Altman film, not only equaled but in many ways eclipsed its progenitor. The black comedy about the Korean War ran for eleven years—nearly four times longer the conflict it depicted—and provided tart commentary that directly correlated with the raging Vietnam War. Alan Alda, the only cast member to appear in every episode, won Emmys for acting, writing, and directing—becoming the only person to win all three awards for one series. In 1983 it would finally take a bow, and its two-and-a-half-hour finale captured 105.9 million viewers, making it the most-watched TV event of all time.

# SEPTEMBER 17 1970

The TV variety show may be alive and well, but watch out: someone's about to "Flip" the script. Tonight comedian Flip Wilson becomes the "host of a different color," the first African American to headline a successful variety hour. During the 1950s, singer Nat King Cole tried but fell victim to low ratings and minimal advertiser support. For Flip, the secret lies in being presold: in the years leading up to *The Flip Wilson Show*, he and his repertoire like Geraldine, Reverend Leroy, and Danny Danger have been all over *The Ed Sullivan Show*, *The Hollywood Palace*, and *Rowan & Martin's Laugh-In*. Two of his comedy albums have been Top 40 best-sellers. During Flip's primetime run, the aforementioned Geraldine popularizes two catchphrases: "The devil made me do it!" and "What you see is what you get."

## SEPTEMBER 18

**1970** Brilliant. Influential. Temperamental. Erratic. Virtuoso guitarist and writer Jimi Hendrix has been spiraling out of control. Financial woes, feuds with managers and band members, regular drug and alcohol abuse, and poorly received concerts have sapped his strength. A couple weeks ago he strode off a stage, declaring, "I've been dead for a long time." Early this morning he leaves a plea on his former manager's answering machine ("I need help bad, man"), takes nine sleeping pills, and crawls into the bed at his girlfriend's basement London apartment. He never wakes up, slipping into unconsciousness and suffocating on his vomit. His extraordinary, uncontrollable run of groundbreaking music, from *Are You Experienced* to *Band of Gypsies*, ends at age twenty-seven. "If I seem free," he said, "it's because I'm always running."

## SEPTEMBER 19

**1970** How will Mary make it on her own? That's the question her self-titled sitcom's theme asks as *The Mary Tyler Moore Show* premieres tonight. Four years removed from housewife Laura Petrie when *The Dick Van Dyke Show* ended, Mary returns as the antithesis of that character: an unmarried, independent woman looking to start a new career in a strange city. Minneapolis may be cold but not to Mary: even when prospective boss Lou Grant tells her, "You got spunk...[and] I hate spunk," he still hires her to associate-produce his TV station's evening newscast, anchored by lovable blowhard Ted Baxter. Although our Mary finds herself in the midst of personality clashes between not only them and various other coworkers and friends, by the end of tonight it's a foregone conclusion that Mary is back. Back for seven much-honored years with three Emmy Awards for best comedy, four for Moore, three apiece for Asner and Valerie Harper, two each for Ted Knight and Betty White.

# SEPTEMBER 20

**1973** Hurry, hurry, step right up to the highly hyped Battle of the Sexes! Master showman, hustler, and former (in the 1940s) world tennis champion Bobby Riggs, fifty-five, has challenged champion Billie Jean King to a winner-takes-all, $100,000 match. Having recently wiped former women's champion Margaret Court off the court, 6-2, 6-1, Riggs has catapulted onto the covers of *Sports Illustrated* and *Time*. In a packed Astrodome, King enters Cleopatra-style, carried aloft in a chair held by four muscular, bare-chested guys dressed like Roman slaves. Riggs follows in a rickshaw pulled by a bevy of buxom, scantily clad models. The unflustered King presents Riggs with a live "male chauvinist" pig. After the showy spectacle it's showtime, but not much of a match as the twenty-nine-year-old King dusts him off in three straight sets. "If I can't play for big money, I play for a little money," says Riggs. "And if I can't play for a little money, I stay in bed that day."

# SEPTEMBER 21

**1970** An institution, *Monday Night Football*, kicks off tonight and scores. And scores and scores. NFL commissioner Pete Rozelle had long wanted a regular primetime Monday night showcase, but couldn't find a network until third-place ABC agrees. Savvy, fast-rising producer Roone Arledge doubles the usual number of cameras, inserts slick graphics packages, and adds another announcer to the standard two-man setup: steady play-by-play man Keith Jackson, dandy Don Meredith, and the voluble Howard Cosell. The league delivers marquee teams, beginning tonight with the Joe Namath-led New York Jets, who lose to the Cleveland Browns, 31-21. When a whopping 35 percent of TV homes tune in, the advertisers paying $65,000 a minute realize that's a bargain. As the season progresses, movie attendance drops nationwide as fans flock for a post-Sunday football fix that will remain an ABC institution for the next thirty-six seasons.

# SEPTEMBER 22

**1976** The more the critics carped ("massage parlor television"), the more the public tuned in. *Charlie's Angels* debuts tonight to a big audience, and soon its sexy, shapely trio—Kate Jackson, Jaclyn Smith, and Farrah Fawcett-Majors—become major stars. Especially Farrah, whose pinup poster becomes all the rage. Unseen John Forsythe provides the melodious voice of the mysterious Charlie, but the real man responsible for this show and lots more is prolific producer Aaron Spelling, Tori's papa. His run of successful young-skewing ABC hits (*The Mod Squad*, *The Love Boat*, and others) leads to a snickering network nickname: "Aaron's Broadcasting Company." Farrah's hubby, Lee Majors, is star of ABC's *The Six Million Dollar Man*.

# SEPTEMBER

# 23

**1976** President Ford's in trouble. Not only is the economy floundering, but he's feeling the backlash for having granted Richard Nixon a post-Watergate pardon. So to shake things up he challenges Democratic presidential candidate Jimmy Carter to a debate, which they hold tonight in Philadelphia. It's the first time since the 1960 JFK-Nixon debates that presidential contenders have met, but it's a rather genteel, uneventful affair—until the audio goes dead near the end. ABC technicians scramble frantically for an agonizing twenty-seven minutes before they can restore power. The whole time the men don't stray from their lectures or acknowledge each other. The culprit? A twenty-five-cent electrolytic capacitor in one of twenty-four amplifiers. "It was like blowing a main fuse," says ABC's embarrassed director of television operations, "and having all the lights go out."

# SEPTEMBER
## 24

**1975** Reading can be done at a leisurely pace, but movies? There the clock's a 'tickin'. Today's taut thriller *Three Days of the Condor* should know— it's taken from a James Grady novel entitled *Six Days of the Condor*. Either way, it's a rousing espionage adventure with a dynamic Robert Redford– Faye Dunaway pairing: he as an on-the-run intelligence desk man since his entire office is wiped out in the film's opening minutes, she as the feisty foil who reluctantly takes him in as the bad guys (Max von Sydow, Cliff Robertson) close in. Director Sydney Pollack keeps the topical tale spinning along, delivering "a neat switch [ending] that mingles liberal humanism with a smidgen of skepticism and a dash of doubt," says David Sterritt of the *Christian Science Monitor*.

> **"Faye carries a cloud of drama round with her. There is something in her at hazard."**
> —Elia Kazan

## SEPTEMBER 25 1979

Fresh off its stunning success in London, Andrew Lloyd Webber's *Evita* opens on Broadway to similar acclaim and attention. Patti LuPone delivers a thundering performance in the title role, matching her dreams with schemes as Eva Duarte climbs from the slums to the pinnacle of power as Argentina's first lady, Eva Perón. Sweeping away all in its path, much like Eva's meteoric rise, *Evita* wins seven Tony Awards including best musical, book (Tim Rice), direction (Harold Prince), score (Lloyd Webber), and actress (LuPone). "*Evita* is a very complex but ultimately satisfying score," writes one English paper. "Although both the authors have gone on to other things, this show is the best they did [together]." Like *Jesus Christ Superstar*, their previous stage hit, *Evita* began as a popular album, with "Don't Cry for Me Argentina" by Julie Covington hitting #1 in the UK before the stage creation.

## SEPTEMBER 26 1978

Like boys chortling in the locker room, a lot of pundits have poked a lot of fun at the case. But while boys will be boys, today the opposite sex has its day when a federal judge rules that all reporters, regardless of sex, must be given equal access to athletes, even in their locker rooms. *Sports Illustrated* writer Melissa Ludtke had filed the suit last year after being banned by the New York Yankees during the World Series versus the Los Angeles Dodgers. An unlikely pioneer, art history major Ludtke had started in sports after a recommendation from ex-player and announcer Frank Gifford. "When the time comes that we no longer read or hear about women in any locker room," says Ludtke, "and instead turn our attention to reading their stories and listening to their accounts of the game, then we will have reached the goal that I set out for."

# SEPTEMBER

# 1973

"I am not a crook." President Nixon won't utter that line in regards to his role in the Watergate morass for another couple months. But it's way too mild for defiant Vice President Spiro Agnew, who seethes today as a federal grand jury convenes in Baltimore to explore allegations of misconduct during his tenure as governor of Maryland. Having transformed over the years from liberal Democrat to law-and-order Republican conservative, Agnew relishes his role as the White House's resident anti-intellectual, hippie-bashing attack dog. But now he's twisting in the wind, which is fast picking up speed. "He will not go quietly," says one unnamed friend, "for that would look like a confession of guilt." But the VP doesn't have a lot of choices, or friends left for that matter. In two short weeks he's gone, breaking his previously adamant refusal to resign by doing just that, a move that elevates House Speaker Gerald Ford to the job from which he'll assume the presidency next August when Nixon resigns. Agnew, who later pleads no contest to tax evasion and money-laundering charges, would have become president had he not first suffered this nasty career-ending tumble.

## SEPTEMBER

**1972** Glam rocker David Bowie and his band, the Spiders from Mars, go through some ch-ch-ch-changes as they sell out Carnegie Hall in their first-ever New York City concert. It's a big step for Bowie, the commercial breakthrough he's been itching for. A pop star back home for a couple of years since "Space Oddity," he hasn't been able to get arrested on the US Top 40 singles or albums charts until *The Rise and Fall of Ziggy Stardust and the Spiders from Mars*. Arguably, singles-wise, the US breakthrough hit for Bowie isn't by him, though he writes, produces, sings backup, and plays guitar on the track. It's "All the Young Dudes" by British glitter-glam rockers Mott the Hoople. Already #3 in England, it entered the US charts earlier this week on its way into the Top 40. The glam anthem punches Bowie's ticket in America, followed by a successful rerelease of "Space Oddity," hit albums *Aladdin Sane*, *Diamond Dogs*, and *Young Americans*, the latter containing his first US chart-topping single, "Fame." While Mott the Hoople fails to repeat its success, "All the Young Dudes" achieves rock-classic status and is discovered by a new generation of fans in 2007 when featured in teen pic *Juno*.

> **"I don't know where I'm going from here, but I promise it won't be boring."**
> **—David Bowie**

## SEPTEMBER

**1976** Living up to his nickname "The Killer," Jerry Lee Lewis celebrates his forty-first birthday by accidentally shooting his bass player, who's rushed to the local Tennessee hospital in critical condition. This kicks off a spree that's pretty wild even by Lewis's crazy bad-ass standards (marrying a thirteen-year-old cousin, six marriages, prodigious drug and alcohol intake…). Early this November he flips his brand-new Rolls Royce and gets charged with drunk driving. The next day he's arrested at the gates of Graceland after waving a pistol and demanding to see Elvis. "I was sitting there with my motor running and a tape playing," says Lewis. "Suddenly I'm surrounded by several squad cars, and before I knew it, I was in jail." Maybe the .38-caliber derringer on his knee had something to do with it. But at least it wasn't a .357 magnum—that gun was confiscated after he shot the bass player.

## SEPTEMBER

**1977** Pandora's box is about to open for crooked Columbia Pictures president David Begelman. Placed on leave today for financial improprieties, he is quietly reinstated a few weeks later by a studio hoping the situation fades away. Uh uh. Actor Cliff Robertson goes public with front-page news: Begelman had cashed a $10,000 check made out to the actor, who hadn't worked on one of the studio's pictures in years. It's the tip of the iceberg, and the resulting scandal exposes a seamy side of Hollywood, with greed, deceit, and cover-ups that inspire a best-seller, *Indecent Exposure*. Begelman resigns in shame, but later resurfaces as president of MGM. Robertson is blackballed, and won't appear again in a major studio film (*Brainstorm*) until 1983.

# OCTOBER

## 1

**1971** The Florida Highway Patrol cancels all leaves and adds extra troopers. Workmen labor 'round the clock. But even with a wave of Tinkerbell's magic wand, Florida's Walt Disney World ("The Magic Kingdom") draws a sparse opening-day crowd. It's a soft opening, though, with much work still to do and the main, celebrity-packed event not planned 'til later in the month. "The first three weeks will be like a shakedown cruise," says a Disney spokesman as the "alohas" of the sarong-clad girls at the Polynesian Village are punctuated by the pounding of workmen's hammers. Most of the kinks are worked out by the time Julie Andrews, working with her choreographer from *Mary Poppins* and *The Sound of Music*, hosts a TV special of the grand opening of the vast resort/theme park complex that grows into the world's busiest vacation destination.

# OCTOBER

## 2

**1971** All aboard: Gladys Knight and the Pips fittingly kick off the first episode of *Soul Train* with "Friendship Train"—and soon young black America rides along every week for not only the latest in sweet soul music but dance moves and hair and fashion tips. "I figured as long as the music stayed hot and important and good," says creator and host Don Cornelius, "there would always be a reason for *Soul Train*." A far more integrated and diverse show than Dick Clark's *American Bandstand*, the ad-libbed but lip-synched *Soul Train* becomes a must-see at a time when blacks have few media role models. (*Julia*, the first sitcom starring an African American, Diahann Carroll, has just ended, and music video–driven BET won't start until 1980.) It's also a must-stop for performers—in its first month alone it features folks like Freda Payne ("Band of Gold") and the Staple Singers ("Express Yourself").

# OCTOBER 3

**1971** Spying Cybill Shepherd on the cover of *Vogue*, film critic turned filmmaker Peter Bogdanovich knows he's found his small-town temptress. Today the ex-model makes her film debut in *The Last Picture Show*, adapted from a novel by Larry McMurtry (*Terms of Endearment*). The claustrophobic black-and-white snapshot of small-town life presents a well-crafted story filled with gentle humor, disillusion, and sexual passions. "One thing I know for sure," says waitress Genevieve (Eileen Brennan). "A person can't sneeze in this town without somebody offering him a handkerchief." It wins eight Oscar nominations and two trophies, for veteran supporting actors Ben Johnson and Cloris Leachman. Shepherd not only smolders onscreen but off, embarking on affairs with costar Jeff Bridges, screenwriter McMurtry, and Bogdanovich, the latter of whom she'll stay with, on and off, for the next seven years.

# OCTOBER 4

**1970** What a voice. What a character. What a star. What a shame. Today it all comes crashing down for outsized, outrageous singer Janis Joplin, discovered dead in a Hollywood motel of a heroin overdose. At twenty-seven, Joplin had been living larger than ever this year with well-received performances at San Francisco's Fillmore West and an antiwar rock festival at Shea Stadium. The bawdy Texas mama had just paid tribute to the past, quietly, by helping buy a tombstone for brassy blues singer Bessie Smith (see Aug. 9). "Maybe I won't last as long as other singers," says Joplin, "but I think you can destroy your now worrying about tomorrow." In Hollywood to record her new album, *Pearl*, Joplin later scores a posthumous #1 with Kris Kristofferson's "Me and Bobby McGee." Though one song she was slated to record the day she died seems more appropriate: "Buried Alive in the Blues."

> **66On stage, I make love to 25,000 people—then I go home alone.99**
> —Janis Joplin

# ALASTAIR COOKING

On October 5, 1970, British journalist Alastair Cooke made a deal with PBS to host its new anthology series. Little did he know that the series, *Masterpiece Theatre*, would end up becoming television's longest-running dramatic program. Cooke likened his role of imparting the social and historical context of the diverse British programs to that of a headwaiter: "I'm there to explain for interested customers what's on the menu, and how the dishes were composed." When *Theatre* premiered the following January, the first dish served was the bawdy *The First Churchills*. The series later cooked up some of television's most prestigious programs including *Upstairs, Downstairs* and *The Jewel in the Crown*. Cooke, who only signed a one-year deal since he was unsure about the show's future, quickly upped his contract for what would become a twenty-two-year run as its erudite, inviting host.

# OCTOBER 5

## 1979

Bad start, strong finish: on the first day of shooting, leading man George Segal bolted after a "difference of opinion" with director Blake Edwards. Good-bye George, hello Englishman Dudley Moore, who is about to receive the most timely of career resuscitations. But it's leading lady Bo Derek who catches the most attention as the title star of *10*. The comedic take on male sexual insecurities opens today, and within a month Derek has not only sold millions of tickets but also a half-million posters. This instant national success validates the views of Moore's besotted character that rates her an eleven. Moore moves on to his signature role as the drunken playboy in *Arthur*. While Derek's career proves fleeting, her fame and fortune remain. "Whoever said money can't buy happiness," she says, "simply didn't know where to go shopping."

# OCTOBER

**1970** Go directly to jail: smuggling hashish out of Turkey proves to be an exceptionally awful idea for cocky young American tourist Billy Hayes. Today he tapes a couple kilos of the drug to his body and is promptly caught by authorities on high alert for terrorist suspects. Convicted and sent to a hellish Turkish prison, he endures five brutal years before managing to escape. Hayes quickly pens a book tailor-made for Hollywood, and exactly eight years to the day of his arrest United Artists' *Midnight Express* arrives onscreen. Relatively unknown Brad Davis plays the reckless, feckless young man who pays a big price for his big mistake. A huge hit among young moviegoers, the 1978 film draws jeers for its harsh stereotyping of Turks but still wins an Oscar for best adapted screenplay for Oliver Stone, and another for Giorgio Moroder for its score. Still relatively unknown, ex-Vietnam vet Stone later writes *Conan the Barbarian* and *Scarface* before hitting directorial heights and eternal fame in the mid-1980s with *Salvador* and *Platoon*.

MEANWHILE...

## OF DIAMONDS AND DENTISTS

Screen villainy drilled down to raw nerve on October 6, 1976, in the taut thriller *Marathon Man*, starring Laurence Olivier. Forced to venture to New York to recover a cache of diamonds, ex-concentration camp commander Dr. Christian Szell (Olivier) uses his dental training to interrogate a grad student (Dustin Hoffman) who he fears knows the reason for his visit. Director John Schlesinger ramped up the tension, especially in a scene on crowded diamond-district streets where the Nazi goes to get an appraisal. "Szell! Szell! Oh my God, he's here!" cries an aging Holocaust survivor, ignored by the crowds who think she's a crazy old woman. (The actress, German-born Lotte Palfi Andor, also had a bit part in *Casablanca*.) Screenwriter William Goldman (*Butch Cassidy & the Sundance Kid*), who masterfully adapted his own novel, won kudos, but not an Oscar—that will come the next year for *All the President's Men*.

# OCTOBER

**1971** Another true drug-smuggling story, on a far more involved, intricate level, roars onscreen today. The crackling *French Connection* features one of film's most riveting chase sequences ever. Everyman cop "Popeye" Doyle (Gene Hackman) races in a car underneath an elevated subway line down New York's 86th Street to catch the hit man of a suave drug kingpin (Fernando Rey). When director William Friedkin first approached NYC authorities, they denied permission for such a dangerous, unprecedented stunt. But one powerful transit boss made Friedkin an offer—$40,000 and a one-way ticket to Jamaica—that he couldn't refuse. The boss got fired, as he'd expected, but Friedkin got his scene, and the movie wins five Oscars.

# OCTOBER

## 1977

Living up to their name, prototype punk rockers the Clash spend this afternoon in a German jail over a hotel bill that a promoter should have paid. With a steady stream of enforcement encounters—arrests for spray-painting graffiti and stealing a hotel pillowcase, among others—the band dubs its latest tour "Out on Parole." Kicking off 1977 with their antagonistic single "White Riot," the band generates undeniable heat and challenges the Sex Pistols as punk's most raging, raw rockers. It takes awhile for the Clash's aggressive act to catch fire stateside; they antagonistically, characteristically make "I'm So Bored with the USA" the opening song at their NYC debut in 1979. Next album *Give 'Em Enough Rope* propels their bad-boy image enough that their label, Columbia, finally releases their first album in the United States two years after its British bow. Soon it's *London Calling* and worldwide fame with high-energy hits like "Should I Stay or Should I Go" and "Rock the Casbah."

# OCTOBER

## 1978

New York City teems with energetic crowds for its annual Columbus Day parade, but tonight an even bigger spectacular unfolds at Madison Square Garden. Progressive rockers Jethro Tull perform for two disparate audiences in one of the first concerts ever broadcast live via satellite. "Thunderous applause and the obvious fanaticism of a 20,000 capacity crowd of new generation Tull freaks made it an impressive demonstration of the group's power and appeal after ten years on the road," writes *Melody Maker*. "But the tension and strain on [Ian] Anderson was obvious, with the knowledge of an estimated potential audience of 400,000,000 TV viewers." On stage madcap Anderson and his lads blast off the forty-five-minute transmission with "Thick as a Brick." Not quite as daunting as D-day, the joint Anglo-British operation nevertheless involves considerable high-tech and nerve-wracking preparations.

# OCTOBER

### 1971
London Bridge is going up, going up, going up, London Bridge is going up in…Arizona?! In an odd mix of ancient pageantry and modern public relations that some liken to a Fellini movie, London Bridge reopens in the planned community of Lake Havasu. The lord mayor of London, in ceremonial black robes, and the governor of Arizona, in a large white Stetson hat, cohost the festivities. Thousands of multicolored balloons and hundreds of white pigeons fly, along with skydivers, rockets, and a hot-air balloon. "It's a super gimmick," says one British newsman. "It's all quite mad—it could happen only in America!" Bought by the town's founder as a tourist attraction, the bridge had been dismantled on site and shipped here for reconstruction over a three-year process.

# OCTOBER

### 1972
When Johnny Carson asks that his weekend reruns (*Best of Carson*) move to select weeknights so he can take yet more time off, NBC casts about for something new and, well, colorful. The Peacock Network taps Canadian producer Lorne Michaels to design a young sketch/musical/variety show, and voila—*NBC's Saturday Night* (later *Saturday Night Live*) debuts tonight with George Carlin hosting. And so kicks off an institution with an edgy blend of satire, skits, star hosts, and top-shelf musical guests, with a resident troupe (the Not-Yet-Ready-for-Primetime Players) of breakout talent: Laraine Newman, John Belushi, Jane Curtin, Gilda Radner, Dan Aykroyd, Garrett Morris, and Chevy Chase in year one alone. "It's better when they laugh," says Michaels, "isn't it?"

## OCTOBER 12 — 1971

Aficionados divide theatrical history into two eras: BC, as in Before *Cats,* and AD—Andrew Dominant. The latter period begins tonight as *Jesus Christ Superstar* opens at the Mark Hellinger Theater. Composer Andrew Lloyd Webber and lyricist Tim Rice had worked previously on *Joseph and the Amazing Technicolor Dreamcoat*, staged in London, but *Superstar* marks their Broadway debut. The rock opera's concept album has already rocked the charts, generating two hits: "Superstar" by Murray Head, playing the part of Judas, and "I Don't Know How to Love Him," performed by Yvonne Elliman's Mary Magdalene (also covered by Helen Reddy, see Dec. 9). Broadway's lights shine bright for more than seven hundred performances, and the religious experience also transfers to the big screen. The only performer to make the transition from record to stage to film is Elliman, who plays the part of Mary Magdalene in all three. Lloyd Webber, of course, follows up with *Evita* and the aforementioned *Cats*, which goes on to displace *A Chorus Line* as Broadway's longest-running show to date.

## OCTOBER 13 — 1972

High in the Andes mountains a plane carrying a Uruguayan rugby team crashes. A dozen members die immediately, and six more succumb to injuries over the next week. With little food, few medical supplies, and no clothing for the bitter-cold weather, the remaining survivors take desperate measures: cannibalism. Two survivors start an arduous trek for help, and the remaining members are rescued two days before Christmas in a story that makes worldwide headlines. The ordeal inspires a 1993 movie, *Alive*, with Ethan Hawke and Vincent Spano starring.

## OCTOBER 14

**1972** Grassy plains grasshopper: a Buddhist monk with a shaved head, Caine (David Carradine) roams the Old West doling out a unique form of frontier justice in ABC's *Kung Fu*, which premieres today. Spurred by the success of martial arts master Bruce Lee, who auditioned unsuccessfully for the role, the series enjoys a short, successful run. Though a pacifist by upbringing, Caine finds his kung fu skills come in handy most every episode. Offscreen the actor, son of veteran character actor John Carradine, draws considerable attention too. Just after season three begins, he breaks into a neighbor's house in the Hollywood Hills. In a drug-induced rampage he overturns furniture and breaks windows, leaving an easily traceable trail of blood. After his arrest his lawyer comments: "He was in a strange house, it was closing in on him, and he had to break out."

## OCTOBER 15

**1971** Ricky Nelson endured tough times in his hits: he was a "Poor Little Fool" and "Stood Up," and saying "Hello Mary Lou" meant "good-bye heart." But truth turns out to be even tougher than fiction when Rick (no "y" anymore) performs at tonight's annual Rock 'n' Roll Revival at Madison Square Garden alongside acts like Chuck Berry, Bo Diddley, and Gary U.S. Bonds. After doing some familiar oldies circa *The Adventures of Ozzie & Harriet* TV days, Rick expands his repertoire with covers of Dylan's "She Belongs to Me" and the Stones' "Honky Tonk Women." The unappreciative crowd literally boos him off the stage. But Rick doesn't get mad, he gets even—and then some—by writing the autobiographical "Garden Party," which puts a fresh spin on the old days and becomes his first million-seller in a decade.

# OCTOBER 16

**1975** Hurry, hurry, step right up, ladies and... well, just ladies mostly. Inspired by women's liberation, the First Women's Bank opens on the site of a former chic Manhattan restaurant. It looks more like an art gallery than a bank with a skylight, plenty of plants, and Turkish rugs adorning the walls. "You walk in and have a gut feeling that it's right," says one new customer. High-profile initial depositors include Bette Davis, Betty Friedan, *Ms.* and *Vogue* magazines, and four women's colleges—Mount Holyoke, Simmons, Smith, and Wellesley. "The bank is totally nondiscriminatory," assures its president. "We're a consumer-oriented bank." A benefit cocktail party caps opening day, attracting Congresswomen Bella Abzug, Elizabeth Holtzman, and Margaret Heckler plus Valerie Harper of CBS's *Rhoda*. The bank changes its name in 1989 after other financial institutions begin targeting women, and folds in 1994.

# OCTOBER 17

**1973** Baby, it's cold outside: better get a sweater, suggests presidential advisor Melvin Laird. And turn down the thermostat four degrees while you're at it, adds the White House. Rattling sabers cause jittering nerves after OPEC Arab nations apply pressure on the United States after a Middle East flare-up ten days ago when Syria struck across a cease-fire line in the Golan Heights, and the United States backed Israel. Today King Faisal of Saudi Arabia announces an immediate 10 percent cutback in oil production. "If these efforts do not produce quick, tangible results," says a Saudi radio broadcast, "Saudi Arabia will stop supplying the United States with oil." Though less than 5 percent of Saudi output goes to the United States, America stands on guard. "The United States, whose phenomenal industrial growth and prosperity have been fueled by abundant, cheap energy," writes Edward Cowan in the *New York Times*, "is being forced to reconsider its high-energy way of life."

# OCTOBER
# 18

**1972** The critics are having a field day. Diana Ross as jazz icon Billie Holiday—who does she think she is? Her only previous acting credit had been playing a nun, along with the other Supremes, on an episode of NBC's *Tarzan*. But the breakout star, who'd departed the Motown group two years before for a solo career, changes a lot of minds when *Lady Sings the Blues* debuts. Her performance wins rave reviews, an Oscar nomination (just like fellow songstress turned actress Bette Midler did in *The Rose*, her debut), and a Golden Globe Award. Also premiering in the film is Richard Pryor as the piano man, while Billy Dee Williams plays her lover—a pairing so successful that they reprise it two years later in the inferior *Mahogany*, though each film does generate successful soundtrack albums.

**"Just because I have my standards they think I'm a bitch."**

—Diana Ross

# CALAMITY PLANE

On October 18, 1974, *Airport 1975* touched down at theaters with an unforgettable line most air travelers pray they'll never hear: "The stewardess is flying the plane!" That would be frazzled Karen Black, who takes radio-tower advice from her pilot-instructor boyfriend (a scenery-chewing Charlton Heston) after a midair collision kills one pilot and blinds the other. It wasn't so safe on the ground, either, as deadly disaster pix multiplied. Here's a sampling of more '70s cinema catastrophique.

- The original *Airport* (1970) paved the way for three campy sequels and nabbed Helen Hayes an Oscar for her role as a sly senior stowaway.
- In *The Poseidon Adventure* (1972), the Irwin Allen production that earned him the nickname "master of disaster," a tidal wave gets the better of a luxury liner.
- *The Towering Inferno* (1974), Allen's follow-up in a burning skyscraper, won Oscars for cinematography, editing, and song— Maureen McGovern's "We May Never Love Like This Again."
- *Earthquake* (1974), inspired by the San Fernando earthquake of 1971, snagged the services of co-writer Mario Puzo, red-hot off *The Godfather*.

"Something hit us... the crew is dead... help us, please, please help us!"

An all **NEW** movie inspired by the film "AIRPORT" based on the novel by Arthur Hailey.

**AIRPORT 1975**

CHARLTON HESTON

KAREN BLACK · GEORGE KENNEDY · GLORIA SWANSON · EFREM ZIMBALIST JR. · SUSAN CLARK · SID CAESAR
DANA ANDREWS · ROY THINNES · NANCY OLSON · ED NELSON · MYRNA LOY · AUGUSTA SUMMERLAND · LINDA BLAIR

---

## OCTOBER 19 · 1977

Blackface in 1927? Acceptable. Blackface today? Uh-uh. That's the shamed-faced lesson the US Postal Service learns today when it's forced to pull a poster of Al Jolson in blackface. Promoting a stamp commemorating the fiftieth anniversary of talking pictures, the poster—shipped to five thousand post offices nationwide—features popular entertainer Jolson in blackface from *The Jazz Singer* with a headline, "You Ain't Heard Nothin' Yet!" Meant to refer to the 1927 movie, which was the first talkie, the postal service does hear something—but it isn't exactly what it expected. Public response is fast and furiously negative. "It wasn't the kind of thing you try to defend or argue with," says a spokesman. "We found that we had offended people and we responded." Fortunately the stamp itself has no image of Jolson, only a vintage movie projector. Good thing, since its initial run is 160 million stamps.

## OCTOBER 20 · 1978

Time to retire: after months of devastating news stories and ten thousand reports about defective tires causing nearly a hundred fatalities and injuries, Firestone announces a recall of 7.5 million steel-belted radial tires—the largest in US history. It also agrees to replace six million more tires at half price. Several months later National Highway Traffic Safety Administration documents reveal that Firestone had known about unsafe tread-separation issues since 1973, though it steadfastly issued public denials that anything was wrong. It stays on the offensive even after the recall, smearing the leak. "We don't think," says a company spokesman, "[that] any purpose is served by an after-the-fact discussion of isolated documents." The nation's second-largest rubber company (behind Goodyear) soon reports a whopping $172 million loss in the fourth quarter, propelling talk of a sale or merger.

## OCTOBER

**1972** One of rock's prime movers, shakers, and shapers, Chuck Berry has been a pivotal force since bursting onto the musical scene with "Maybellene" back in 1955. Since then he's been true to his blues rockin' roots, churning out hits like "Sweet Little Sixteen" and "Johnny B. Goode," and influencing the sound and maturation of preeminent bands like The Beatles and Rolling Stones. So it's off to merry olde England as Chuck goes to record a rude little ditty called "My Ding-A-Ling," which hits #1 today—the only chart-topper of the pioneering singer-songwriter's long career. "I may go down sometimes," he says, "but I always come back rocking." Better tell Tchaikovsky the news.

## OCTOBER

**22**

**1977** Rock me two times: coming off a pair of extravagant, best-selling albums named for Marx Brothers films—*A Night at the Opera* and *A Day at the Races*—Queen faces a challenge: how to top the six-minute opus "Bohemian Rhapsody," which has just been voted Best British Pop Single of the past quarter century. Fabulous Freddie Mercury and company go for a pair of queens: side one, "We Will Rock You," transitions into the flip side, "We Are the Champions." Today the double-sided single simultaneously enters the US and UK charts en route to Top 10 status in both countries. Prodigious live performers, Queen hones its lush, multilayered, glam-meets-metal sound with massive tours, and later smashes a world record by playing a concert in Brazil before 130,000 adoring fans. "I won't be a rock star," says Mercury. "I will be a legend."

## OCTOBER 23

**1978** Last year the spiky-haired, black-lipsticked, safety pin–clad Sex Pistols ruled the earth. Their *Never Mind the Bollocks, Here's the Sex Pistols* album produced the outrageous seminal singles "God Save the Queen" and "Anarchy in the UK." But in January, front man Johnny Rotten quit the band during its US tour, telling a sellout San Francisco crowd, "Ha! Ha! Ever got the feeling you've been cheated? Good night." Bassist Sid Vicious spirals even deeper out of control, with his multiple arrests, accidents, and overdoses culminating in his being charged earlier this month with the stabbing death of his companion, Nancy Spungen. Today writes another chapter in the strange saga of the mother of all punk bands when Sid, released on bail and staying in his mother's hotel room, attempts suicide and is admitted to a psychiatric ward. His life ends, not surprisingly, next February of complications caused by a heroin overdose.

## OCTOBER 24

**1973** A New York City detective needs something to kick the habit, so he turns to lollipops. And so is born one of the more endearing, ongoing aspects of tough (on the outside) Inspector Theo Kojak (Telly Savalas). He also devises a trademark catchphrase that enters pop lexicon: "Who loves ya, baby?" The answer, apparently, is viewers, as CBS's *Kojak* premieres tonight and vaults into the Top 10 in its first season. In the ratings race, streetwise Kojak bypasses shapely Angie Dickinson (*Police Woman*), flabby Frank Cannon (*Cannon*), and folksy Buddy Ebson (*Barnaby Jones*). Though he can't quite catch cool Jack Lord, who patrols a far different home turf in *Hawaii Five-O* than Kojak's gritty Big Apple. The ultimate outsider, Kojak chafes while working within the system and isn't above a little rule-breaking if it helps him solve the case. Savalas stays on the case for five seasons, then returns after a decade's hiatus to star in new *Kojak* films for a different network, ABC.

**1978** Hallowed haunting: shooting in three weeks with an unknown lead actress and a minuscule budget of $325,000, the film wasn't expected to have much of an impact. But that lead, Jamie Lee Curtis (paid $8,000 for this, her screen debut), capitalizes on her famous parentage—particularly her mother, Janet Leigh, known forever for her shower scream scene in Alfred Hitchcock's *Psycho*. B-movie master John Carpenter borrows liberally from that and other horror classics, and with savvy, timely promotion, *Halloween* opens today and torches the box office for $47 million. And so is born the horny-teen slasher movie genre, spawning umpteen sequels and a horrid horde of imitative franchises like *Friday the 13th* and *Nightmare on Elm Street*. Beware of things that go slash in the night.

# OCTOBER

**1970** A cartoon strip with a decidedly countercultural slant makes its nationally syndicated debut today in a couple dozen newspapers. Garry Trudeau's *Doonesbury*, a revamped version of his strip from his undergraduate days at the *Yale Daily News*, quickly makes its presence felt. Its topical, timely social and political humor is vastly unlike the mass of gentle, family-friendly strips, and some papers opt to run it outside of the "funny pages." In 1975 it wins a Pulitzer Prize for editorial cartooning, the first strip to be so honored. The year after it breaks yet more bounds and grounds by introducing the first cartoon character to come out of the closet. As if its conservative critics didn't have enough to already hate, what with its irreverent liberal tone and freewheeling attitudes toward sex, drugs, and rock 'n' roll—not heretofore standard comic pages fare.

# OCTOBER 27

**1979** Like father, unlike son. A generational clash erupts between a tough-as-nails Marine fighter pilot (Robert Duvall) and his loyal but conflicted eldest son (Miles O'Keefe) in *The Great Santini*. Adapted from Pat Conroy's best-seller, the Southern drama veers toward melodrama with a ponderous subplot about racial tolerance, but wins plaudits for its two leads, each of whom wins Oscar nominations. The movie, filmed in the same house where much of *The Big Chill* (in 1983) will take place, propels the career of novelist Conroy who later enjoys two successive movies based on his work: the Southern military academy drama *The Lords of Discipline* (1983), which surprisingly shoots mostly in England; and the Southern family drama *The Prince of Tides* (1991), costarring Nick Nolte and Barbra Streisand (who also directs).

# OCTOBER

**1977** School kids and singers of all ages have someone new to blame for America's musically challenging "The Star-Spangled Banner"—an Englishman! A scholar retired from the Library of Congress unearths an eighteenth-century document that clears up the song's long contested compositional provenance. No one disputes that Francis Scott Key wrote the words in 1814, or that he set it to a British drinking song—what's never been established is who wrote *that* song. Today the composer is unveiled as John Stafford Smith, a member of a London gentleman's club renowned for its "music and mirth." But the scholar downplays its reputation as a haven for rakes and roués, insisting that the melody that has become the US National Anthem had less intoxicating roots: "It was not a barroom ballad, a drinking ditty to be chorused with glasses swung in rhythm."

# OCTOBER

**1971** Life offers a roller-coaster, up-and-down ride for the Allman Brothers Band. Guitarist Duane Allman plays lead guitar on King Curtis's Grammy-winning album, and the next thing you know he's playing at the murdered King's funeral. The Southern boogie rockers help close one of New York City's most fabled venues, and turn that finale into a searing two-disc album, *The Allman Brothers Band at Fillmore East*, with wicked takes on standards like "Stormy Monday" and an extended, life-is-tough number, "Whipping Post." In it lead singer Gregg sings that sometimes he feels like he's dying. Today his brother sadly does just that when motorbiking Duane crashes and dies while trying to avoid a turning truck. In the eeriest of coincidences, just over a year later, bassist Berry Oakley dies in a motorcycle accident not three blocks away. Duane and Berry's last studio recordings together are featured on the double album *Eat a Peach*.

# DIVIDED THEY STAND

Although John Lennon was singing, "I don't believe in Beatles," the fans still did. The Fab Four may have been no more, but this just meant that there were now four distinct careers to follow. Besides "Imagine," here's a review of what the broken-up band did solo.

- George Harrison turned out to be the not-so-silent Beatle, with six albums and a dozen Top 40 hits. The triple-disc *All Things Must Pass* made George the first to steer an album to #1 for seven straight weeks. (Unfortunately, the album's chart-topping single, "My Sweet Lord," became famous for having lifted its melody from the Chiffons' 1963 chart-topper "He's So Fine.") George also organized the Concert for Bangladesh (see Aug. 1), the album of which reached #2 and won a Grammy.

- One-time "cute Beatle" Paul McCartney became the prolific one, with nine studio albums and fourteen Top 10 singles. In 1971 Paul, wife Linda, and former Moody Blues guitarist Denny Laine formed a new band, Wings. They flew highest with the James Bond movie theme "Live and Let Die," the album and single titled "Band on the Run," and 1976's hit, "Silly Love Songs." They perhaps swooped the lowest, however, with the 1979 disco hit "Goodnight Tonight."

- Don't expect silly love songs from The Beatles' resident iconoclast John Lennon. He and his Plastic Ono Band forged their own path with six studio albums, each showing flashes of brilliance if not radio friendliness. High points included the cathartic "Mother" and two timeless classics, the aforementioned "Imagine" and the holiday standard "Happy Xmas (War Is Over)." Lennon was the last of the four to score a solo #1, but with the help of friend Elton John, "Whatever Gets You Through the Night" did the trick.

- Who'd have thought that low-key Ringo Starr would have gotten the fastest start out of the gate? The drummer scored Top 10 hits in "It Don't Come Easy" and "Back Off Boogaloo" before back-to-back chart-toppers "Photograph" and "You're Sixteen." But he was still getting by with a little help from his friends: George produced his first two hits and co-wrote "Photograph," while Paul played kazoo on "You're Sixteen."

**1971** An instant hit, a classic, a plea for peace—John Lennon's "Imagine" is simultaneously all these. Subsequently, and sadly, this signature tune will also become an epitaph, but today it's all aces as the album *Imagine* reigns at #1 in both the United States and UK. Lennon dislikes the added syrupy strings, describing the sound as "chocolate coated," but the album clicks with fans even more than his successful first solo effort, *John Lennon/Plastic Ono Band* (let's forget Yoko's screechy companion album, shall we?). But it's not all sweetness and light: *Imagine* also contains two thinly veiled attacks on former friend and partner Paul, "How Do You Sleep?" and "Crippled Inside."

# OCTOBER **1974**

Joking that the weekly grind was cutting into his drinking and golfing schedule, Dean Martin hosts the first of an occasional series of specials, the *Dean Martin Celebrity Roast*. Having ended his nine-year run hosting his weekly NBC comedy variety series last May, Martin emerges to torment pal Bob Hope. It's all in good fun, and he gets a considerable helping hand, make that hands, from the likes of Howard Cosell, Phyllis Diller, Zsa Zsa Gabor, Secretary of State Henry Kissinger, and California governor Ronald Reagan. The hour-long special, expanded from a popular segment from the weekly series, goes on to future installments skewering personages including Lucille Ball, Sammy Davis, Jr., Jackie Gleason, and Telly Savalas. Martin ends the run the following season with a two-hour roast of himself, with Don Rickles assuming Roast Master duties amid another Hollywood who's who and a bipartisan political pair, Senators Barry Goldwater and Hubert Humphrey.

# NOVEMBER 1972

**III**

The love that dares not speak its name gets extraordinary primetime exposure tonight in ABC's *That Certain Summer*. Hal Holbrook plays a dad determined to tell his visiting teenage son (Scott Jacoby) that he's gay and living with his partner (Martin Sheen). Written and produced by the team of Richard Levinson and William Link (*Mannix*, *Murder She Wrote*), the movie presents an honest portrayal of homosexuality in a time before AIDS. Critics rave ("A giant step for television," says Judith Crist of *New York* magazine), but at award time the industry shows its usual timidity. Nominated for seven Emmy Awards, it wins but one for supporting actor (Jacoby). Nevertheless Sheen neatly skewers a hoary Hollywood adage. "I'd robbed banks, kidnapped children, raped women and murdered people, you know, in any number of shows," he says. "Now I was going to play a gay guy and that was considered a career ender? Oh, for Christ's sake! What kind of culture do we live in?"

# NOVEMBER 1974

Salinger speaks! Though it may not have quite the dramatic impact as the talkies' 1930 introduction of the legendary Greta Garbo ("Garbo talks!"), it's a landmark occasion nevertheless for reclusive author J.D. Salinger. He hasn't spoken publicly in more than twenty years, since shortly after the publication of *Catcher in the Rye*, his classic, oft-banned novel of teen rebellion and defiance. His literary fame has risen, perhaps fueled in part by his determined inaccessibility. Today he breaks that self-imposed silence by talking by phone from his home in Cornish, New Hampshire, to denounce an unknown publisher's release of some circa-1940s magazine stories he'd written. "I'm not trying to hide the gaucheries of my youth," says Salinger. "I just don't think they're worthy of publishing." The FBI soon becomes involved in the strange case, unsuccessfully trying to locate the man responsible for peddling an estimated thirty thousand unauthorized editions.

# NOVEMBER 3 1976

Bad dreams come true for an odd, ostracized high schooler (Sissy Spacek) who makes her mean high school classmates pay dearly in director Brian De Palma's bloody *Carrie*. As the onset of the girl's puberty coincides with the onset of her paranormal powers, the movie jaggedly juxtaposes both romantic and horrific elements. Based on Stephen King's first published novel, it becomes an instant pop-culture classic, especially for its blood-drenching climax. *Carrie* torches the box office and, rare for a horror flick, nets two Oscar nominations, for best actress (Spacek) and supporting actress (Piper Laurie, as her religiously demented mother). It also notably features a young, deliciously evil John Travolta. The movie ignites Spacek's career, which soon includes an Oscar and Golden Globe for *Coal Miner's Daughter*. Not bad for a gal who'd started out as a country singer and, under the name Rainbo, released an extremely minor single about John Lennon entitled "John, You Went Too Far This Time."

# NOVEMBER

## 1978

Amiable pop/country singer Kenny Rogers has had lots of success with the ladies: "Ruby, Don't Take Your Love to Town" (with the First Editon) and "Lucille." Today he releases what'll become his signature song, "The Gambler." The first of five straight country #1s, it also wins a Grammy and enjoys pop culture longevity with the forthcoming boom in poker, especially Texas (Rogers's birthplace) hold 'em. Soon he's back wooing the women with "She Believes in Me," "Don't Fall in Love with a Dreamer" (with Kim Carnes), and his first pop chart-topper, "Lady." When the hits stop, Kenny branches out into fast food, opening Kenny Rogers Roasters. His street cred rises even higher after a store plays a prominent role on an episode of *Seinfeld,* though Kenny himself loses a bit of luster when he can't identify his roasted chicken on a blind taste test conducted on *Late Night with Conan O'Brien.*

# NOVEMBER

# 5

## 1972

Overdose Overview: Miss Christine, a member of Frank Zappa's backing groupie group, the GTOs, dies today of a heroin overdose. And so begins two weeks of bizarre rock deaths. Tomorrow New York Dolls drummer Billy Murcia dies on tour in London from a drug overdose. On November 11, Allman Brothers bassist Berry Oakley crashes his motorcycle and dies three blocks from the site of Duane Allman's fatal accident last year. Finally, on November 18, Crazy Horse guitarist Danny Whitten, after having been fired by Neil Young from an upcoming tour, flies to Los Angeles, buys some heroin, and checks out permanently.

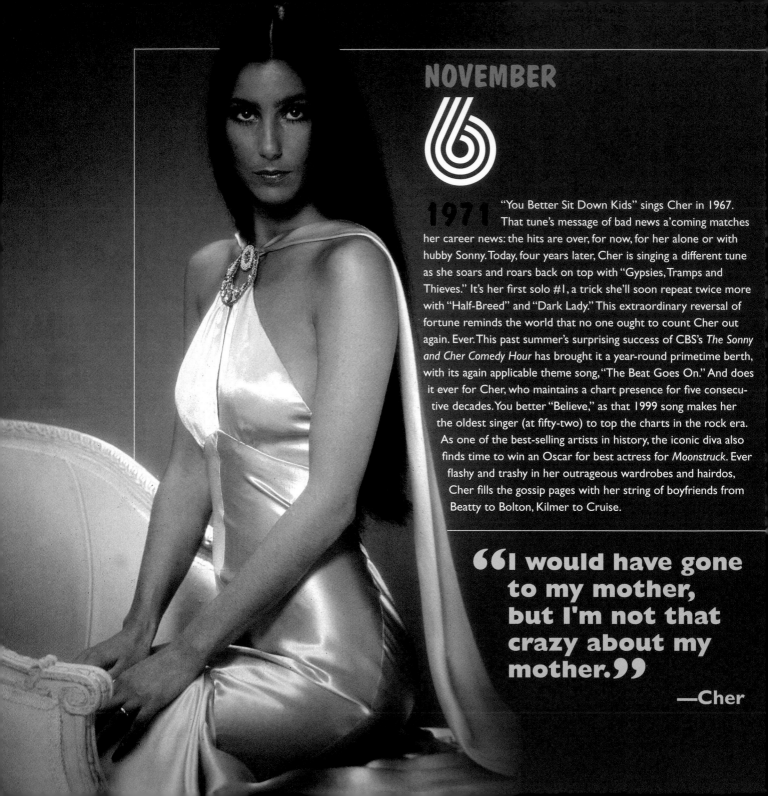

# NOVEMBER

## 6

### 1971

"You Better Sit Down Kids" sings Cher in 1967. That tune's message of bad news a'coming matches her career news: the hits are over, for now, for her alone or with hubby Sonny. Today, four years later, Cher is singing a different tune as she soars and roars back on top with "Gypsies, Tramps and Thieves." It's her first solo #1, a trick she'll soon repeat twice more with "Half-Breed" and "Dark Lady." This extraordinary reversal of fortune reminds the world that no one ought to count Cher out again. Ever. This past summer's surprising success of CBS's *The Sonny and Cher Comedy Hour* has brought it a year-round primetime berth, with its again applicable theme song, "The Beat Goes On." And does it ever for Cher, who maintains a chart presence for five consecutive decades. You better "Believe," as that 1999 song makes her the oldest singer (at fifty-two) to top the charts in the rock era. As one of the best-selling artists in history, the iconic diva also finds time to win an Oscar for best actress for *Moonstruck*. Ever flashy and trashy in her outrageous wardrobes and hairdos, Cher fills the gossip pages with her string of boyfriends from Beatty to Bolton, Kilmer to Cruise.

> **"I would have gone to my mother, but I'm not that crazy about my mother."**
>
> —Cher

# NOVEMBER 7

**1972** Promising that peace is at hand in Vietnam, President Richard Nixon steamrolls Democratic challenger George McGovern. The incumbent carries forty-nine states, representing a whopping 520 electoral votes, and buries the man derided as the candidate of "acid, amnesty, and abortion." McGovern's anti-war platform falls flat, though his vice-presidential blunder doesn't help—selecting, then jettisoning Senator Thomas Eagleton after reports surface that he had undergone shock therapy for depression. Eagleton later says that he was just "one rock in a landslide," and within a couple years it's President Nixon who has every right to feel depressed as the unpopular war and burgeoning Watergate scandal cause the roof to cave in on his presidency.

# NOVEMBER 8

**1972** Home Box Office lifts off today, premiering via terrestrial microwave to a few hundred wired cable homes in Wilkes-Barre, Pennsylvania. The service begins with an NHL game live from Madison Square Garden and the prophetically titled movie *Sometimes A Great Notion*, cowritten by Ken Kesey from his novel and starring and directed by Paul Newman. Until now, cable systems are delivering only existing broadcast signals to rural homes with poor or nonexistent on-air reception. Today pioneering Chuck Dolan unveils this other, infinitely more promising (and profitable) application: a pay channel offering sports, Hollywood movies, and other original fare. Ushering in the brave new world of cable television (see Sept. 7), Time, Inc., soon acquires the fledgling network while Dolan goes on to build his own cable system and programming (Bravo, AMC) empire.

# NOVEMBER

**1973** Growing up in London, son of a Greek restaurateur and Swedish mother, Cat Stevens always followed his own path. His good looks, good voice, and good songwriting skills ("The First Cut Is the Deepest") made him a teen pop favorite. But after recovering from a serious bout with tuberculosis, Stevens embarks on a deeper musical journey. An informal concert telecast locally in LA in 1971 hints at his future success. "[He] is an exceptional singer and artist whose highly distinctive voice has the rare ability to combine the strength, fragility and sometimes mystery of his highly personal compositions," writes Robert Hilburn in the *Los Angeles Times*. Stevens's star ascends and today, two years later, he makes his national US television debut on ABC's weekend series *In Concert*. It features both a Hollywood Bowl appearance and a years-before-MTV clip for "Moonshadow," featuring animated versions of the characters on the cover of his *Teaser and the Firecat* album. Later he'll abandon his pop success, convert to Islam, and change his name to Yusuf Islam.

# NOVEMBER 10 1975

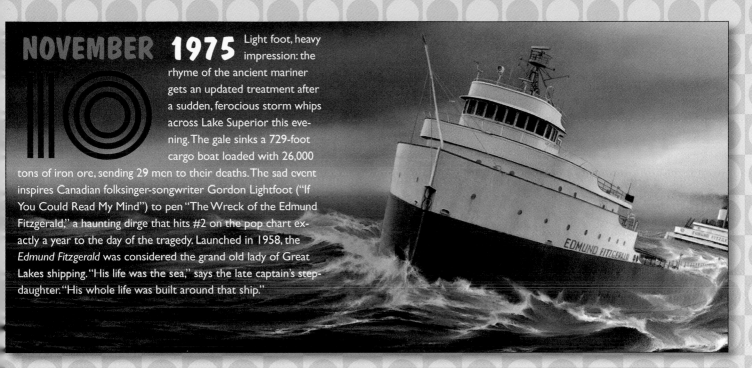

Light foot, heavy impression: the rhyme of the ancient mariner gets an updated treatment after a sudden, ferocious storm whips across Lake Superior this evening. The gale sinks a 729-foot cargo boat loaded with 26,000 tons of iron ore, sending 29 men to their deaths. The sad event inspires Canadian folksinger-songwriter Gordon Lightfoot ("If You Could Read My Mind") to pen "The Wreck of the Edmund Fitzgerald," a haunting dirge that hits #2 on the pop chart exactly a year to the day of the tragedy. Launched in 1958, the *Edmund Fitzgerald* was considered the grand old lady of Great Lakes shipping. "His life was the sea," says the late captain's step-daughter. "His whole life was built around that ship."

# NOVEMBER 11 1971

Destruction. Degradation. Drugs. Embodying the new term "gonzo journalism" (coined by a friend), intrepidly incomparable Hunter S. Thompson explodes onto the literary scene with *Fear and Loathing in Las Vegas: A Savage Journey to the Heart of the American Dream*. Today *Rolling Stone* publishes the first part of what Tom Wolfe calls a "scorching epochal sensation" that follows the deranged, drug-fueled exploits of journalist Raoul Duke and his three-hundred-pound Samoan attorney, Dr. Gonzo, in and around a narcotics officers' convention. Featuring equally crazed, brilliant artwork by Ralph Steadman, it becomes a Random House book that catapults eternal rebel Thompson to fame, more fear, and fiction (Duke in *Doonesbury*). "A word to the wise," says Thompson, "is infuriating."

# NOVEMBER 12 1973

Many trace the roots of hip-hop to today's formation of the Universal Zulu Nation by a South Bronx community leader, deejay, and former gang member named Afrika Bambaataa. Gathering a disparate group of rappers, break-dancers, and graffiti artists, he begins organizing block parties and club dates that spread the hip-hop word and gradually expand into white new wave circles. His spinning evolves into recording, and his 1982 release "Planet Rock" becomes one of the earliest and most influential rap songs. But the first hip-hop group to break into mainstream prominence is the Sugarhill Gang, formed by an enterprising producer turned on by the burgeoning street-party circuit. The Gang produces the first pop-chart success, "Rapper's Delight," released in the waning days of 1979. It's the record's opening rap of "I said a-hip, hop" that helps give the hottest musical movement of the next quarter century its name.

# NOVEMBER 13

## 1974

On a desolate stretch of Oklahoma highway, late at night, state police discover a lone car crashed into a culvert. The twenty-eight-year-old driver, Karen Silkwood, is dead. Considered just another routine traffic fatality, it gathers passing local attention and no national interest. Then, slowly, word begins to seep out. An employee at a nuclear plant, Silkwood had been investigating possible falsification of safety records and procedures, and had recently tested positive for plutonium exposure. The night she died she was driving to meet a union official and a reporter from the *New York Times*. The death is ruled an accident, but her family files a civil suit against her employer Kerr-McGee for inadequate health and safety programs. A jury awards her estate $10.5 million, later reduced on appeal to $5,000. As it's about to go to trial again, Kerr-McGee settles out of court for $1.3 million without admitting any liability. The mystery remains, dramatized in the 1983 film *Silkwood* starring Meryl Streep.

## MEANWHILE...

## MAN VERSUS MACHINE

On a bright desert highway, cool wind in his hair, big truck out of nowhere gives him a major scare. Steven Spielberg made his directorial debut on November 13, 1971, with a white-knuckles ABC movie, *Duel*, about an ordinary traveling salesman (Dennis Weaver, who previously played Chester Goode on *Gunsmoke*) whose life is about to get less ordinary—and possibly lethal. A malevolent truck of unknown origin and its driver menace the increasingly panicked businessman in an illogical but mesmerizing duel to the death, years before the term "road rage" came into vogue. "The best made-for-TV movie of the year, and possibly the best such TV film yet created," crowed Norman Mark of the *Chicago Daily News*. Indeed, Spielberg's taut direction, multi-angled road shots, and tight editing fueled its success.

# NOVEMBER 14

## 1972

Happy days are here again! Champagne corks fly as usually staid financial firms let their hair (but not guard) down to celebrate a momentous first: the Dow Jones Industrial Average's first close ever above 1,000 points. "I think the significance is basically psychological," says a Paine, Webber, Jackson & Curtis representative. "The public investor should come back in, and that's a real plus. They're doing it gradually and slowly, but convincingly." On the heels of President Nixon's landslide victory last week (see Nov. 7), the market is buoyed by an improving economy and prospects of peace in Indochina. The Dow continues a steady ascent with only occasional downturns, but hopes for peace fade and economic uncertainties continue. "I look for a higher market over the next few months," says an analyst at E.F. Hutton & Company, "with the usual profit taking pauses," i.e., business as usual. Say, is there any bubbly left in that bottle?

# NOVEMBER

# 15

**1975**   Adored by the masses and abhorred by the critics, ABBA brings their rhythmic, harmonizing sound stateside as they debut today on Dick Clark's *American Bandstand*. Singing "S.O.S." and "I Do, I Do, I Do, I Do, I Do," the Swedish quartet, matching husbands and wives, deliver in grand style. About to become the biggest international pop act of the decade, they'll chart oodles of hypnotic hits like "Take a Chance On Me," "Fernando," their sole #1 in the US "Dancing Queen," and the one that years later would give rise to a Broadway and movie musical, "Mamma Mia." In short succession come sold-out tours near and far, a command royal performance, a movie, and a *Guinness Book of World Records* mention. With that kind of success, who needs (or heeds) the critics?

## IT'S ALL IN THE NAME

"Brandy" had already been the subject of a #1 song several years earlier with Looking Glass's "Brandy (You're a Fine Girl)." So when budding singer Barry Manilow was first shown a schmaltzy song called "Brandy," he decided a little name change was in order. The result, "Mandy," debuted in November 1974, and quickly reached #1. "Who knew that this little album cut would turn out to be the beginning of my career?" the crooner would later say. Pre-"Mandy," the New York native worked as a piano accompanist to Bette Midler at the Continental Baths bathhouse/nightclub, and also helped produce her first two albums. Afterward, he shouldered aside similar song stylist Engelbert Humperdinck with a string of adult contemporary hits like "Could It Be Magic," "I Write the Songs," and "Looks Like We Made It." The peak of his long career would come in the late '70s, when Manilow would have five albums on the charts simultaneously—a feat matched only by Frank Sinatra and Johnny Mathis.

## NOVEMBER

## 1976

From penning songs for a disparate East Coast crowd from Velvet Underground chanteuse Nico to folkie Tom Rush, LA native Jackson Browne covers a pretty wide range. His major label debut album, *Jackson Browne, Saturate Before Using*, goes gold today, cementing his position as a literate, melodic force to be reckoned with. Co-writing the Eagles' "Take It Easy" further fuels his reputation, but only so-so sales and a low-key performing persona keep him a mostly cult figure. Browne keeps on delivering solid albums like *Late for the Sky* and *The Pretender*, but it's *Running on Empty*, an album of songs performed live or inspired by the road—recorded in halls, hotel rooms, on the tour bus, and backstage—that finally ups his profile. Both the album's title cut opener and its closing medley of "The Load-Out" and "Stay" (the latter a remake of the Maurice Williams #1 hit of 1960) become Top 40 hits and help make Jackson Browne a household name.

**1976**   Just because he's been dead for centuries doesn't mean that the ancient boy-king Tutankhamun can't still attract a crowd. His tomb, first discovered by Egyptologist Howard Carter in 1922, made King Tut an instant celebrity. "As my eyes grew accustomed to the light, details of the room within emerged slowly from the mist, strange animals, statues and gold," wrote Carter. "Everywhere the glint of gold." Today that's the glint anticipated in the eyes of the huge crowd that wraps around the National Gallery of Art as *Treasures of Tutankhamun* opens in Washington, DC. The fifty-five objects on display from the tomb include his solid-gold funeral mask, a gilded wood figure of the goddess Selket, lamps, jars, jewelry, and furniture. More than 800,000 visitors attend the four-month exhibition, and over the next four years the traveling show attracts some 8 million visitors in the United States alone. A proliferation of Tut paraphernalia follows, and the ancient revival gets a comedic slant with Steve Martin's take on vinyl and *Saturday Night Live.*

# NOVEMBER

## 1971

In riveting testimony before Congress last summer, a helicopter pilot told of hundreds of eagles—plus countless antelope, coyotes, elk, deer, geese, and wolves—shot and killed from the air by marksmen hired by ranchers in Wyoming and Colorado. An enraged public and the growing environmental movement mobilizes, decrying what journalist Wade Greene calls "a macabre parody on frontier vigilantism." With only around ten thousand golden and two thousand bald eagles nationally, the need for action is immediate. "Some predators as individuals will have to be got rid of, but there is no justification for exterminating a whole species," says the director of the Institute for Environmental Quality. Today President Nixon signs the Airborne Hunting Act, which prohibits shooting, attempting to shoot, or harassing any bird, fish, or other animal from an aircraft.

# NOVEMBER

## 1975

Inspired asylum antics reign as director Milos Forman's rollicking *One Flew Over the Cuckoo's Nest* opens. Based on Ken Kesey's dark, satiric novel, it pits crafty new guy in the asylum (Jack Nicholson) against severe Nurse Ratched (Louise Fletcher). It wows the crowds and later rakes in Oscar gold—the top five trophies, for the first time since *It Happened One Night* in 1934: best picture, director (Forman), lead actor (Nicholson), actress (Fletcher), and adapted screenplay. Jack's especially grateful for this, his first Oscar, having lost the two previous years with *The Last Detail* and *Chinatown*. Fletcher brings the house down as she signs a tearful tribute to her deaf parents. She signed on only a week before production began; the role was passed up by Anne Bancroft, Ellen Burstyn, Colleen Dewhurst, Jane Fonda, Angela Lansbury, and Geraldine Page.

# NOVEMBER 20

## 1973

Is there a drummer in the house? So asks the Who's Pete Townshend after manic Keith Moon collapses for the second and last time at a concert at San Francisco's Cow Palace. Up steps one Thomas Scot Halpin, in low-slung bell-bottoms, a tight T-shirt, and a mod hair-cut, to grab his fifteen minutes of fame. The skinny nineteen-year-old settles onto the drummer's stool and plays on the last three numbers including "Won't Get Fooled Again." Invited backstage, he receives the rock-opera tour's official *Quadrophenia* jacket that's promptly stolen when he leaves it to visit the buffet table. "The Who was the most drum-driven band in rock, with Moon an unorthodox showman who did flips and walked on his drums," says the *San Francisco Examiner*. "He would pound the air and contort his face, but he never missed a beat." Moon's over-the-top lifestyle catches up to him five years later when he dies of a drug overdose.

# NOVEMBER 21

## 1970

"Ladies and gentle-men, America's latest success story, the Partridge Family." Those words, spoken by Johnny Cash on the sitcom's debut episode less than two months ago, have proved prophetic: not only is *The Partridge Family* ABC's highest-rated new series, but today the prefab pop act's inaugural single, "I Think I Love You," tops the charts. Real-life family act the Cowsills provided inspi-ration, right down to the music: "I Think I Love You" comes from the writer of their hit "Indian Lake." Only two "family members" actually appear on the record-ing: Mom Shirley Jones, who starred in the film version of *Oklahoma*, and her stepson, David Cassidy—that is, Keith Partridge—who sings lead. Like TV-created pop predecessors the Monkees and the Archies, the Partridges also enjoy a string of Top 40 hits, and teen heartthrob Cassidy (see May 11) launches a successful solo recording career. While none of the other Par-tridges excel at singing, two of the show's five kids re-surface in later years: Susan Dey as a take-no-prisoners D.A. on *L.A. Law*, and smart aleck Danny Bonaduce as a radio host, reality-TV star, and all-around train wreck.

# NOVEMBER

## 22

**1975** Touting the arrival of nothing less than the future of entertainment, Sony premieres its first Betamax product: a combination color TV/videocassette recorder listing for $2,295. "Schedule conflicts are a thing of the past," promises a slickly produced promotional video, equal parts vintage clips and futuristic, state-of-the-art technology. The name comes from the tape path inside the one-hour cartridges that resembles the Greek letter β (beta). Revolutionary in its day, Betamax soon locks into a fierce battle with VHS for format supremacy. The cumbersome Betamax has a bit sharper picture, but VHS can hold two hours on one tape and is easier to use. VHS wins, though both are later replaced by the next generation of technology, DVD. Sony makes its last Betamax recorder in 2002.

## GADGETRY GALORE

Betamax may not have ended up to be the future of entertainment, but it was just one of the many high-tech additions to life in the 1970s (note: pet rocks, mood rings, and lava lamps don't qualify). Here, some other new advances in technology, some of which led to more advanced products, and some of which were never heard from again.

- IBM 8-inch floppy diskette (1970): Acclaimed for its portability, affordability, and high-density data storage; the 5-inch consumer disk from Shugart came five years later.
- Polaroid SX-70 Land Camera (1972): Point, shoot, and watch the image develop before your eyes: single-lens reflex beauty.
- Hamilton Pulsar watch (1972): Look Ma, no gears, springs, or hands! Even though you had to push a button to see the time, the first LED watch was revolutionary, and imitators quickly followed.
- Texas Instruments SR-10 calculator (1973): The first heavy-duty handheld to do slide-rule calculations.
- CB radios (1977): The craze in vehicle-to-vehicle communication surged beyond truckers to millions of ordinary drivers as the technology improved, prices dropped, and top manufacturers like General Electric, Motorola, and Panasonic entered the fray.
- Konica C35-AF camera (1977): The first compact, point-and-shoot, auto-focus camera.
- Atari Video Computer System (1977): Later renamed the Atari 2600, these wood-paneled consoles brought early-generation video games like Combat and Air-Sea Battle—and later arcade classics like Space Invaders and Pac-Man—into people's homes.
- Magnavox Magnavision Model 8000 videodisc player (1978): Decades before DVDs, Magnavox premiered the first consumer optical-disc player and its often-renamed discs, which were almost one foot in diameter.
- Milton Bradley's Simon (1978): A popular memory game with lots of flashing and blipping, often to a disco beat.
- Sony Walkman TPS-L2 (1979): Originally called a "Soundabout," this sharp-looking blue and white portable cassette player was the first player that was portable and had no speaker, just lightweight headphones.

# NOVEMBER

## 23

**1976** The sky isn't falling, but it is about to change. Today the Food and Drug Administration (FDA) proposes that labels be affixed to aerosol sprays warning that fluorocarbons may harm the environment by reducing the ozone layer. It comes on the heels of last night's surprise vote by a small, recently formed government agency. The Consumer Product Safety Commission voted 5-0 to take the first steps to ban fluorocarbon aerosols, saying they "present an unreasonable risk of injury to consumers." Both actions send shock waves across the bows of deodorant, hair spray, household cleaner, and pesticide companies. The actual ban on manufacture comes two years later on October 15, 1978, by which time many companies have switched to other propellant gases or mechanical pumps.

# NOVEMBER

## 24

**1971** Leaving on a jet plane, don't know when I'll be back again: departing with a light load of thirty-six passengers and six crew, a Northwest Orient Airlines flight embarks at 2:58 p.m. PST from Portland, Oregon, en route to Seattle—and history. For among the passengers is a nondescript fellow in a dark raincoat, suit, neatly pressed white shirt, and black necktie. He carries a briefcase, which he claims holds a bomb. He's one D.B. Cooper, or at least that's what it says on the ticket he purchased for $19.46. After careful instructions the plane lands in Seattle, picking up $200,000 in small bills and four parachutes. After the passengers are released and the plane's again airborne, the mystery man parachutes to eternal fame but unknown ends. Exhaustive FBI ground searches discover nothing, though in 1980 an eight-year-old boy vacationing with his family in the mountains of Washington discovers $5,800 in decaying bills that's determined to be from the ransom.

# NOVEMBER 1976

## 25

**1976** Save the last waltz for me: a thirty-eight-piece orchestra plays on a stage dressed with the set of *La Traviata* from the San Francisco Opera. Seven imported cut-glass chandeliers hang to impart a more regal tone to the city's famed Winterland Ballroom. So begins tonight's celebration of the last public performance of the Band. They'd emerged as Bob Dylan's backing band after recording their seminal album, *Music from Big Pink*, named for the house near Woodstock in which it was created, featuring "The Weight." Now they're takin' a load off as the orchestra fades and the main event begins with "Up on Cripple Creek" and more Band favorites. Then it's on to the starry guests, one by one: Dr. John, Paul Butterfield, Muddy Waters, Eric Clapton, Neil Young, Joni Mitchell, Neil Diamond (not as warmly received as Neil Young), Van Morrison, and finally, old friend Bob, and a group finale of "I Shall Be Released." But wait, there's more as Ringo Starr and the Band's drummer, Levon Helm, begin a drum duet. Soon they're joined by guitarists Stephen Stills and Ron Wood. And the Band plays on.

## NOVEMBER

**1978** A year after her adopted mother's death, disinherited daughter Christina Crawford gets some sweet revenge. *Mommie Dearest*, her scathing exposé about her famous actress mother Joan Crawford, tops the best-seller lists. Old Hollywood immediately divides into two camps. Supporters of the late actress, like longtime friend Myrna Loy, call it exaggerated lies by a spoiled brat. Yet others who witnessed Joan's ultra-controlling behavior voice support for Christina. "Joan was not quite rational in her raising of children," says Helen Hayes. "You might say she was strict or stern—but cruel is probably the right word." About the only thing Hollywood can agree on is business as usual, i.e., ka-ching! The book spawns the inevitable biopic three years later, with icy Faye Dunaway chewing up the scenery as the fearsome movie queen.

## NOVEMBER

**1976** "I'm mad as hell, and I'm not going to take this anymore!" So cries mad prophet of the airwaves Howard Beale (Peter Finch), urging viewers at home to open their windows and scream out those words. Director Sidney Lumet's savage satire, *Network*, gleefully skewers television's shameless search for ratings. After Walter Cronkite and Henry Fonda had turned down the role, Finch gladly accepted. "I love being a mouthpiece for Paddy Chayefsky," says Finch of the writer whose prophetic script wins an Oscar. Faye Dunaway, Beatrice Straight and Finch each win Oscars too, but he's not around to receive his. Finch died of a heart attack while on a promotional tour for the movie, so his Jamaican, mink-clad widow accepts the trophy and gives a moving acceptance speech, later revealed as having been written by…Chayefsky.

# NOVEMBER

## 1974

Payback lands some lucky fans the concert of a lifetime. For at Madison Square Garden tonight, John Lennon unexpectedly joins Elton John onstage. Why? Because when Elton played several months earlier on the session for "Whatever Gets You Through the Night," he extracted a promise if it hit #1. Last week it did just that, making Lennon the last of the four Beatles to have a solo chart-topper. Man of his word, he appears to a tumultuous, Beatlemania-ish welcome, joining Elton and his band on the hit plus, "I Saw Her Standing There" and "Lucy in the Sky with Diamonds." "Elton wanted me to do 'Imagine,' but I didn't want to come on like Dean Martin doing my classic hits," says Lennon. "I wanted to have some fun and play some rock and roll." It's a rockin' good night into which Lennon goes noisily. Unbeknownst to all, it'll be the last concert appearance he ever makes.

# NOVEMBER

## 29

**1979** As Iranian revolutionaries continue to hold fifty-two American diplomats hostage at the US embassy in Tehran that they seized on November 4, ABC continues its late-night news coverage, *The Iran Crisis: America Held Hostage, Day __*. As the days increase, President Carter's popularity decreases. Tonight regular anchorman Frank Reynolds takes the night off, so into the top spot steps smooth, soothing diplomatic correspondent Ted Koppel. Though it's not called that yet, *Nightline* emerges from the crisis to become a landmark late-night news program that Koppel winds up anchoring for a quarter century. After 444 days the hostages are released, moments after President Reagan assumes office. The timing spurs talk of a negotiated, prearranged but never confirmed "October surprise."

## NOVEMBER 30

**1977** One of pop music's most surreal pairings ever surfaces today—The Thin White Duke meets Mr. White Christmas—as Bing Crosby's posthumous special *Merrie Olde Christmas* airs tonight on CBS. (Crosby died last month of a heart attack after playing eighteen rounds at a golf course in Madrid.) Gamely trying to attract younger viewers, he'd met David Bowie back in September while on tour in London. After some frantic rewriting by composers backstage, they sang duets on "Peace on Earth" and "The Little Drummer Boy." Mightily impressed, Bing later said he considered Bowie "a clean-cut kid and a real fine asset to the show. He sings well, has a great voice, and reads lines well. He could be a good actor if he wanted." Their appearance becomes a perennial chestnut played in heavy radio rotation at Christmastime, and a CD, DVD, and later YouTube favorite. While only Bing and Bowie make the video cut, tonight's two-hour special also includes guests Twiggy, *Oliver!* star Ron Moody, and the Trinity Boys Choir.

# DECEMBER

## 11

**1973** After Aerosmith's first single recently hit #1 in their hometown of Boston, can nationwide fame be far behind? To quote its title, Dream On: today it stalls at a nightmarish #59. Having opened for bands like John McLaughlin's Mahavishnu Orchestra and Mott the Hoople, will the bad boys from Boston move from second string to top tier? Their second album fails to generate a hit, but the third time's indeed the charm. Riding on "Sweet Emotion," the album *Toys in the Attic* also delivers the FM rock monster "Walk This Way," prompting Columbia Records to rerelease "Dream On." This time it's Top 10 material, and Aerosmith, fronted by Jagger-like lead singer Steven Tyler, becomes a big-time national act. Sweet dreams are made of this.

# DECEMBER 1972

## 2

A little bit of mystery never hurts. Today Carly Simon's "You're So Vain" enters the charts, on a collision course with #1, triggering immediate mass speculation over the story's subject. New husband James Taylor? Kris Kristofferson? Cat Stevens? Warren Beatty? Or is the joke on the song's nasal-y backup singer, Mick Jagger? Who, if any of them, looks best wearing apricot? "I can't possibly tell you who it's about," says Simon, "because it wouldn't be fair." Nearly thirty years later she breaks her silence, whispering the name of Mr. Vain into the ear of sports producer Dick Ebersol. He'd submitted a successful $50,000 bid for charity to gain such exclusive, elusive knowledge—but mum's the word from him, too.

## THE KIDS AREN'T ALRIGHT

What a year 1979 was for the Who. Their *Quadrophenia* movie had a boffo box-office. In back-to-back months they played sold-out shows at London's Wembley Stadium and NYC's Madison Square Garden. And in November, their *The Kids Are Alright* album went platinum. But December 3 was a band's worst nightmare, as eleven concert-goers were trampled to death and scores were injured at Riverfront Coliseum in Cincinnati. Waiting in near-freezing temperatures with general-admission tickets, the crowd turned into a deadly crush as it surged toward the only two doors opened. "I can't stop shaking," said fan Jon Holmstrom. "I don't know how I got out. Somebody was on top of me. I couldn't breathe." Fearing a riot, officials let the show proceed as scheduled, and the band wasn't informed of the fatalities until afterward. In the aftermath, open "festival seating" at venues nationwide came under close scrutiny.

# DECEMBER 3 1971

Outspoken. Outrageous. Outstanding. Idiosyncratic avant-garde artist Frank Zappa attracts a devoted cult following whilst confounding the masses. A best-selling black-and-white poster of the day shows the longhaired freak perched on the toilet, with a simple label: "Phi Zappa Krappa." Tonight when his band, the Mothers of Invention, plays the Montreux Casino in Switzerland, a fan fires a flare that sets the roof ablaze. The joint burns down, and though no one is hurt the band loses $50,000 of equipment. Deep Purple, recording nearby, appropriates the event for their hit "Smoke on the Water." Zappa's bad luck continues a week later when the jealous boyfriend of an ardent female fan pushes him off the stage.

# DECEMBER  1971

Move over, Fellini: today the pop chart has its own 8½. The eight-and-a-half-minute song that's as praised (and as tough to figure out) as that film, Don McLean's "American Pie" enters the Top 40 today, touching off national debate: Who's the jester? And that king and queen? One thing we know for sure: the February that makes Don shiver is February 3, 1959—the day a plane crash claimed the young lives of Buddy Holly, Ritchie Valens, and the Big Bopper, a.k.a. "the day the music died." Over those glorious eight-plus minutes Don allegorically retells the history of popular music from Holly to, well, McLean. During the song's four-week reign at #1, countless newspaper and magazine articles dissect each verse, but as Don himself tells *Life* magazine, "I can't necessarily interpret 'American Pie' any better than you can."

# DECEMBER
# 5

**1970** Off the cuff, and off the charts. Jazz musicians often gather for informal, improvisational jam sessions. But can the same freewheeling approach work for blues-based rock 'n' rollers? On one night in May 1968 it can, and does, for guitarist extraordinaire Mike Bloomfield and singer/organist Al Kooper, late of the Electric Flag and Blood, Sweat and Tears, respectively. Their searing *Super Session*, a 1960s virtuoso benchmark, goes gold today. After one marathon nine-hour session, impulsive Bloomfield split, so Kooper recruited old pal Stephen Stills to finish up. "It's hard to get the right people at the right time," says Michael Thomas. "The very spontaneity and rashness of a jam depends on the good luck of one night, any night, but no night in particular. A jam is, must be, a fugitive occasion."

# DECEMBER 1979

The original NBC series ended more than a decade ago. Long forgotten? Hardly. Today Paramount launches *Star Trek—The Motion Picture* and reignites *Trek*-mania everywhere. Between syndicated re-runs and an animated series, the series' fanatical fan base has been thirsting for a fresh take. Off the box-office success of films like *Star Wars* and *Close Encounters of the Third Kind*, creator/producer Gene Roddenberry has finally gotten a big ($20 million) budget go-ahead. He re-attracts all the major players including William Shatner (Captain Kirk), Leonard Nimoy (Mr. Spock), DeForest Kelley (Bones), James Doohan (Scotty), and more, all of whom know a Klingon—and a career-making franchise—when they see it. Four more big-budget sequels follow in the 1980s, with more after that, as well as an unprecedented deluge of *Trek*-related products, spinoffs, and conventions. All from what Roddenberry first termed: "*Wagon Train* in the sky."

**DECEMBER 1978** In a medium where rhyme is king, two New York musicians take it a step further by applying it to both song title and group name. Today Chic's sleek "Le Freak" goes platinum, topping the charts two days later for a five-week reign. An infectious disco era–defining dance number, the hypnotic tune rockets the group to international fame—which was always the plan. "We didn't want to be a small band playing bar mitzvahs the rest of our lives," says cofounder Nile Rodgers of the early days with partner Bernard Edwards. "So we got into disco." And disco proves to be very, very good to them.

**DECEMBER 1975** **8** The ragtag, traveling circus that is the Rolling Thunder Revue wraps up its first leg with a star-studded benefit tonight for imprisoned boxer Rubin "Hurricane" Carter at Madison Square Garden. And who answers the phone when the ex-boxer calls in? None other than the Greatest, Muhammad Ali. Organized by Bob Dylan, the tour kicked off last fall in a string of mostly Northeast concerts at small venues with little publicity. Its eclectic lineup includes Joan Baez, *Nashville* star Ronee Blakley, Roger McGinn (Byrds), Joni Mitchell, Bowie guitarist Mick Ronson, beat poet Allen Ginsberg, and more. It's an enthusiastic, somewhat disjointed affair, with Dylan appearing on some nights in whiteface makeup or wearing a plastic mask. Still the music's top notch, as one critic lauds its "rugged and inspired reworkings of many Dylan standards."

**1973** Few take much notice when obscure Congressman Harold Froehlich (R-Wisc.) takes to the House floor today. He warns that manufacturers' bids to supply the federal government with toilet paper "fell far short of the total quantity needed." He adds that a possible toilet paper crunch would be "no laughing matter." Yet that's exactly what Johnny Carson uses it for, poking fun at a toilet paper shortage a week later on *The Tonight Show Starring Johnny Carson*. His erroneous comments set off an unfounded and unprecedented run (not to be confused with the runs) as people empty store shelves everywhere. Though the American Paper Institute quickly reiterates there is no shortage, rumors and buying continue apace. Asked if his hotel is suffering from a shortage, a spokesman for a Marriott hotel in Atlanta replies, "Are you putting me on?"

**DECEMBER** **1972** Hear her roar: her version of "I Don't Know How to Love Him" from the rock opera *Jesus Christ Superstar* has given Aussie Helen Reddy a toehold in America. An early and passionate supporter of women's liberation, she co-writes a song called "I Am Woman." But radio play is minimal, prompting her aggressive manager/husband Jeff Wald to line up for lots of TV appearances. "Television forced radio to play it," says Reddy. "Women started calling up radio stations and requesting it." Today "I Am Woman" is strong, invincible, and #1. Reddy and Wald receive countless offers to license the song for commercials, but they refuse, instead giving the United Nations use for its International Women's Year for a token fee of one dollar. At the Grammys early next year, Helen accepts the award for best pop female performance by thanking her label, her husband, and "God, because She makes everything possible." Feminists cheer, fundamentalists fume.

## DECEMBER 12

**1976** MIT graduate, an MS in mechanical engineering, a product designer for Polaroid. Not the kind of qualifications you'd expect to see on a rock star's resume, right? Yet that's the curriculum vitae of Tom Scholz, who in his spare time applies his scientific background to producing tracks he cut with musician friends in his homemade basement studio. CBS Records, upon hearing the demo tapes, signs Scholz to a recording contract. Even though the album is finished in LA, the group is named for the city where it all began, Boston. Today both Boston's self-titled debut album and single, "More Than a Feeling," make the Top 10. The album receives the RIAA's relatively new "platinum" certification for one million copies, going on to become the biggest selling debut album in history. Not bad for an MIT nerd.

## DECEMBER 1976

Revered for years in his hometown of Detroit, Bob Seger has found wider success elusive. He came close in 1969 with a respectable Top 20 hit, "Ramblin' Gamblin' Man," but eight years and six albums later, still no breakout. Earlier this year, though, *Live Bullet,* a double album from his last tour, brought new fans eager for the next studio effort. Today that album's title track, "Night Moves," enters the charts en route to #4, his biggest hit yet. Bob Seger and the Silver Bullet Band's bittersweet look back at teenage sex "in the back seat of my '60 Chevy" isn't the only hit on *Night Moves*. Nostalgic "Mainstreet" and hard-drivin' "Rock and Roll Never Forgets" find singles success, while the suggestive, sexy album cut "The Fire Down Below" torches FM radio. The wait is over, Seger is hot. *Night Moves* becomes the first of seven consecutive Top 10 albums. Although he writes most of his songs, it's one Seger doesn't write from his next album that becomes an enduring party standard: "Old Time Rock and Roll," immortalized when Tom Cruise dances to it in his skivvies in *Risky Business.*

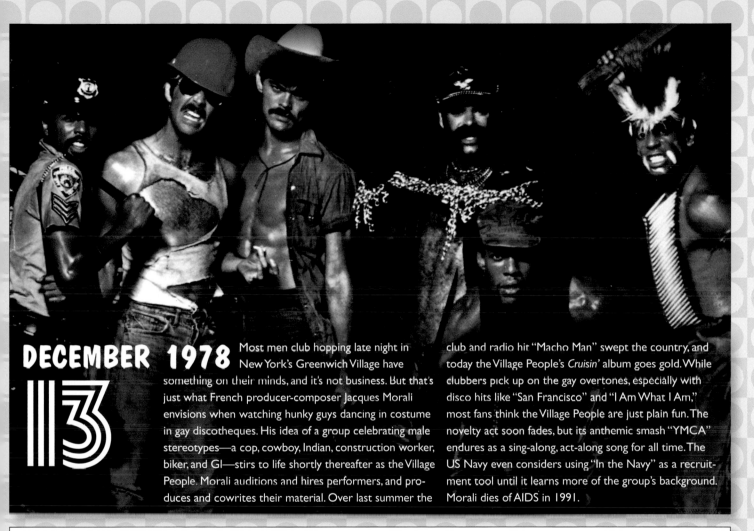

# DECEMBER 13 1978

Most men club hopping late night in New York's Greenwich Village have something on their minds, and it's not business. But that's just what French producer-composer Jacques Morali envisions when watching hunky guys dancing in costume in gay discotheques. His idea of a group celebrating male stereotypes—a cop, cowboy, Indian, construction worker, biker, and GI—stirs to life shortly thereafter as the Village People. Morali auditions and hires performers, and produces and cowrites their material. Over last summer the club and radio hit "Macho Man" swept the country, and today the Village People's *Cruisin'* album goes gold. While clubbers pick up on the gay overtones, especially with disco hits like "San Francisco" and "I Am What I Am," most fans think the Village People are just plain fun. The novelty act soon fades, but its anthemic smash "YMCA" endures as a sing-along, act-along song for all time. The US Navy even considers using "In the Navy" as a recruitment tool until it learns more of the group's background. Morali dies of AIDS in 1991.

# DECEMBER 14 1971

Good cop, bad cop: whistle-blowing detective Frank Serpico testifies today about police corruption in New York City, stirring up a hornet's nest of charges and recriminations. Earlier in the year he'd been shot in the face during a botched drug raid, but, ignored by his fellow officers, only a 911 call by a neighbor saved his life. Stonewalled and ostracized, Serpico recounts one police captain's warning that he keep quiet or "before it was all over I might be found floating in the river." His damning charges make sensational front-page headlines nationwide. Author Peter Maas, no stranger to cops and robbers thanks to his book about a mobster informant, *The Valachi Papers*, writes a biographical best-seller that's immediately snapped up by Hollywood. Director Sidney Lumet's *Serpico* opens two years later with Al Pacino as the idealistic, alienating cop.

# FAST AS LIGHTNING AND GONE JUST AS QUICK

In December 1974, no song was hotter than pop culture classic "Kung Fu Fighting." Cashing in on the martial arts craze was singer Carl Douglas, not to be confused with Carol Douglas, who made #11 a month later with "Doctor's Orders." Here are some other one-hit wonders and their chart-topper.

- The Five Stairsteps, "O-o-h Child" (1970)
- Bobby Bloom, "Montego Bay" (1970)
- Brewer & Shipley, "One Toke Over the Line" (1971)
- Jean Knight, "Mr. Big Stuff" (1971)
- Commander Cody & His Lost Planet Airmen, "Hot Rod Lincoln" (1972)
- King Harvest, "Dancing in the Moonlight" (1973)
- Vicki Lawrence, "The Night the Lights Went Out in Georgia" (1973)
- George McCrae, "Rock Your Baby" (1974)
- Dave Loggins, "Please Come to Boston" (1974)
- Billy Swan, "I Can Help" (1974)
- Minnie Riperton, "Lovin' You" (1975)
- Sammy Johns, "Chevy Van" (1975)
- Van McCoy & the Soul City Symphony, "The Hustle" (1975)
- Vicki Sue Robinson, "Turn the Beat Around" (1976)
- Wild Cherry, "Play That Funky Music" (1976)
- Debby Boone, "You Light Up My Life" (1977)
- Steve Martin, "King Tut" (1978)
- Alicia Bridges, "I Love the Nightlife" (1978)
- Amii Stewart, "Knock on Wood" (1979)
- Anita Ward, "Ring My Bell" (1979)

## DECEMBER 16 1970

The screenplay looked so promising that the producers had author Erich Segal pen a novel to release first. The strategy pays off spectacularly as *Love Story* topped the best-seller lists for more than thirty weeks. Today the Paramount movie version arrives and duplicates that success onscreen. The schmaltzy, simple tale of two attractive youngsters (Ryan O'Neal, Ali McGraw) falling in love but suffering an unhappy ending, runs away with moviegoers' hearts—and dollars. *Love Story* not only becomes the year's highest-grossing movie, its $50 million take is more than triple that of second-place finisher *Little Big Man*. Tommy Lee Jones makes his film debut as O'Neal's Harvard University roommate — in real-life, Jones did attend Harvard, and his roommate was Al Gore, Jr.

## DECEMBER 15 1978

Ever since the demise of the late 1960s campy *Batman* TV series, studios have shied away from adapting comic book heroes for major motion pictures. Until today, that is, when up on the screen, up in the sky, it's…Superman as director Richard Donner's big-budget action-adventure *Superman* takes flight. During its long gestation a virtual who's who of major Hollywood names flitted in and out, with the final mega-star wattage—Marlon Brando, Gene Hackman, Glenn Ford, Trevor Howard—supporting the handsome, strapping Man of Steel, unknown Christopher Reeve. It's not only the year's top moneymaker, pulling in more than $80 million—it also shoots a flashy sequel simultaneously, paving the way for the advent of the superhero film genre with the forthcoming *Batman* series, and *Spiderman* series, and *X-Men* series, and…you get the picture(s).

## DECEMBER 17 1976

Before ESPN, Nickelodeon, C SPAN, and just about every other national basic cable channel, there was WTCG (for "watch this channel grow"). Known better by its later name, WTBS, it's a tiny UHF Atlanta station run by the entrepreneurial Ted Turner. Today he upgrades its microwave delivery to the latest technology: satellite transmission via Satcom 1. Instantly its rerun-heavy lineup, starting with an old Dana Andrews movie, *Deep Waters*, appears on cable systems in Alabama, Kansas, Nebraska, and Virginia. Soon renamed SuperStation TBS, it paves the way for the burgeoning cable revolution (see Sept. 7) and turns Ted into a major media mogul. He buys the Atlanta Braves and Hawks before lightning strikes twice. In 1980 he starts a shoestring 24-hour news network that doubters dub "chicken noodle news," which morphs into the groundbreaking powerhouse CNN. Turner, dubbed the Mouth of the South, laughs last.

# DECEMBER

**1975** A politically active white girl singing the blues, Bonnie Raitt never exactly set the charts on fire. But she'd built up enough momentum, after years of touring, a devoted fan base and five mostly praised Warner Bros. albums, to merit the cover of *Rolling Stone* today ("Daughter of the Blues"). Yet her bluesy R&B style, mean slide guitar, and strong songwriting skills won't produce that elusive commercial success for another fourteen years. In 1989 her tenth album, *Nick of Time*, soars to the top of the album charts and wins three Grammy Awards. For an encore she wins a fourth for her duet, "In the Mood," with John Lee Hooker. "There's nothing like living a long time," says Raitt, "to create a depth and soulfulness in your music."

# DECEMBER 19

**1971** Scathing satire and ritualistic violence so extreme that the publication of Anthony Burgess's novel introduced a new catchword, "ultraviolence." Today Stanley Kubrick's film version of *A Clockwork Orange* explodes onscreen and immediately triggers controversy and condemnation. Set in a bleak futuristic world, it catapults mesmerizing lead Malcolm McDowell to stardom. Kubrick cut thirty seconds to achieve an "R" instead of "X" rating, but later approves the film's ban in England after several real-life copycat assaults that mimic the attacks of Alex (McDowell) and his "droogs" (mates).

# DECEMBER
## 20

**1971** A generationally challenged black comedy opens to withering reviews. "He begins the film in a gross and macabre manner, and never once deviates from that concept," says *Variety* of director Hal Ashby's *Harold and Maude*. But audiences warm to its unusual couple, an 80-ish swinger (Ruth Gordon) and a death-obsessed teen (Bud Cort), and his hilarious phony suicide attempts. Cat Stevens provides the music. The script helps establish its writer, Colin Higgins, who moves on to *Silver Streak*, *Nine to Five*, and *The Best Little Whorehouse in Texas*. Over the years, *Harold and Maude* reaches cult status, a sweet sleeper "in which the laughs stick in your throat," writes *Rolling Stone* film critic Peter Travers.

# DECEMBER
## 21

**1970** Elvis is in the (White) House: a fawning note penned by Elvis Presley nets him a meeting today with President Nixon. It's not just a social call—Presley wants to be appointed a "federal agent-at-large" in the service of the administration's war on drugs. Apparently unsearched, Elvis brings along a present for the prez: a World War II–era Colt .45 pistol. Two years later, Nixon moves from the King to the Hardest Working Man in Show Business. Soul shouter James Brown had visited LBJ in the White House in 1968, and later performed for the troops in Vietnam, but after throwing his support to Nixon in 1972 gets a presidential invite and visits the White House in October 1972. Two years later, in the midst of a thirty-date tour, George Harrison stops by to meet President Ford, and Peter Frampton stops by shortly thereafter to chat up Ford and his son Jack.

# DECEMBER

## 22

**1971** Known as the man with no name for his tight-lipped portrayals in spaghetti westerns like *The Good, the Bad, and the Ugly,* Clint Eastwood assumes today a new, longer-lasting moniker: *Dirty Harry.* He plays an iconoclastic cop prowling the alleys and streets of San Francisco in search of a serial killer. Law and order filmmaking of the first order, *Dirty Harry* touches a nerve in a nation anxious about urban crime and presages a torrent of tough-cop flicks. Though he later reprises the role in four sequels, Eastwood never equals one of the most oft-quoted lines in movie history. With a suspect sprawled on the sidewalk, he explains that he, too, has forgotten how many shots he's fired: "But being as this is a .44 Magnum, the most powerful handgun in the world, and would blow your head clean off, you've got to ask yourself one question: 'Do I feel lucky?' Well do ya, punk?"

# DECEMBER

## 23

**1978** Sexy, rich, and generous to boot—a nice combination. Today Rod Stewart, planning to perform "Do Ya Think I'm Sexy" at an upcoming benefit concert at the United Nations headquarters, announces he'll donate all royalties from the song to UNICEF. That'll generate a tidy sum as the song soon rises to #1, the third (after "Maggie May" and "Tonight's the Night") for the blond, raspy-voiced mod English rocker. One of the decade's most popular showmen, Stewart gets an affirmative answer to his "sexy" question five months later when he marries for the first time. The lucky gal? Former model Alana Hamilton, George Hamilton's ex-wife, with whom he'll have two children before splitting up five years later.

# DECEMBER
24

## 1979

What is it good for? Tens of thousands of Soviet troops begin pouring over the border into Afghanistan. The Russian army quickly deposes and executes the current leader and installs a puppet, communist dictatorship. The occupying force eventually expands to more than 100,000 as entrenched guerrilla fighters, the mujahideen, battle with clandestine help from the United States and other Western nations. Calling the invasion "the most serious threat to peace since the Second World War," President Carter places a trade embargo against the USSR and boycotts the Olympic Games next year. The quagmire continues. "The Russians can't stay in Afghanistan," says one guerrilla. "Even the animals hate them." After nine years of mounting losses and no end in sight, the USSR withdraws, paralleling America's ignominious experience in Vietnam a decade earlier.

## MEANWHILE...

## A FOOTBALL FIRST

With Christmas fast approaching, the Pittsburgh Steelers gladly accept a gift from the Oakland Raiders on December 23, 1972. Trailing by one point with twenty-two seconds left and no timeouts, Steelers quarterback Terry Bradshaw passed the ball from his own 40-yard line to receiver Frenchy Fuqua. But when Fuqua collided with Raider safety Jack Tatum, the ball deflected back to Steeler running back Franco Harris, who scooped it up mid-air and continued into the end zone. When Tatum argued that the touchdown was invalid due to the rule that two receivers in a row can't touch the ball in a single play, for the first time the referee had backup: NFL supervisor of offcials Art McNally was in the press box watching the instant replay on TV. The play, later voted the greatest of all time by NFL Films, was immediately dubbed the "Immaculate Reception," and the Steelers won the game, 13-7.

PAUL NEWMAN · ROBERT REDFORD
ROBERT SHAW

IN A BILL/PHILLIPS PRODUCTION OF
A GEORGE ROY HILL FILM

**THE STING**

A RICHARD D. ZANUCK/DAVID BROWN PRESENTATION

...all it takes is a little Confidence.

Written by       Directed by       Produced by
DAVID S. WARD · GEORGE ROY HILL · TONY BILL, MICHAEL and JULIA PHILLIPS
Music Adapted by MARVIN HAMLISCH · A UNIVERSAL PICTURE · TECHNICOLOR®

## DECEMBER 26 1973

Possession is nine-tenths of the plot: demonic possession, a popular box-office theme, made a hit out of *Rosemary's Baby*. Today comes an even more sensationalistic and shocking horror tale, *The Exorcist*. Voted the scariest movie ever by *Entertainment Weekly*, this adaptation of a William Blatty novel by director William Friedkin features a head-turning, stomach-churning debut by Linda Blair as a young girl possessed by Satan. It causes such a commotion—audience hysteria and fainting and such—that the studio provides free barf bags. An insider commotion erupts when Mercedes McCambridge complains at her lack of screen credit for providing the demon's voice. "[Her] outrageous attempt to detract from Linda Blair's portrayal and push herself into the spotlight," says Friedkin, "is the most unjustifiable and unprofessional action I have ever encountered as a filmmaker." The film's overdubbed instrumental theme, *Tubular Bells*, becomes a Top 10 hit for Mike Oldfield. Possession resurfaces several years later in director Richard Donner's horror-suspense summertime smash, *The Omen*.

## DECEMBER 25 1973

The con is on: with their wildly successful pairing as Butch Cassidy and the Sundance Kid, respectively, Paul Newman and Robert Redford reunite on the big screen in director George Roy Hill's *The Sting*. Set in Prohibition-era Chicago, the rollicking yarn pits two small-time, sweet-talking con artists against a high-rolling low-life (Robert Shaw). "The movie has a nice, light-fingered style to it," says Roger Ebert. "It's good to get a crime movie more concerned with humor and character than with blood and gore." The year's biggest box-office draw, it goes on to nab seven Oscars including best picture, director, original screenplay and score (Marvin Hamlisch). *The Sting* also sparks a national revival of the melodic ragtime music of Scott Joplin.

## DECEMBER 27 1975

Although they've done well in their homeland, English band Roxy Music has been known more in America for their racy album covers than their music. In fact, it's one such cover that propels their *Country Life* album to the US Top 40. Today the band, led by charismatic Bryan Ferry, lets the music do the talking as the textured "Love Is the Drug" becomes their first American chart record. Listeners quickly "catch that buzz," sending the quirky pop-dance track into the Top 30. The cover of *Siren*, the album including the hit single, features a leggy young Texas model named Jerry Hall, to whom Ferry is romantically linked, but not for long. Mick Jagger soon falls for this siren's song, marrying her after divorcing his first wife, Bianca.

# THE LOOKS OF BOOKS

While *The Gulag Archipelago* shook the world's foundations, many less-weighty, but also influential, works of both fact and fiction impacted the 1970s. Here's a sampling.

- Richard Bach's novella about a seagull's fight and plight, Jonathan Livingston Seagull, became a spiritual parable about reaching one's goals (1970).

- E.M. Foster's Maurice was published sixty years after the manuscript was begun and a year after the author's death. While dated, it elucidates gay relationships in early-twentieth-century England (1971).

- Perfectly named Alex Comfort reapplied the principles of popular cooking books in The Joy of Sex, a groundbreaking sex manual that ushered in a new era of heterosexuality (1972).

- From cult classic to cultural phenomenon, Anne Rice's Interview with the Vampire stirred a potent brew of ruminations from a philosophical immortal (1973).

- Erica Jong's Fear of Flying explores a post—women's liberation way of coexisting with the opposite sex, with a raunchy frankness that has both shocking and somewhat serious tones (1973).

- The first Book-of-the-Month Club main selection written by an African American since Richard Wright's *Native Son* in 1940, Toni Morrison's Song of Solomon follows a young black man's journey of discovery (1977).

- The first book in Armistead Maupin's six-volume Tales of the City series introduced readers to a wondrous tableau of sexually liberated life in San Francisco (1978).

- An absurdist, outlandish world awaited in Douglas Adams's sci-fi classic, The Hitchhiker's Guide to the Galaxy (1979).

## DECEMBER

**1973** A new work by Alexander Solzhenitsyn appears today in the bookstalls of Paris. From there *The Gulag Archipelago* explodes into worldwide consciousness, exposing the brutal network of Soviet forced labor and prison camps for all the world to see. Trained as a mathematician, Solzhenitsyn, while serving in the Soviet army in 1945, had been arrested and imprisoned for criticizing Stalin. He later won a Nobel Prize for literature, then devoted his time to assiduously researching and exposing the prison system's shrouded history through the testimony of more than two hundred former prisoners. Three months after it appears in Paris, the USSR strips him of his citizenship and deports him. But his collective memoir has shone a light on one of the world's darkest places, and no one will ever forget. "Blow the dust off the clock," he says. "Your watches are behind the times. Throw open the heavy curtains which are so dear to you—you do not even suspect that the day has already dawned outside."

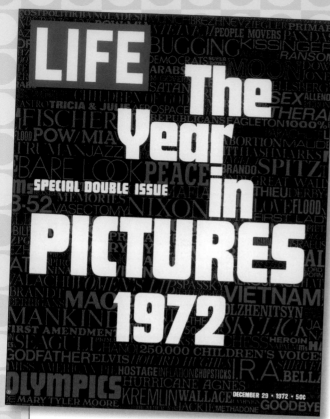

# DECEMBER

## 29

**1972** Life cycle: for millions of Americans each week, it just isn't life without *Life*. For nearly four decades *Life* has been the preeminent weekly magazine, known primarily for its of-the-moment photographs evoking the American experience. But over the past few years circulation and advertising have fallen with the rise of more specialized periodicals like the news-oriented weeklies *Time* (from the same parent company) and *Newsweek*. Television and radio, too, of course, are simultaneously turning readers into viewers and listeners, respectively. *Life*'s main competitor in the mass appeal magazine field, *Look*, folded last year. Today's issue of *Life* is its last. There is *Life* after *Life*, however: Time Inc. continues to publish occasional special and/or monthly issues, and *Life* later has a brief run as a weekly supplement to Sunday newspapers.

# DECEMBER

## 30

**1976** Ask one generation *Where the Wild Things Are*, and their Jimi Hendrix or Troggs album collections might come to mind. Ask another, and they'll mention the classic children's storybook by author-illustrator Maurice Sendak. Today his horned and fanged characters decorate the Christmas tree on the cover of *Rolling Stone*. Sendak's popularity has soared during the 1970s, with his artwork filling a dozen children's books, appearances on *Sesame Street*, and in an animated TV special with songs by Carole King. Before the decade is over, Sendak's creations will gnash their terrible teeth and show their terrible claws live in a stage adaptation of *Wild Things*. With all this attention from the media, has Sendak gone pop? Any fan'll tell you it's more like *Higglety Pigglety Pop!*

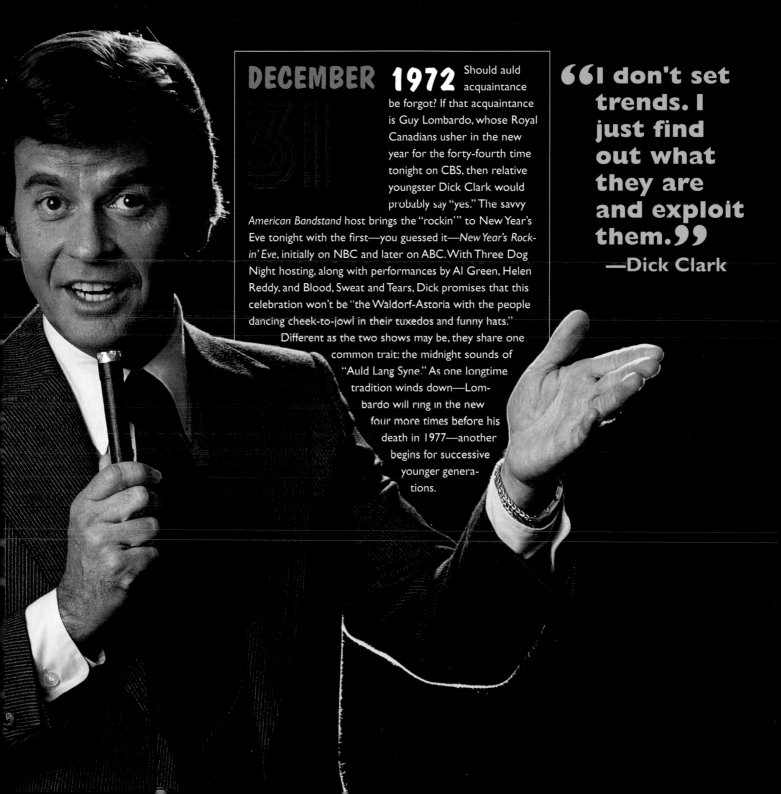

**DECEMBER 1972**
**31**

Should auld acquaintance be forgot? If that acquaintance is Guy Lombardo, whose Royal Canadians usher in the new year for the forty-fourth time tonight on CBS, then relative youngster Dick Clark would probably say "yes." The savvy *American Bandstand* host brings the "rockin'" to New Year's Eve tonight with the first—you guessed it—*New Year's Rockin' Eve*, initially on NBC and later on ABC. With Three Dog Night hosting, along with performances by Al Green, Helen Reddy, and Blood, Sweat and Tears, Dick promises that this celebration won't be "the Waldorf-Astoria with the people dancing cheek-to-jowl in their tuxedos and funny hats." Different as the two shows may be, they share one common trait: the midnight sounds of "Auld Lang Syne." As one longtime tradition winds down—Lombardo will ring in the new four more times before his death in 1977—another begins for successive younger generations.

> **"I don't set trends. I just find out what they are and exploit them."**
> —Dick Clark

## OSCAR WINNERS

### 1970

Picture . . . . . . . . . . . . . . *Patton*

Actor . . . . . . . . . . . . . . . George C. Scott *(Patton)*

Actress . . . . . . . . . . . . . Glenda Jackson *(Women in Love)*

Supporting Actor . . . . . . . John Mills *(Ryan's Daughter)*

Supporting Actress . . . . . Helen Hayes *(Airport)*

Director . . . . . . . . . . . . . Franklin Schaffner *(Patton)*

Adapted Screenplay . . . . Ring Lardner, Jr. *(M*A*S*H)*

Original Screenplay . . . . . Francis Ford Coppola,
Edmund H. North *(Patton)*

### 1971

Picture . . . . . . . . . . . . . . *The French Connection*

Actor . . . . . . . . . . . . . . . Gene Hackman *(The French Connection)*

Actress . . . . . . . . . . . . . Jane Fonda *(Klute)*

Supporting Actor . . . . . . . Ben Johnson *(The Last Picture Show)*

Supporting Actress . . . . . Cloris Leachman *(The Last Picture Show)*

Director . . . . . . . . . . . . . William Friedkin
*(The French Connection)*

Adapted Screenplay . . . . Ernest Tidyman *(The French Connection)*

Original Screenplay . . . . . Paddy Chayefsky *(The Hospital)*

### 1972

Picture . . . . . . . . . . . . . . *The Godfather*

Actor . . . . . . . . . . . . . . . Marlon Brando *(The Godfather)*

Actress . . . . . . . . . . . . . Liza Minnelli *(Cabaret)*

Supporting Actor . . . . . . . Joel Grey *(Cabaret)*

Supporting Actress . . . . . Eileen Heckart *(Butterflies Are Free)*

Director . . . . . . . . . . . . . Bob Fosse *(Cabaret)*

Adapted Screenplay . . . . Francis Ford Coppola, Mario Puzo
*(The Godfather)*

Original Screenplay . . . . . Jeremy Larner *(The Candidate)*

### 1973

Picture . . . . . . . . . . . . . . *The Sting*

Actor . . . . . . . . . . . . . . . Jack Lemmon *(Save the Tiger)*

Actress . . . . . . . . . . . . . Glenda Jackson *(A Touch of Class)*

Supporting Actor . . . . . . . John Houseman *(The Paper Chase)*

Supporting Actress . . . . . Tatum O'Neal *(Paper Moon)*

Director . . . . . . . . . . . . . George Roy Hill *(The Sting)*

Adapted Screenplay . . . . William Peter Blatty *(The Exorcist)*

Original Screenplay . . . . . David S. Ward *(The Sting)*

### 1974

Picture . . . . . . . . . . . . . . *The Godfather, Part II*

Actor . . . . . . . . . . . . . . . Art Carney *(Harry & Tonto)*

Actress . . . . . . . . . . . . . Ellen Burstyn *(Alice Doesn't Live
Here Anymore)*

Supporting Actor . . . . . . . Robert De Niro *(The Godfather, Part II)*

Supporting Actress . . . . . Ingrid Bergman *(Murder on the Orient
Express)*

Director . . . . . . . . . . . . . Francis Ford Coppola
*(The Godfather, Part II)*

Adapted Screenplay . . . . Francis Ford Coppola, Mario Puzo
*(The Godfather, Part II)*

Original Screenplay . . . . . Robert Towne *(Chinatown)*

## 1975

Picture . . . . . . . . . . . . . . . *One Flew Over the Cuckoo's Nest*

Actor . . . . . . . . . . . . . . . Jack Nicholson *(One Flew Over the Cuckoo's Nest)*

Actress . . . . . . . . . . . . . Louise Fletcher *(One Flew Over the Cuckoo's Nest)*

Supporting Actor . . . . . . George Burns *(The Sunshine Boys)*

Supporting Actress . . . . . Lee Grant *(Shampoo)*

Director . . . . . . . . . . . . Milos Forman *(One Flew Over the Cuckoo's Nest)*

Adapted Screenplay . . . . Bo Goldman, Lawrence Hauben *(One Flew Over the Cuckoo's Nest)*

Original Screenplay . . . . . Frank Pierson *(Dog Day Afternoon)*

## 1976

Picture . . . . . . . . . . . . . . *Rocky*

Actor . . . . . . . . . . Peter Finch *(Network)*

Actress . . . . . . . . . . . . . Faye Dunaway *(Network)*

Supporting Actor . . . . . . Jason Robards *(All the President's Men)*

Supporting Actress . . . . . Beatrice Straight *(Network)*

Director . . . . . . . . . . . . John Avildsen *(Rocky)*

Adapted Screenplay . . . . William Goldman *(All the President's Men)*

Original Screenplay . . . . . Paddy Chayefsky *(Network)*

## 1977

Picture . . . . . . . . . . . . . . *Annie Hall*

Actor . . . . . . . . . . . . . . . Richard Dreyfuss *(The Goodbye Girl)*

Actress . . . . . . . . . . . . . Diane Keaton *(Annie Hall)*

Supporting Actor . . . . . . Jason Robards *(Julia)*

Supporting Actress . . . . . Vanessa Redgrave *(Julia)*

Director . . . . . . . . . . . . Woody Allen *(Annie Hall)*

Adapted Screenplay . . . . Alvin Sargent *(Julia)*

Original Screenplay . . . . . Woody Allen, Marshall Brickman *(Annie Hall)*

## 1978

Picture . . . . . . . . . . . . . . *The Deer Hunter*

Actor . . . . . . . . . . . . . . . Jon Voight *(Coming Home)*

Actress . . . . . . . . . . . . . Jane Fonda *(Coming Home)*

Supporting Actor . . . . . . Christopher Walken *(The Deer Hunter)*

Supporting Actress . . . . . Maggie Smith *(California Suite)*

Director . . . . . . . . . . . . Michael Cimino *(The Deer Hunter)*

Adapted Screenplay . . . . Oliver Stone *(Midnight Express)*

Original Screenplay . . . . . Nancy Dowd, Waldo Salt, Robert C. Jones *(Coming Home)*

## 1979

Picture . . . . . . . . . . . . . . *Kramer vs. Kramer*

Actor . . . . . . . . . . . . . . . Dustin Hoffman *(Kramer vs. Kramer)*

Actress . . . . . . . . . . . . . Sally Field *(Norma Rae)*

Supporting Actor . . . . . . Melvyn Douglas *(Being There)*

Supporting Actress . . . . . Meryl Streep *(Kramer vs. Kramer)*

Director . . . . . . . . . . . . Robert Benton *(Kramer vs. Kramer)*

Adapted Screenplay . . . . Robert Benton *(Kramer vs. Kramer)*

Original Screenplay . . . . . Steve Tesich *(Breaking Away)*

## TOP 25 MOVIES

Most-watched films based on box-office receipts.

1. *Airport*
2. *American Graffiti*
3. *Blazing Saddles*
4. *Close Encounters of the Third Kind*
5. *Every Which Way But Loose*
6. *The Exorcist*
7. *The Godfather*
8. *Grease*
9. *Jaws*
10. *Jaws 2*
11. *Kramer vs. Kramer*
12. *Love Story*
13. *M*A*S*H*
14. *National Lampoon's Animal House*
15. *One Flew Over the Cuckoo's Nest*
16. *Patton*
17. *The Poseidon Adventure*
18. *Rocky*
19. *Smokey and the Bandit*
20. *Star Wars*
21. *The Sting*
22. *Summer of '42*
23. *Superman*
24. *The Towering Inferno*
25. *Young Frankenstein*

# TELEVISION

## EMMY WINNERS

### 1970

Drama . . . . . . . . . *Marcus Welby, M.D.* (ABC)

Comedy . . . . . . . . *My World and Welcome to It* (NBC)

Actor Drama . . . . Robert Young, *Marcus Welby, M.D.* (ABC)

Actress Drama    Susan Hampshire, *The Forsyte Saga* (PBS)

Actor Comedy    William Windom, *My World and Welcome to It* (NBC)

Actress Comedy. . . Hope Lange, *The Ghost and Mrs. Muir* (ABC)

### 1971

Drama . . . . . . . . . *The Senator, The Bold Ones* (NBC)

Comedy . . . . . . . . *All in the Family* (CBS)

Actor Drama . . . . Hal Holbrook, *The Senator, The Bold Ones* (NBC)

Actress Drama    Susan Hampshire, *The First Churchills, Masterpiece Theatre* (PBS)

Actor Comedy    Jack Klugman, *The Odd Couple* (ABC)

Actress Comedy    Jean Stapleton, *All in the Family* (CBS)

### 1972

Drama . . . . . . . . . *Elizabeth R, Masterpiece Theatre* (PBS)

Comedy . . . . . . . . *All in the Family* (CBS)

Actor Drama . . . . Peter Falk, *Columbo, NBC Mystery Movie* (NBC)

Actress Drama    Glenda Jackson, *Elizabeth R, Masterpiece Theatre* (PBS)

Actor Comedy    Carroll O'Connor, *All in the Family* (CBS)

Actress Comedy    Jean Stapleton, *All in the Family* (CBS)

## 1973

Drama . . . . . . . . . . *The Waltons* (CBS)

Comedy. . . . . . . . . *All in the Family* (CBS)

Actor Drama. . . . . Richard Thomas, *The Waltons* (CBS)

Actress Drama . . . . Michael Learned, *The Waltons* (CBS)

Actor Comedy . . . . Jack Klugman, *The Odd Couple* (ABC)

Actress Comedy . . . Mary Tyler Moore,
*The Mary Tyler Moore Show* (CBS)

## 1974

Drama . . . . . . . . . . *Upstairs, Downstairs, Masterpiece Theatre* (PBS)

Comedy. . . . . . . . . *M*A*S*H* (CBS)

Actor Drama. . . . . Telly Savalas, *Kojak* (CBS)

Actress Drama . . . . Michael Learned, *The Waltons* (CBS)

Actor Comedy . . . . Alan Alda, *M*A*S*H* (CBS)

Actress Comedy . . . Mary Tyler Moore,
*The Mary Tyler Moore Show* (CBS)

## 1975

Drama . . . . . . . . . *Upstairs, Downstairs, Masterpiece Theatre* (PBS)

Comedy. . . . . . . . . *The Mary Tyler Moore Show* (CBS)

Actor Drama. . . . . Robert Blake, *Baretta* (ABC)

Actress Drama . . . . Jean Marsh, *Upstairs, Downstairs,
Masterpiece Theatre* (PBS)

Actor Comedy . . . . Tony Randall, *The Odd Couple* (ABC)

Actress Comedy . . . Valerie Harper, *Rhoda* (CBS)

## 1976

Drama . . . . . . . . . . *Police Story* (NBC)

Comedy. . . . . . . . . *The Mary Tyler Moore Show* (CBS)

Actor Drama. . . . . Peter Falk, *Columbo* (ABC)

Actress Drama . . . . Michael Learned, *The Waltons* (CBS)

Actor Comedy . . . . Jack Albertson, *Chico and the Man* (NBC)

Actress Comedy . . . Mary Tyler Moore, *The Mary Tyler Moore
Show* (CBS)

## 1977

Drama . . . . . . . . . . *Upstairs, Downstairs, Masterpiece Theatre* (PBS)

Comedy. . . . . . . . . *The Mary Tyler Moore Show* (CBS)

Actor Drama. . . . . James Garner, *The Rockford Files* (NBC)

Actress Drama . . . . Lindsay Wagner, *The Bionic Woman* (ABC)

Actor Comedy . . . . Carroll O'Connor, *All in the Family* (CBS)

Actress Comedy . . . Beatrice Arthur, *Maude* (CBS)

## 1978

Drama . . . . . . . . . . *The Rockford Files* (NBC)

Comedy. . . . . . . . . *All in the Family* (CBS)

Actor Drama. . . . . Ed Asner, *Lou Grant* (CBS)

Actress Drama . . . . Sada Thompson, *Family* (ABC)

Actor Comedy . . . . Carroll O'Connor, *All in the Family* (CBS)

Actress Comedy . . . Jean Stapleton, *All in the Family* (CBS)

## 1979

Drama . . . . . . . . . . *Lou Grant* (CBS)

Comedy . . . . . . . . *Taxi* (ABC)

Actor Drama. . . . . Ron Leibman, *Kaz* (CBS)

Actress Drama . . . . Mariette Hartley, *The Incredible Hulk* (CBS)

Actor Comedy . . . . Carroll O'Connor, *All in the Family* (CBS)

Actress Comedy . . . Ruth Gordon, *Taxi* (ABC)

## TOP 25 TELEVISION SHOWS

The most-watched shows of the decade based on Nielsen ratings.

1. *60 Minutes*
2. *Alice*
3. *All in the Family*
4. *The Bionic Woman*
5. *Bridget Loves Bernie*
6. *Charlie's Angels*
7. *Chico and the Man*
8. *The Flip Wilson Show*
9. *Gunsmoke*
10. *Happy Days*
11. *Hawaii Five-O*
12. *Here's Lucy*
13. *Ironside*
14. *The Jeffersons*
15. *Laverne & Shirley*
16. *M*A*S*H*
17. *Marcus Welby, M.D.*
18. *Maude*
19. *Mork & Mindy*
20. *Phyllis*
21. *Rhoda*
22. *Sanford and Son*
23. *That's Incredible*
24. *Three's Company*
25. *The Waltons*

## GRAMMY AWARD WINNERS FOR RECORD OF THE YEAR

1970 . . . . . . . . . . . . . . "Bridge Over Troubled Water," Simon & Garfunkel

1971 . . . . . . . . . . . . . . "It's Too Late," Carole King

1972 . . . . . . . . . . . . . . "The First Time Ever I Saw Your Face," Roberta Flack

1973 . . . . . . . . . . . . . . "Killing Me Softly With His Song," Roberta Flack

1974 . . . . . . . . . . . . . . "I Honestly Love You," Olivia Newton-John

1975 . . . . . . . . . . . . . . "Love Will Keep Us Together," The Captain & Tennille

1976 . . . . . . . . . . . . . . "This Masquerade," George Benson

1977 . . . . . . . . . . . . . . "Hotel California," Eagles

1978 . . . . . . . . . . . . . . "Just The Way You Are," Billy Joel

1979 . . . . . . . . . . . . . . "What A Fool Believes," Doobie Brothers

## TOP 25 SONGS

Most popular songs, based on total points earned during chart runs on *Billboard* and *Cashbox*.

1. "You Light Up My Life," Debby Boone (1977)
2. "Night Fever," Bee Gees (1978)
3. "Shadow Dancing," Andy Gibb (1978)
4. "Joy to the World," 3 Dog Night (1971)
5. "Le Freak," Chic (1978)
6. "The First Time Ever I Saw Your Face," Roberta Flack (1972)
7. "Stayin' Alive," Bee Gees (1978)
8. "My Sharona," The Knack (1979)
9. "Alone Again (Naturally)," Gilbert O'Sullivan (1972)
10. "Tonight's the Night," Rod Stewart (1976)
11. "I Just Want to Be Your Everything," Andy Gibb (1977)
12. "Bridge Over Troubled Water," Simon & Garfunkel (1970)
13. "I'll Be There," Jackson 5 (1970)
14. "Maggie May," Rod Stewart (1971)
15. "It's Too Late," Carole King (1971)
16. "Raindrops Keep Falling on My Head," B.J. Thomas (1970)
17. "Hot Stuff," Donna Summer (1979)
18. "Best of My Love," Emotions (1977)
19. "Bad Girls," Donna Summer (1979)
20. "How Deep Is Your Love," Bee Gees (1977)
21. "My Sweet Lord," George Harrison (1971)
22. "American Pie," Don McLean (1972)
23. "Tie a Yellow Ribbon Round the Ole Oak Tree," Dawn featuring Tony Orlando (1973)
24. "I Think I Love You," The Partridge Family (1970)
25. "(They Long to Be) Close to You," The Carpenters (1970)

## ACADEMY AWARD WINNERS FOR BEST SONG

1970 . . . . . . . . . . . . . . . "For All We Know," Lovers and Other Strangers

1971 . . . . . . . . . . . . . . . "Theme from Shaft," Shaft

1972 . . . . . . . . . . . . . . . "The Morning After," The Poseidon Adventure

1973 . . . . . . . . . . . . . . . "The Way We Were," The Way We Were

1974 . . . . . . . . . . . . . . . "We May Never Love Like This Again," The Towering Inferno

1975 . . . . . . . . . . . . . . . "I'm Easy," Nashville

1976 . . . . . . . . . . . . . . . "Evergreen," A Star Is Born

1977 . . . . . . . . . . . . . . . "You Light Up My Life," You Light Up My Life

1978 . . . . . . . . . . . . . . . "Last Dance," Thank God It's Friday

1979 . . . . . . . . . . . . . . . "It Goes Like It Goes," Norma Rae

# ABOUT THE AUTHORS

Dreading the next day's 7 a.m. starting whistle at his summer job in a corrugated cardboard box factory, college junior **Harvey Solomon** nevertheless drives an hour to Boston to see the matchless (though definitely not jointless) Bob Marley (see July 16). So continues a lifelong interest in music and the arts. After college he tops the masthead at a publisher of millions of monthly cable TV program guides. But the muse favors freelance over full-time employment, so he embarks on an itinerant literary life: hundreds of articles for trades from *Adweek* to *Variety*, newspapers from *The Boston Globe* to *The Los Angeles Times*. Answering Hollywood's siren call, he writes for *Law & Order* and options a screenplay. He even braves choppy corporate waters, writing speeches and scripts and such. About the only writing he doesn't attempt, thank God, is poetry. Back on that long ago summer, he sets a record on a box-folding machine and wins a much sought-after prize: S&H Green Stamps.

When **Rich Appel** doesn't win a fortune in a McDonald's contest (see July 20), it becomes clear to the junior high schooler that he's going to have to actually work for a living, preferably as a writer or a radio DJ. There's one problem: no one's hiring eighth graders. So Appel carries golf bags for the summer, hoping a club member turns pro and takes him along for the ride. Instead, our caddy's inadvertent dial twist on a pocket transistor radio sends up the volume of James Taylor's "You've Got a Friend" (see July 31) so high that what should be an easy fairway shot lands in a brook, costing his golfer a stroke (maybe causing him one, too). Somehow, Appel still goes on to higher learning, then work as a DJ, club performer, TV and record company researcher, album liner notes writer, and editor of radio/music e-zine *Hz So Good*. Proving he holds no grudges, Appel still gets a Big Mac once in awhile. But he only takes golf carts when out on the links.

# PHOTOGRAPHY CREDITS

Alamy Photos: 100 © Photos 12; 8, 26, 123, 130, 190, 202 © Pictorial Press Ltd.

© AP Photos: 27, 71, 86, 98-99, 108, 147, 161; 164 © C-SPAN; 132 © Nihon Denpa News

The Bridgeman Art Library: 72 © Universitatsbibliothek, Gottingen, Germany/ Bildarchiv Steffens

© Corbis: 17, 36, 54-55, 57, 63, 64, 75, 87, 93, 110-111, 134, 157, 171, 184, 187, 194 (George), 208, 231; 92 © Jeff Albertson; 104-105 © Henry Diltz; 6 (David Bowie), 149, 176-177 © Lynn Goldsmith; 185 © Group of Survivors; 204 © Images.com; 6 (Dick Clark), 233 © Douglas Kirkland; 191 © Dieter Klar/ dpa; 106 © Wally McNamee; 79 © Richard T. Nowitz; 40 © Alan Pappe; 6 (Elton John), 50-51, 77, 133, 211 © Neal Preston; 183 © Roger Ressmeyer; 229 © Patrick Robert

The Everett Collection: 10 (*Three's Company* Cast), 21, 22, 24, 28, 32, 38, 43, 52 inset, 52-53, 58, 65, 70, 81, 82, 101, 102, 116, 117, 119, 120, 126, 135, 136, 137, 138, 140, 142, 154, 155, 158, 159, 165, 170 left, 179, 181, 182, 188, 195, 201, 205 inset, 212, 215, 217, 226 right, 230; 10 (*M*A*S*H* Cast), 35, 90, 129, 170 right © 20th Century Fox; 15, 131, 214 © ABC; 156 © Embassy Pictures; 31 © Chris Foster; 118 © Henson Associates; 213 © Steve Morley; 219 © Paramount Pictures; 34 © Rex Features; 95 © Jerry Tavin; 62, 80 © United Artists

© Getty Images: 48, 133 inset, 160, 166; 88-89 © John Bryson/Time Life Pictures; 60 © Columbia Tristar; 18 © John Dominis/Time Life Pictures; 112-113 © Ron Galella/ Wirelmage; 19 © Walter Iooss, Jr.; 178 © Yale Joel/Time Life Pictures; 148 © David Hume Kennerly; 146 © Ronald C. Modra; 139 © Museum of the City of New York; 76 © NASA/Time Life Pictures; 23 bottom © NFL; 162 © Terry O'Neill; 73 © Herb Scharfman; 232 © Time Life Pictures; 194 (John) © Chris Walter/Wirelmage; 14 © Susan Wood

The Image Works: 25 © ArenaPal/Topham; 61 © L. Degraces & P. Ladet/Topham; 16 © John Hedgecoe/Topham; 163 © W. Schmitt; 83 © Topham

iStockphoto.com: 210 joystick © Denise Campione; 210 console © Edward Dron; 14 flag © Stefan Klein; 5 © Steven Rohrer

Kimballstock.com: 12 © Ron Kimball

The Kobal Collection: 59, 89 inset, 190; 97 © 20th Century Fox; 209 © ABC; 103 © Lucasfilm/20th Century Fox; 7, 23 top, 112, 174-175 © Paramount Pictures; 47, 189, 198 © Universal Pictures; 6 (Christopher Reeve in *Superman*), 37, 225 © Warner Bros.

Landov: 9, 20, 169 © CBS Broadcasting

© London Features International: 227; 42 © CV; 85 © Peter Mazel

Photofest: 6 (Cher), 109, 115, 200, 218, 220; 150 © 20th Century Fox; 114 © ABC; 74 © Capitol Records/EMI; 84 © Columbia Pictures; 192 © Compass International Pictures; 145

© New World Pictures; 199, Pathfinder; 33, 128 © United Artists; 68-69 © Warner Bros.

© Redferns: 144, 205, 223, 226 left, 228; 121, 222 © Richard E. Aaron; 49 © Howard Barlow; 14 © BBC; 66-67 © David Corio; 111 inset © Fin Costello; 39 © David Warner Ellis; 153 © GAB Archives; 216-217 © GEMS; 29 © Fraser Gray; 127 © Keith Morris; 44-45 © Jan Persson; 107 © Gesine Petter/Fotex; 56 right, 192 (Paul) © RB; 194 (Ringo), 206 right © David Redfern; 221 © Tony Russell

Retna Ltd.: 56 left, 91 © Richard E. Aaron; 172-173, 186, 196-197 © ABC; 10 (*Mork and Mindy* Cast), 168 © Jim Britt/ABC; 207 © R. Stonehouse/Camera Press; 124-125 © Holland; 94-95 © Patrick Lichfield; 96 © Jan Persson; 128-129, 141 © Michael Putland; 152 © RB; 198-199, 224 © David Redfern; 206 left © Barry Schultz/Sunshine; 46 © Gai Terrell; 180 © Baron Wolman

© Captain C. "Bud" Robinson: 203